Doubt, Conflict, Mediation

Journal of the Royal Anthropological Institute Special Issue Series

The Journal of the Royal Anthropological Institute is the principal journal of the oldest anthropological organization in the world. It has attracted and inspired some of the world's greatest thinkers. International in scope, it presents accessible papers aimed at a broad anthropological readership. We are delighted to announce that from 2014 the annual special issues will also be available from the Wiley Blackwell books catalogue.

Previous special issues of the JRAI:

DOUBT, CONFLICT, MEDIATION

THE ANTHROPOLOGY OF MODERN TIME

EDITED BY LAURA BEAR

Library of Congress Cataloging-in-Publication Data

Doubt, conflict, mediation : the anthropology of modern time / edited by Laura Bear.
     pages cm. – (Journal of the Royal Anthropological Institute special issue series)
   Includes bibliographical references and index.
   ISBN 978-1-118-90387-2 (alk. paper)
   1. Time–Philosophy.   2. Civilization, Modern–Social aspects.   I. Bear, Laura, author, editor of compilation.
   BD638.D68 2014
   304.2'37–dc23

                                                                                    2014007123

A catalogue record for this book is available from the British Library.

Journal of the Royal Anthropological Institute
Incorporating MAN
Print ISSN 1359-0987
All articles published within this special issue are included within the ISI Journal Citation Reports® Social Science Citation Index. Please cite the articles as volume 20(Supp) of the Journal of the Royal Anthropological Institute.

Cover image: Cross-section of a sequoia tree at the American Museum of Natural History, New York City. (Courtesy of the American Museum of Natural History Library.)

Cover design by Ben Higgins

Set in 10 on 12pt Minion by Toppan Best-set Premedia Limited

Printed in Singapore by C.O.S. Printers Pte Ltd

1   2014

Contents

To Stephan Feuchtwang
In gratitude for his great contribution to this collective project.
We only follow where his open questioning leads.

Notes on contributors

Simone Abram is Reader at Leeds Metropolitan University and at Durham University. In much of her work, she has explored the political processes that shape the landscape and built environment through the planning system, examining the policies and practices of public participation and relations of governing. An account of this work was published in collaboration with Jonathan Murdoch in *Rationalities of planning: development versus environment in planning for housing* (Ashgate, 2002) and a range of articles and book chapters relate broader reflections on this work. Simone's recent monograph *Culture and planning* (Ashgate, 2011) synthesizes many of the observations and theoretical questions that were raised through empirical research and teaching in Britain and Norway. A particular challenge has been to open up a space in anthropological thinking for domestic state planning, a field that has until recently not been considered fully 'anthropological', and she began this process with the publication of an edited volume with Jacqueline Waldren, *Anthropological perspectives on local development* (EASA: Berghahn, 1998), and more recently she co-edited *Elusive promises: planning in the contemporary world* (Berghahn, 2013) with Gisa Weszkalnys. Alongside this, her work on tourism and outdoor life ranges from early articles and editorship (*Tourists and tourism*, Berg, 1997) to recent work on Norwegian hiking (with Gro Ween). She has been visiting professor in Paris, Gothenburg, and Tromsø and visiting researcher at Oslo University. *International Centre for Research in Tourism, Events and Hospitality, Leeds Metropolitan University. Correspondence to: 18 Lees Hall Road, Sheffield S8 9JH, UK. S.Abram@leedsmet.ac.uk*

Laura Bear is Associate Professor of Social Anthropology at the London School of Economics and Political Science. She is the author of two monographs: *Lines of the nation: Indian railway workers, bureaucracy and the intimate historical self* (Columbia University Press, 2007); and *Navigating austerity: state debt policy and popular economies on a South Asian river* (Stanford University Press, 2014). She has written twelve articles and book chapters which have appeared in journals such as *Economy and Society*, *Focaal*, and edited volumes for Duke University Press. Reflecting a commitment to forging public debate, she is also the author of a novel, *The Jadu house* (Doubleday, 2000), and has made four films in collaboration with river workers on the Hooghly. *Department of Social Anthropology, London School of Economics and Political Science, Houghton Street, London WC2A 2AE, UK. L.Bear@lse.ac.uk*

Sarah Franklin holds the Chair in Sociology at the University of Cambridge, where she is Director of the Reproductive Sociology Research Group (ReproSoc). Professor Franklin was among the first social scientists to investigate new reproductive technologies and is one of the founders of the 'new kinship studies' as well as the anthropology of bioscience. Over the past three decades, she has conducted fieldwork on IVF, cloning, preimplantation genetic diagnosis (PGD), and stem cell research in the UK. Her work combines ethnography with science studies, gender theory, and the analysis of visual culture. Her major publications include *Embodied progress: a cultural account of assisted conception* (Routledge, 1997), *Dolly mixtures: the remaking of genealogy* (Duke University Press, 2007), and *Biological relatives: IVF, stem cells and the future of kinship* (Duke University Press, 2013). *Department of Sociology, University of Cambridge, Free School Lane, Cambridge CB2 3RQ, UK. sbf25@cam.ac.uk*

Matt Hodges is Senior Lecturer in Social Anthropology at the University of Kent. He has a long-term interest in the anthropology of time, and has conducted fieldwork related to this theme in Southwest Europe, principally concerning the social impact of rural restructuring, and corporate influence on public sector research in agricultural biotechnology development. Recent articles exploring the relevance of time studies to contemporary anthropology have appeared in *American Ethnologist* **37: 1** (2010), *Anthropological Theory* **8: 4** (2008), *BioSocieties* **7: 1** (2012), and *Comparative Studies in Society and History* **55: 2** (2013). *School of Anthropology and Conservation, University of Kent, Canterbury, Kent CT2 7NR, UK. m.hodges@kent.ac.uk*

Sian Lazar is Lecturer in Social Anthropology at the Department of Archaeology and Anthropology, University of Cambridge. She has conducted research on collective politics and citizenship in Bolivia and Argentina. She is the author of *El Alto, rebel city: self and citizenship in Andean Bolivia* (Duke University Press, 2008) and editor of *The anthropology of citizenship: a reader* (Wiley-Blackwell, 2013). *Department of Archaeology and Anthropology, Division of Social Anthropology, University of Cambridge, Free School Lane, Cambridge CB2 3RF, UK. sl360@cam.ac.uk*

Nayanika Mathur holds a British Academy Postdoctoral Fellowship at the Division of Social Anthropology, University of Cambridge. She is also a Research Fellow on the Leverhulme funded 'Conspiracy & Democracy' project at the Centre for Research in the Arts, Social Sciences, and Humanities (CRASSH). Her research interests are centred upon the study of the state, law, bureaucracy, human-big cat conflict, materiality, and the role of new technologies in the working of government. She is currently completing a monograph on the developmental Indian state, provisionally entitled *Paper tiger: bureaucratic everydayness and the law in Himalayan India. Centre for Research in the Arts, Social Sciences, and Humanities, University of Cambridge, Alison Richard Building, 7 West Road, Cambridge CB3 9DT, UK. nm289@cam.ac.uk*

Morten Nielsen is associate professor at Aarhus University. His first major fieldwork project was in Recife, Brazil (2000-1), among community leaders in poor urban neighbourhoods. Since 2004, he has been working in Mozambique doing ethnographic research in peri-urban areas of Maputo, as well as in rural areas of Cabo del Gado, the northernmost region. Based on his fieldwork in Brazil and Mozambique, he has published on issues such as urban aesthetics, time and temporality, materiality, relational ontologies, and political cosmologies. In 2013, he commenced a new research project on land rights and 'collapsed futures' in Islay, the southernmost island of the Inner Hebrides. He is currently completing a book manuscript with Morten A. Pedersen and Mikkel Bunkenborg, University of Copenhagen, based on a comparative ethnographic research project on Chinese infrastructural interventions in Mozambique and Mongolia. His monograph *Bricks of time: inverse governmentality through informal house-building projects in Maputo, Mozambique* is forthcoming with Berghahn. *Department of Culture and Society, Aarhus University, Moesgaard Allé 20 DK – 8270, Denmark. etnomn@cas.au.dk*

Felix Ringel is Assistant Professor at the University of Vienna and holds a Ph.D. in Social Anthropology from the University of Cambridge (2012). He works on knowledge, time, and urban regeneration in medium-sized European cities. His primary research focus is on how people envision the future in times of post-industrial change. He has published several articles on his fieldwork in the former East German socialist model city of Hoyerswerda in journals such as *Focaal* and *Critique of Anthropology*. A monograph entitled *Back to the post-industrial future: a presentist ethnography of Germany's fastest-shrinking city* is in preparation. *Department of Social and Cultural Anthropology, Universitätsstr. 7, 1010 Vienna, Austria. felix.ringel@univie.ac.at*

Introduction

Doubt, conflict, mediation: the anthropology of modern time

LAURA BEAR *London School of Economics and Political Science*

In this introduction, I argue that in spite of recent discussions of global and neoliberal time, the anthropology of modern time remains under-explored. Modern time here is understood to be a complex historical product. At its centre is the abstract time-reckoning of capitalism, which acts as a universal measure of value, but which always comes into conflict with concrete experiences of time. Its social disciplines emerge from Christian practice, but the ethics of these routines are marked as secular and universal. Its politics is founded on representations of the natural connections of communities through a homogeneous historical time. Its science and technology tightly link social, human time to external non-human rhythms. It is important for anthropologists to reflect on modern time because our discipline has been profoundly influenced by the discoveries of its depth, secularity, and relativity. The controversies that emerged in relation to Darwin's and Einstein's insights still provide the framework for many of our theories, especially when we draw on phenomenological philosophy. In this introduction, I suggest that the key resources for overcoming this significant absence in anthropology lie in a *rapprochement* between Alfred Gell's epistemology of time and the approaches of Marxist political philosophers. This combination, along with an emphasis on the labour in/of time, gives rise to new questions and reveals new aspects of modern time in the present.

In recent years, anthropologists have reopened the question of capitalist time. In particular, they have entered into an interdisciplinary dialogue with sociologists about neoliberal and global time. Suggestions have been made that the present is characterized by time-space compression, cultures of speed or uncertainty (Comaroff, Comaroff & Weller 2001; Harvey 1989; Hope 2006; Mains 2007; Tomlinson 2007). Futures are described as particularly problematic and as radically uncertain, evacuated, or sites of nostalgia (Guyer 2007; Hell & Schonle 2010; Piot 2010; Rosenberg & Harding 2005; Wallman 1992). All of this work rebalances the sole focus on the past that characterized the *rapprochement* between anthropology and history in the 1980s (Munn 1992). It also goes beyond the spatial metaphors that dominated debates about globalization in the 1990s, unsettling their emphasis on scale, scape, and distance (Law 2004). Yet in this special issue we argue that these dialogues need to be more ambitious in their scope. Here ethnographies of economic, political, and bureaucratic social time are used as the foundation for a rigorous rethinking of modern time and to develop new anthropological theories.

Journal of the Royal Anthropological Institute (N.S.), 3-30
© Royal Anthropological Institute 2014

To understand the challenge that faces us, it is useful to start with an ethnographic example. In 2008, during my fieldwork in Kolkata, the city was filled with public speculation about schemes for economic prosperity. Liberalization (the opening of the economy to foreign direct investment in 1991), especially since 2000, had brought new public-private partnerships and volatile enterprise to West Bengal. The most debated issue at that time was the question of whether a factory that would produce the world's cheapest car, the Nano, would be built by the global TATA company at Singur. Most discussions were sympathetic to the small land-holders who had their property forcibly taken away from them or to the agricultural labourers who had not been retrained for industrial work. Their cause had been taken up by Mamata Banerjee and Trinamul Congress through picketing and demonstrations, but their supporters included people who were critical of this politics. Yet once rumours began to spread that TATA was going to pull out of the project, opinion swung in favour of the factory. Colleges and schools mounted spontaneous public petitions and marches supporting it. The informal sector shipbuilders and dockworkers who were my fieldwork companions bitterly regretted the loss of the prospect of *poriskar kaj*, or clean, respectable high-tech factory work. When TATA finally announced its withdrawal and intention to build the plant in Gujarat, Kolkata was stunned.

The news of this decision came on a day when the citizens of the city were celebrating Durga Puja. In this annual festival the goddess Durga returns to earth to destroy demons and restore productive order. It is at once an explicit enactment of the civic, an expression of patronage relationships, and a celebration of cosmogony (Bhattacharya 2007; McDermott 2011). Political figures as well as neighbourhood groups set up elaborate *pandals* (mixtures of stages, temples, and homes) to the goddess on every street that often reflect contemporary themes. The city becomes manifest to itself as people also take pleasure in watching the crowds as they tour famous *pandals*. The stated aim of the festival is to create *annondo* or joy. This is a sentiment of elation that permeates workplaces and homes for weeks afterwards. The timing of the TATA announcement during Durga Puja prompted widespread speculation that it had been intentionally made on a day when the emotions of the city would be least likely to be affected.

The *pandal* that received the most extensive media coverage and largest footfalls that day was that in Santosh Mitra Square. This depicted in perfect detail the decaying, ruined factories of the city and the proposed plant at Singur tied up with an enormous lock and chain. According to the president of the puja committee, Pradip Ghosh, it was designed to bring the industrialization debate to the masses. His speech about this was broadcast outside the *pandal*. He claimed that in the last few decades 50,000 industries had shut down and that the factories in the city were all locked up just as the plant in Singur was now. People, like myself, who made their way to the *pandal* travelled from the spectacle of a past of decay in ruined factories and a vanished future of 'clean' prosperous work on the outside of the structure (Fig. 1). We then entered the inside, where the annual return of the goddess Durga was being celebrated with drumming and offerings of fire (Fig. 2). Only in front of the goddess did we grow still and gather to experience the *aarti* (fire blessing). Everyone froze the image of the goddess in mobile phone photographs to be shown later to relatives and friends. Here in front of the goddess there was a peak of *annondo* that overcame the disappointment of the day. What drew the large crowds was the portrayal of cosmogony alongside a past of economic decay and a thwarted future, all in one place. Laid out in space juxtaposed

Figure 1. Factory ruins and Singur plant with Nano car, Durga Puja *pandal*, Santosh Mitra Square, 2008. (Photo: Laura Bear.)

Figure 2. *Aarti* worship of Durga, inside Santosh Misra Square *pandal*, 2008. (Photo: Laura Bear.)

with each other, these times could be simultaneously manifest. At the heart of the *pandal*, the time of cosmogony could overcome with its *annondo* the sense of loss manifest in the images of ruined and lost future factories. In this timespace, crowds of citizens drew on representations of sacred and economic time in order to give shape to the uncontrollable event that had just occurred.

We could add this day and the Santosh Mitra Square *pandal* to our catalogue of cases of neoliberal uncertain times and lost futures. But to do so would be to ignore the diversity of the chronotopes present here and the multiple temporal rhythms that converged in this timespace. How could we draw a diachronic section through this event in which the single truth of the present epoch would be expressed (Althusser 1970; Harris 2004; 2006; Osborne 1995)? Even if we look solely at the representations of time in the *pandal*, we can see that the present and future are certain at its centre, less certain on its outside. Nor can we see this timespace event of the crowds at the *pandal* as a 'response' to neoliberal uncertainty. It is a shaping of the meaning of an event that emplaces it within the civic and the divine, extracting it from other institutional framings (Greenhouse 1996; W. James & Mills 2005). Clearly we have a more challenging task in our analysis of current forms of social time than that proposed in work that emphasizes the new, singular characteristics of neoliberal or global time (Johnson-Hanks 2005).

This volume takes up the challenge by developing an anthropology of modern social time. After the many discussions of postmodernism (Harvey 1989; Jameson 2003) and the argument that we have never been modern (Latour 1993), why do we return here to the term 'modern' time ? This is for two reasons. First, we argue that the qualities and characteristics of modern social time require further investigation. Secondly, we show that its representations and techniques endure in the present. What do we mean by modern social time? Here we focus on economic, political, and bureaucratic representations and techniques of time. At first we might appear to be treading on territory already well covered by Marx (1992 [1885]), Weber (2008 [1922]), Beck (1992), and Luhmann (1993). All of these authors trace the management of time within modern institutions. But our approach builds on this work to make a different point. We argue that institutions *mediate* divergent representations, techniques, and rhythms of human and non-human time. As a result, modern time is characterized by unprecedented doubt about, and conflict in, representations of time. Time thickens with ethical problems, impossible dilemmas, and difficult orchestrations. To capture this reality fully, we argue that we must focus on the labour in/of time. The guiding emblem for our approach is the complex civic event of the Durga Puja *pandal* through which the meaning of another event, the withdrawal of TATA, was shaped by the citizens of Kolkata. We take it as characteristic of current timespaces. Multiple representations and social rhythms form a dynamic simultaneity from which further representations and experiences unpredictably emerge through human labour (Massey 2005; Munn 1986; 1992).

Our longer-term perspective on the social time of the present is driven by theoretical as well as empirical concerns. We do not only wish to demonstrate that modern time is diverse and complex. We also suggest that, without acknowledging the fact, anthropologists have used theories of time profoundly shaped by practices of modern social time. As this introduction and the specific studies in this volume will show, we need to confront directly the analytical impasses caused by the foundation of our discipline in debates about, and experiences of, modern time. To overcome these barriers we need to state explicitly an epistemology of time as the basis for our analysis (Hodges, this volume). We also have to develop tools that allow us to examine dominant representations of time and the social rhythms, conflict, mediation, and heterochrony that unpredictably emerge in relation to them (Greenhouse 1996; Shove, Trentmann & Wilk 2009). This introduction will proceed by addressing each of these issues in turn, drawing on insights from papers in the volume. First, it will define the qualities of modern time. Secondly, it will examine the origins of anthropological approaches in debates about modern time. Thirdly, it will construct an explicit epistemology of time. Fourthly, it will develop a theoretical framework that can make the complexity of social time intelligible. Our collective endeavour in this volume ultimately aims to provide resources for anthropologists that can help them to ask open, new questions about

Journal of the Royal Anthropological Institute (N.S.), 3-30
© Royal Anthropological Institute 2014

modern time, make their epistemology of time explicit, and develop new theoretical tools. Although the papers in this volume take diverse approaches, our analysis is centrally informed by a critical reworking of the approaches of Alfred Gell and Marxist political philosophers. Here in the introduction, I turn first to the definitional question of the specific qualities of modern time.

Modern time and its qualities

What is this modern time, then, that we are attempting to bring into view? We would identify it through a series of circulating representations, social disciplines, and technologies of time (similar to the global forms described by Ong and Collier [2004]). These are contingent historical products. They generate unpredictable effects and are subject to alteration, especially since they are associated with contradictory social rhythms (May & Thrift 2001). Most dominant in modern time is the abstract time-reckoning of capitalism, which acts as the basis for the universal measure of value in labour, debt, and exchange relationships. This always comes into conflict with concrete experiences and social rhythms of time (Glennie 2009; Innis 2004; Landes 2000; Marx 1992 [1885]; Postone 1993). Also important are the routines of state bureaucracies and productive institutions such as the factory, bank, and corporation. These social disciplines emerge from Christian routines and military regimes, but are represented as secular, humane, and universal practices (Foucault 2012; Weber 2008 [1922]). Politics is founded on representations of the natural connections of communities through a homogeneous deep historical and cultural time that is entangled in metaphors of biological life and kinship (Allen 2008; Bear 2007; Kaplan 2009; Stoler 1995). Science and technology tightly link social, human time to external non-human rhythms; frame time as a radically other secular force; and project a deep history of natural time (Gould 1987; Mackenzie 2001; Pickering 1995; Pickering & Guzik 2008). Importantly, the practices of modern time attempt to order hierarchically, separate, and adjudicate between 'other' social times (Ssorin-Chaikov 2006). An important role for institutions becomes the normative mediation between conflicting representations, technologies, and rhythms in time (see Bear, Mathur, Abram, this volume).

The dense, mixed qualities of this modern social time are traceable even if we just consider its representations. We assume, following the adaptation of Einstein's theory by Bakhtin (1981), that images of time often take the form of chronotopes. Or, in other words, they are representations that materialize timespace in a manner that enables the dimension of time to become visible. They achieve this through thickening the dimension of time by a layering of the effects of images and narrative structures. Importantly, in Bakhtin's analysis these representations are related to forms of agency. All the papers in this volume follow this approach, linking representations of time to their connected concepts of agency. But as explained later in the introduction, we depart from Bakhtin in two ways. First, developing arguments made by Gell, we refine the concept of chronotopes by placing these in a wider spectrum of time-maps. Secondly, we draw on Marxist political philosophy to examine the heterochrony of chronotopes and the unresolved experience of agency that emerges from their contradictory social effects. For now let us pause to consider the complexity of the mixed, layered chronotopes of modern time, as this is one of our key points (see also Strathern 1992).

A good place to start is with the historical time charts that emerged through the nineteenth and twentieth century. These are not of a single, homogeneous, linear temporality, as older analyses of modern time suggested (Kaplan 2009). They are heterochronic. They knot together many diverse forms of social and non-human time. Here I will draw on Rosenberg and Grafton's important 2009 book and take three examples that illustrate the times of social discipline, politics, and biology. The first example, Auguste Comte's *Calandrier positiviste* from 1849, illustrates the mixed qualities of the social discipline of the citizen-subject (Fig. 3). This calendar organized a cycle of reflection through the year, mimicking prayer books such as the priest's office. This time discipline also inscribed the homogeneous linear time of the nation into daily observances. The events and personages to be remembered each day were organized in the sequence they occurred in historical time. This time-reckoning wove together religious, secular, cyclical, and linear representations of time into a practice of social discipline. The second example, revealing of the complexity of the political time of the nation, is the popular chart produced by Henry Bostwick in 1828 (Fig. 4). This illustrated the progress of national history as an accretion of simultaneously historical, religious, and genealogical time. Its title (see caption) illustrates these complex qualities clearly.

The mixed natural, productive, and historical time of the nation is visible in the maps of political events that existed within the stream of time, following the course of a river-like flow (Fig. 5). Our third and final example reveals the layering of natural, human, and scientific time. Exhibited in the American Museum of Natural History, the cross-section of a huge sequoia tree acted as a 'natural' measure for the human history of politics and science. Marked on its rings were intervals of a hundred years and events such as the invention of the telescope used by Galileo, the founding of Yale College, and Napoleon's accession to power (Fig. 6). The large scale of this object and its time produce a sense of the extended duration of biological, natural time that enfolds our human life-spans. The knotting together of all of these political, economic, human, and natural heterogeneous social times is perhaps most visible in the over-determined reproductive time of kinship, which is at once intimate, productive, national, universal, religious, scientific, natural, and social (Bear 2007; Cannell & McKinnon 2013; Franklin, this volume). Each of these chronotopes can be related to practices of time in economics, politics, and science. They contribute to the generation of the contradictory experience of being a worker, citizen, or secular rationalist. Neither the internal multiplicity of these representations nor the diversity of social practices of modern time has been fully explored. We intend this volume to be the beginning of a much wider conversation on these themes.

The papers in this volume follow this complexity within the present, focusing in particular on the social time of economics, politics, and bureaucracy. Recent work has argued that there have been dramatic changes in these arenas. Capital is now shaped by the social disciplines of shareholder value, financialization, and consumption (Ho 2009; Shove *et al.* 2009; C. Zaloom, pers. comm., 2012). Bureaucratic time has turned to a focus on projections of the future in risk analysis and scenario planning (Adam & Groves 2007; Lakoff 2006; Reith 2004). Politics has become focused on new social movements beyond and above the nation-state. The papers in this volume take these arguments seriously, engaging with them, but they pause to analyse the complex, everyday uses of social time within bureaucracies, political movements, workplaces, and by citizens before attempting to chart new forms. Our approach comes from our awareness of how little we yet know about modern time. This raises the important question, to which the introduction now turns, of why it is that modern time has not been an object of analysis in anthropology.

Journal of the Royal Anthropological Institute (N.S.), 3-30
© Royal Anthropological Institute 2014

Modern time and anthropology: doubt and analytical impasses

Time 'exists' for academic discussion, speculation, and comparison, only in the interplay of idioms we provide or invent for it through our languages, ceremonies, cultural codes and technical inventions.

W. James & Mills 2005: 14

But, a day is not an abstract measure; it is a magnitude which corresponds to our concern and to the world in which we are thrown ... it is a time of labours and days.

Ricoeur 1980: 173

As Wendy James and David Mills suggest, we only ever access time through idioms that attempt to enfold and act on it. They also alert us to the fact that academic discussions of time are as subject to this condition as any other human practice. Here I will argue that approaches to time in anthropology have been profoundly shaped by the discoveries of its depth, secularity, and relativity in the late nineteenth and early twentieth century. This period was increasingly characterized by the sense of doubt and tension about time enunciated by Ricoeur in the quote that heads this section. An uncertainty about the relationship between abstract measures of time, human experiences of time, and the relativity of time raised analytical questions. It was these that anthropologists pursued and that they often continue to ask in the present. But such a pursuit closes off investigation of the context that generates research questions. Modern time does not become an object of inquiry; it provides the foundational questions for inquiry.

It would be a project beyond the scope of an introduction to describe fully this entangled history of the anthropological study of time and modern time. Yet I will illustrate this point with one key example that should make us reflect on how to borrow from philosophy in our theoretical analysis of time. The disciplinary controversies that emerged in relation to Darwin's and Einstein's insights still provide the source of many of our questions and theories. Science had provided a new ground from which to doubt the authority of religion and philosophy over matters of time generating wide speculation. This development contributed to heated debates between philosophy and science. From the exploration of social time by the Durkheimian school to more recent interventions, anthropologists have often developed their approaches in relation to these hard-fought encounters.

The encounters were most dramatically manifest in the public debates between Bergson and Einstein. From 1922 to 1929 they met in forums including the Société Française du Philosophie de Paris and the International Commission for Intellectual Co-operation of the League of Nations to contest the status of scientific versus philosophical knowledge (Canales 2005). Widely reported in the press at the time, commented on at length in three appendices to Bergson's *Durée et simultaneité*, and followed subsequently by Bachelard, Deleuze, Heidegger, and Whitehead, these forums contributed to a crisis within philosophy about the grounds for its disciplinary authority. Wading into the controversies, Durkheim and Hubert also debated with Kant and Bergson (Munn 1992). They argued for the novel concept of socially produced categories of time from the position of analysts who had transcended these through their own knowledge of secular, scientific time. The anthropological study of time therefore began with the borrowing of the authority of science in order to investigate key philosophical questions provoked by the new radical split between human and scientific time. Later work such as that of Munn and Das drew on Heidegger's and Ricoeur's

CALENDRIER POSITIVISTE,

POUR UNE ANNÉE QUELCONQUE;
OU

TABLEAU CONCRET DE LA PRÉPARATION HUMAINE.

PREMIER MOIS. MOÏSE. LA THÉOCRATIE INITIALE.	DEUXIÈME MOIS. HOMÈRE. LA POÉSIE ANCIENNE.	TROISIÈME MOIS. ARISTOTE. LA PHILOSOPHIE ANCIENNE.	QUATRIÈME MOIS. ARCHIMÈDE. LA SCIENCE ANCIENNE.	CINQUIÈME MOIS. CÉSAR. LA CIVILISATION MILITAIRE.	SIXIÈME MOIS. SAINT-PAUL. LE CATHOLICISME.	SEPTIÈME MOIS. CHARLEMAGNE. LA CIVILISATION FÉODALE.
1 Prométhée.	Hésiode.	Anaximandre.	Théophraste.	Miltiade.	Saint-Luc. ... Saint-Jacques.	Théodoric-le-Grand.
2 Hercule. ... Thésée.	Tyrtée. ... Sapho.	Anaximène.	Hérophile.	Léonidas.	Saint-Cyprien.	Pélage.
3 Orphée.	Anacréon.	Héraclite.	Érasistrate.	Aristide.	Saint-Athanase.	Othon-le-Grand. ... Henri-l'Oiseleur.
4 Ulysse.	Pindare.	Anaxagore.	Celse.	Cimon.	Saint-Jérôme.	Saint-Henri.
5 Lycurgue.	Sophocle. ... Euripide.	Démocrite. ... Leucippe, Galien.	Xénophon.	Saint-Ambroise.	Villiers. ... La Valette.
6 Romulus.	Théocrite. ... Longus.	Hérodote.	Avicenne. ... Averrhoès,	Phocion. ... Épaminondas.	Sainte-Monique.	Don Juan de Lépante. Jean Sobieski.
7 NUMA.	ESCHYLE.	THALÈS.	HIPPOCRATE.	THÉMISTOCLE.	SAINT-AUGUSTIN.	ALFRED.
8 Bélus. ... Sésostris.	Scopas.	Solon.	Euclide.	Périclès.	Constantin.	Charles-Martel.
9 Sésostris.	Zeuxis.	Xénophane.	Aristée.	Philippe.	Théodose.	Le Cid. ... Tancrède.
10 Menou.	Ictinus.	Empédocle.	Théodose-de-Byzance.	Démosthènes.	Saint-Chrysostome. ... Sainte-Basile.	Richard. ... Saladin.
11 Cyrus.	Praxitèle.	Thucydide.	Héron. ... Ctésibius.	Ptolémée Lagus.	Saint-Pulchérie. ... Saint-Paris.	Jeanne-d'Arc.
12 Zoroastre.	Lysippe.	Archytas.	Pappus.	Philopœmen.	Saint-Geneviève-de-Grand.	Albuquerque. ... Walter Raleigh.
13 Les Druides. ... Ossian.	Apelles.	Apollonius de Tyane. ... Philolaus.	Diophante.	Polybe.	Saint-Grégoire-le-Grand.	Bayard.
14 BOUDDHA.	PHIDIAS.	PYTHAGORE.	APOLLONIUS.	ALEXANDRE.	HILDEBRAND.	GODEFROI.
15 Fo-Hi.	Ésope. ... Pilpaï.	Aristippe.	Eucloxe. ... Aratus.	Brutus. ... Junius-Brutus.	Saint-Benoît. ... Saint-Antoine.	Saint-Léon-le-Grand. ... Léon II.
16 Lao-Tseu.	Plaute.	Antisthènes.	Pythéas. ... Néarque,	Camille. ... Marquis.	Saint-Boniface. ... Saint-Austin.	Gerbert. ... Pierre Damien.
17 Meng-Tseu.	Térence. ... Ménandre.	Zénon.	Aristarque. ... Bérose.	Fabricius. ... Régulus.	Saint-Isidore-de-Séville. ... Ste-Bruno.	Pierre-l'Ermite.
18 Les théocraties du Tibet.	Phèdre.	Cicéron. ... Pline-le-Jeune.	Ératosthène.	Annibal.	Lanfranc. ... Saint-Anselme.	Suger. ... Saint-Éloi.
19 Les théocraties du Japon.	Juvénal.	Épictète. ... Arrien.	Ptolémée.	Paul-Émile.	... Beatrix.	Alexandre III. ... Thomas Becket.
20 Manou-Capac. ... Temochama,	Lucien.	Tacite.	Albaténius. ... Nassir-Eddin.	Marius. ... Les Gracques.	Les archiv.du moyen âge.S.-Robert,	St-François-d'Ass. ... St-Dominique.
21 CONFUCIUS.	ARISTOPHANE.	SOCRATE.	HIPPARQUE.	SCIPION.	SAINT-BERNARD.	INNOCENT III.
22 Abraham. ... Joseph.	Ennius.	Xénocrate.	Varron.	Auguste. ... Mecène.	St-François Xav.. ... Ignace-de-Loyola.	Sainte-Clotilde.
23 Samuel.	Lucrèce.	Philon d'Alexandrie.	Columelle.	Vespasien. ... Titus.	St-Charles-Borrom.. ... Fred. Borrom.	Ste-Isabelle. Ste-Math.-de-Toscane.
24 Salomon. ... David.	Horace.	Saint-Jean-l'Évangéliste.	Vitruve.	Adrien. ... Nerva.	Ste-Thérèse.Ste-Cather.-de-Sienne.	St-Étienne-de-Houg. Math. Corvin.
25 Isaïe.	Tibulle.	Saint-Justin. ... Saint-Irénée.	Strabon.	Antonin. ... Marc-Aurèle.	St-Vinc.-de-Paule. L'abbé-de-l'Épée.	Saint-Elisabeth-de-Hongrie.
26 Saint-Jean-Baptiste.	Ovide.	Saint-Clément-d'Alexandrie.	Frontin.	Papinien. ... Ulpien.	Bourdaloue. ... Claude Fleury.	Blanche de Castille.
27 Haroun-al-Raschid. Abdérame III.	Lucain.	Origène. ... Tertullien.	Plimsergue.	Alexandre-Sévère.	W. Penn. ... G. Fox.	Saint-Ferdinand III. ... Alphonse X.
28 MAHOMET.	VIRGILE.	PLATON.	PLINE-l'ANCIEN.	TRAJAN.	BOSSUET.	SAINT-LOUIS.

Catéchisme Positiviste ; page 332.

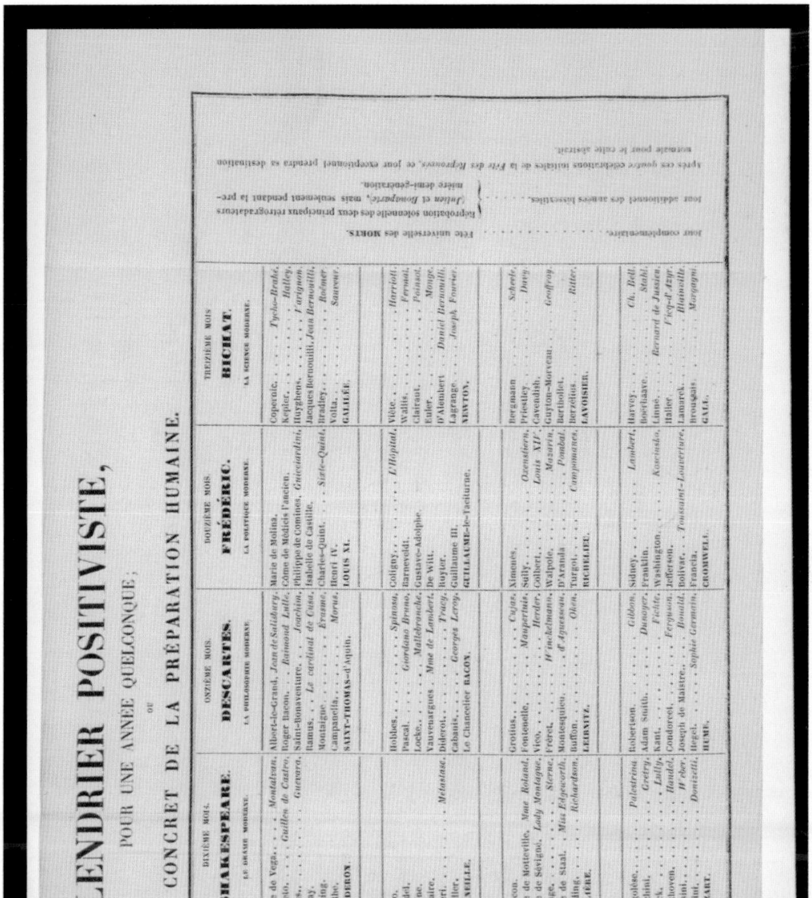

Figure 3. Auguste Comte, *Calandrier positiviste*, from *Catechisme positiviste*, 1852. (Courtesy of Department of Rare Books and Special Collections, Princeton University Library.)

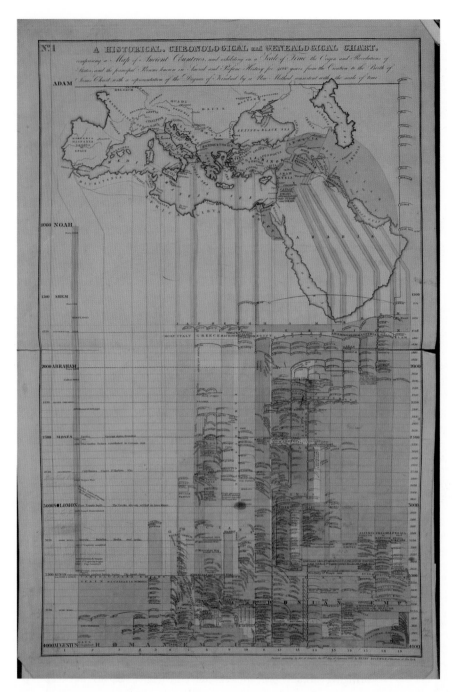

Figure 4. Henry Bostwick, *A historical, chronological and genealogical chart, comprising a map of ancient countries, and exhibiting a scale of time the origins and revolutions of states and the principal persons known in sacred and profane history for 4000 years from the creation to the birth of Jesus Christ and a representation of the degrees of kindred by a new method consistent with the scale of time,* Historical Chart and Atlas, 1828. (Courtesy of Department of Rare Books and Special Collections, Princeton University Library.)

Figure 5. Thomas Clarkson, Stream Chart from *The history of the rise, progress and accomplishment of the abolition of the African slave-trade by the British Parliament* [1808], 1836 New York Edition. (Courtesy of Department of Rare Books and Special Collections, Princeton University Library.)

emphasis on the human consciousness of time and intersubjective narrative. This was developed to reinstate the authority of philosophy rather than science over questions of human time. More recent approaches, by using Deleuze, revive the encounters between Bergson and Einstein over whether philosophers or scientists should have the final say on the true nature of time (Pandian 2012). The point here is that philosophy alone, especially that which emphasizes becoming or emergence, is not a sufficient basis for our investigation of modern social time. This is because its questions are posed in relation to debates that have arisen from experiences of it. Anthropologists can draw on philosophy as a source of epistemologies. Yet if they do so they need to make explicit their origin and be committed to moving beyond the particular foundational assumptions of philosophers into other social constellations of time.

This special issue makes visible the foundational framing of our disciplinary questions by addressing modern time as an object of direct inquiry. Ultimately, our approach allows the papers in this volume to apply new perspectives to a core anthropological question – first posed by Durkheim – of what is time in society and human experience. By bringing modern time into explicit consideration within our discipline, we can remake our questions about time, our theories of time, and our empirical objects. We no longer have to ask questions only about temporality or relative senses of time or about abstract versus experienced time. Instead we can map a complex field of representations, technologies, and social disciplines of time. Once we have done this we can then relate both institutional mediations and phenomenological experiences of time to this field.

Journal of the Royal Anthropological Institute (N.S.), 3-30
© Royal Anthropological Institute 2014

Figure 6. Cross-section of a sequoia tree at the American Museum of Natural History, New York City. The tree was cut down in California in 1891 and its rings date it to the mid-sixth century. This photograph was taken in the 1950s. On the tree are placed historical events marking the passage of a century. These include: the invention of the telescope used by Galileo; the founding of Yale College; and Napoleon's ascent to power. (Courtesy of the American Museum of Natural History Library.)

In the section that follows I demonstrate that the first step in mapping this social field is the construction of an epistemology that clearly states our analytical assumptions about time. It is through the construction of such an ideal type against which other social constellations of time can be compared that their diverse forms and effects become visible. Without such an explicit statement, we are at risk of unconsciously borrowing theories of the subject-in-time from philosophy provoked by practices of modern time. Modern time in all its diversity and complexity would be likely to continue to remain invisible.

Resources for an epistemology of time

> In time's passage we only encounter the flux of our own spiritual powers, which we reify and project onto the cosmos, which simply is and knows nothing of past, present and future.
>
> Gell 1992: 237

From this discussion it has become clear that the first step in our analyses of social time must be the adoption of an explicit commitment to a specific epistemology of time. Without this it is impossible to identify, by contrast, other social framings of time. We would also be at risk of mistaking our models of time as non-human time in the world. Hodges in this volume identifies this problem in turns to process in the practice theory that became predominant across the social sciences from the 1980s. In writers as diverse as Sahlins, Giddens, Ortner, and Bourdieu, time as the passage of history and process provides the dynamic container for social life. I began this introduction by describing a more recent epochal turn in which anthropologists seek to trace the signs in the real world of neoliberalism and postmodernism, without reflecting on the models of time that such claims rely on. In addition, Ringel in this volume suggests that some recent uses in anthropology of Deleuzian philosophy privilege the new and emergent without explicitly addressing the theoretical limits of such an approach. We need to engage, therefore, in a more sustained reflection on our models of time before we can deploy them to analyse current forms of modern social time. Otherwise our models of time become the universal truths of time. We would not be able to see the diversity of epistemologies and practices of social time at work in the world, especially not those of modern time. Instead time would be analysed as 'really' only process, history, neoliberal, or becoming and as incapable of being anything else.

The only anthropologist who has given us an example of how to construct an explicit epistemology of time is Alfred Gell, in *The anthropology of time* (1992). Importantly, his approach is developed from modern scientific concepts of time and philosophical responses to them. As the quotation heading this section illustrates, he makes explicit what only remains implicit in anthropology and philosophy. We reflect on questions about time from within a post-Einsteinian understanding of the cosmos. Gell creates an ideal type through which our discipline's tacit model of agency and time becomes visible to ourselves. Once we have acknowledged this, we can analyse by contrast other intellectual models and formations of social time, including those within modernity. We can even adopt, as do some papers in this volume, alternative epistemologies of time different from dominant modern forms (Hodges, Ringel, Bear; also see Harms' [2011] use of Gell). In Gell's ideal type, time exists in three forms: as a non-human timespace phenomenon traced in Einsteinian physics; as a social framing of time; and as a personal experience of time. This separation prevents the confusions that have beset the anthropology of time. Frequently, anthropologists have used hermeneutical philosophies of personal experiences of time to analyse the social life of time (see Ringel, this volume, for a discussion of this). In such approaches, social practices of time are collapsed into internal, personal experiences of time, or qualities of personal or social time are seen as expressions of the real force of time in and of itself.

The construction of an ideal type in which non-human, social, and personal time are separated from each other allows Gell to reflect more broadly on the techniques people use to act on and with time. Through such an approach, we can break out of the specific idioms of philosophy that are used to encompass time within other epistemologies. Gell argues that in order to navigate in time, humans develop representations or time-maps. These time-maps only have a partial relationship to the passage of real time, yet they mediate and shape personal experiences of it. With the aid of this concept, we can turn towards an analysis of the representations of time with which humans act in the world. It also allows us to examine how different personal experiences of time might emerge in relation to the forms these time-maps take. Thereby it permits us to step outside a philosophy into a concrete anthropology of time. Gell makes one final helpful move. He reflects on the different qualities of various kinds of time-maps. These do not all have the same relationship to the passage of non-human time. Some time-maps mimic the qualities of the human experience of the flux of life as we move through successive pasts, presents, and futures ('A' series time). Others heighten the sense of before and after or periods in time ('B' series time). Still others strain to mimic the qualities of non-human time. Time-maps will vary in the degree to which they mimic the other of non-human time or human time experiences. For example, technologies of time such as navigational devices will be closely tied to non-human forces. Historical records and personal mementos, by contrast, can improvise freely with both the flux of life and experiences of before and after, largely unconstrained by non-human time. Environmental plans, meanwhile, attempt to project and combine human and non-human forms of time, whereas economic models make social time-maps of other social time-maps that bear little relation to human or non-human time.

In two pioneering chapters of his book, Gell demonstrates how to analyse such economic models. He examines Shackle's simulation of the market, which suggests it is composed of lone businessmen locked in the moment of time producing an emergent economy from the anticipatory joy of profits. Gell's point here is that time-maps based on either the time of becoming and flux ('A' series time) or the time of before and after ('B' series time) cannot in themselves guarantee authenticity, liberation, or truth (unlike the recent suggestions of the philosophers Agamben [1993] and Casarino [2008], for example). To create such models is simply to be human and to be acting within the timespace of the world according to representations of it. Most importantly, Gell starts to bring into view a highly diverse arena of representations of time. It is this arena that the papers in this volume explore further. Our terrain is the old Durkheimian one of social time. Yet we can now approach this differently. We can move beyond the old epistemologies of philosophy into an anthropology of social time.

But what do we need to add to Gell's discussion? We need to develop his understanding of time-maps. He only analyses these as short-term, pragmatic tools used by individuals. The discussion of the chronotopes of modern time earlier in this introduction raises questions about such an approach. These collective representations thicken time-maps with affect and deep temporal depth. One of our key research questions must be how time-maps knot together pragmatic concerns about navigating in time to the long-term fate of ethical and political relations (Bear, Franklin, this volume). We must also explore the full range of time-maps and their different social effects. These exist along a continuum from practical forms of technology tied to non-human rhythms to the other extreme, more chronotopic, aesthetic representations of the past, present, and future or of the flux of time. The papers in this volume explore these varieties of form and their affective and ethical life. They also, unlike Gell, focus on individual and collective long-term projects (Bear, Nielsen, Abram, Mathur, Ringel, this volume). Here we are inspired by other anthropologists who have focused on predictive devices (Lakoff 2006; Miyazaki 2003; Riles 2004; Zaloom 2009). Ultimately, Gell's focus on individual rather than collective social navigation in time means that he cannot build a framework that captures the complexity of labour in/of time (S. Feuchtwang, pers. comm., 2012). As we navigate time, we co-ordinate various time-maps at once in relation to diverse social and non-human rhythms. To help us theorize this complex action in relation to collective projects of social time, it is useful to turn to a different tradition of analysis, Marxist political philosophy.

Marxist approaches to modern time: hierarchy, conflict, and heterochrony

My thesis is that time's many forms are cultural propositions about the nature and distribution of agency across social space – cultural propositions cast as normative claims.

Greenhouse 1996: 82

Only Marxism ... takes up ... a time that is always internal-external – hence collective foundational – and at once antagonism.

Negri 2003: 62

Here I turn to Marxist traditions of analysis not because these are free from the influence of the intellectual controversies provoked by modern social time. On the contrary, I do so because they directly engage with the idealism of philosophical debates from an opposed, materialist perspective. In addition, they confront the question of what modern social time is through their analysis of capitalism. Everything about time that is excluded from consideration in anthropology and philosophy is addressed within this tradition of analysis. My use of it here and the engagements of other papers in this volume with the work of Harvey, Arendt, Negri, and Badiou is therefore strategic, but critical (Bear, Hodges, Lazar, Ringel, this volume). The central Marxist insights we draw on arise from its analysis of the effects of abstract time in capitalism. As the quotations from Negri and Greenhouse above suggest, this approach brings the collective, antagonistic, and normative nature of time-maps into view. We are able to ask questions about the hierarchical ordering of time-maps within society. We can explore how they interact with multiple social and non-human rhythms in time. We can trace diversity and clashes among these representations. We can also examine how representations of time within institutions produce divergent social rhythms. Hierarchy, conflict, and heterochrony in representations of time and among their various social effects become visible.

The foundation for our approach is not Marx's well-known discussion of the use of clock time in factories (Ingold 1995; May & Thrift 2001; Parry 1999; Thompson 1967). Instead it is his diachronic analysis of circulation time in *Capital*, Volume 2, on which Postone, Althusser, and Negri have built. Here Marx takes his claim that abstract time acts as the measure of the value of objects and labour and he turns it into a broader argument about the social time of capitalism. In this volume the irreconcilable social rhythms produced by the use of abstract time are laid bare. It is these and the attempts by workers, factory owners, banks, entrepreneurs, financial markets, and governments to mediate them that are discussed. The volume is an extended reflection on how human labour in the world attempts to bring into congruence time-maps, social rhythms, and non-human time.

Marx shows that for the social relationships of capitalism to continue, capital must pass through a circuit from money to productive to commodity capital and back to money again, generating surplus value along the route. But the human labour that achieves this is full of instabilities. In particular, there is a contradiction between the rhythms of production and consumption and those of financial markets. Infrastructures of production are imperilled by the rhythms of credit and money markets. Natural processes of decay of non-human time along with the wear and tear of labour mean that infrastructure needs to be renewed. But such infrastructure requires the withholding of capital from circulation for the long term, which runs counter to the drive to keep capital in fluid metamorphosis in the 'castle in the air' of 'active, usurious, proliferating capital' in the money markets (Marx 1992 [1885]: 468). In addition, credit inevitably leads to a further contradictory social rhythm of overproduction. Overproduction will always occur because it becomes impossible to sell commodities to workers whose wages are kept down to create relative surplus value. Credit supports overproduction because long-term instabilities such as this one are temporarily fixed through loans to businesses and workers (Harvey 1989). Acts of labour by capitalists, traders, financiers, and workers mediate these contradictions in social rhythms by redistributing value and generating surplus value. The most complex mediation is that of workers (whether their labour is paid industrial, informalized, or unpaid domestic work). They both generate the virtual money market from the surplus value they produce in the circuit of capital and are most subject to its anti-productive rhythms. In addition, their bodily movements and their pacing through the day determine the fate of the circulation of capital. Their tiredness, health, employment, unemployment, consumption, all secure or undermine its future. What is important, therefore, about abstract time in capitalism is that it produces a form of reckoning value. This time-map creates contradictory social rhythms that have to be mediated by acts of concrete labour in the world. It is Postone (1993) who has most fully explored the contradictions produced by the use of abstract time measurement in capitalism. He analyses how abstract time acts both to produce and to conceal the concrete social content of time. Most importantly, Postone argues that abstract time increasingly becomes a teleological necessity of uniform, homogeneous empty time. It becomes an objective temporal norm a, 'now independent of activity ... an absolute measure of motion and of labour' that can itself be further commodified in credit relationships and futures trading, for example (Postone 1993: 278). Concrete time is experienced in contrast to this as a time of qualitative good and bad and as events and periodicities of human life.

So how are these analyses helpful to anthropologists in their investigation of modern social time? Building on Marx and Postone, we are able to refine further our theory of time-maps. Some of these will be quite distinct in kind. They will be dominant representations of time that anchor the measure of value, concepts of productive agency, and social relationships. These will in turn produce conflictual social rhythms and experiences. These important differences between representations of time and their effects are too often glossed with the single term 'temporality'. Or, in Actor Network Theory, all representations and technologies of time are described as having a similar obdurate agency. It is very important, however, that we distinguish various types of time-maps from each other. This can be achieved by attention to their significance to measures of value; how crucial they are to the definition of agency; and the degree of contradiction and/or inequality they contribute to. The papers in this volume identify and hierarchically organize the different time-maps at work in various social settings. They trace dominant forms such as process (Hodges); legal conservation regimes (Mathur); public deficit repayment (Bear); biological deep time (Franklin); and decline and sustainability (Ringel). They also pay attention to the specific social rhythms and relationships associated with them. In addition, the papers focus on the attempts by people to bring incommensurable rhythms and representations into synchronicity. Following Marx's example, we place hierarchy, social effects, and conflict at the centre of our analysis of social time.

Once this complexity is brought into view, we also have to explore how different social rhythms in time are related to each other. Althusser, building on the diachronic analysis of circulation in *Capital*, Volume 2, provides resources to think about this issue. He develops a complex model of the temporalities of capitalist society, arguing that various economic, political, and social institutions have 'peculiar rhythms and can only be known on condition that we have defined the concept of the specificity of ... [their] ... historical temporality and its punctuations' (Althusser 1970: 94). Each of these institutions is part of a wider social field, and he argues that we should track the 'intertwining of the different times, i.e. the type of "dislocation" and torsion of the different temporalities produced by the different levels of the structure' (Althusser 1970: 94). We have not fully developed the implications of Althusser's insight. This is that it is not enough to trace diverse institutional representations and practices of time. We have to track how these produce social rhythms and follow the relationships of these rhythms to each other. Even May and Thrift's important (2001) discussion of social time, which we draw on in this volume, does not attempt such a relational analysis. Their formulation of the concept of timespaces that contain diverse representations, technologies, disciplines, and rhythms of social time that form dispersed networks is typical of recent approaches in this respect (e.g. Bestor 2001). We have not yet developed any theoretical tools for describing relationships within and between these rhythms. The papers in this volume take an exploratory approach to this issue by following how various institutional temporalities are in tension; the relationship between social rhythms; the convergent and divergent effects of multiple representations; and contingent causalities (Mathur, Lazar, Bear, Abram, Nielsen). Recognizing the heterochrony of modern time, we start to chart the effects of this diversity in various social situations.

This heterochrony also has implications for the subjective experience of time that are not fully drawn out by Marx, Postone, or Althusser. It makes our navigation of time in capitalism particularly tense and full of dilemmas. Negri takes up this theme. He suggests that the contradictory rhythms of circulation create divergent experiences of social time that are a product of the 'clash of diverse and antagonistic temporalities' (Negri 2003: 68). Intellectually and pragmatically, we constantly reflect on and attempt to overcome these contradictions in social time. As Negri puts it, 'The crisis is in circulation, at every point, and does not so much concern the path of needs, of commodities, and information as the emergence of plural, multiversal ... times of subjects' (2003: 55). This claim becomes clearer if we take as an example recent ethnographies of indebtedness relationships in Chile and South Africa (Han 2011; 2012; D. James 2012). These show that the urban poor attempt to use monetary credit to open up potential futures for social reproduction and family relations. Seeking to overcome the staccato rhythms of precarious work that threaten the long-term continuity of kinship affect and obligation, they are drawn into another temporal rhythm of debt. Living in plural social rhythms, they attempt to control them using credit, making themselves subject to yet another tempo. From this work and that of Negri, it is clear that capitalist time-maps produce an increasingly irreconcilable and unpredictable series of localized, emergent dialectics. In these, time is so thickened with representations and practices that it becomes the core contradiction of life. The central problem that we reflect on and labour with is how to make and manage time.

The key point here is that within capitalism time is the key site for attempts to develop legitimacy and agency. Yet this centrality of time is a symptom of inequalities in social relationships. We cannot overcome the tension in time by invoking alternative non-linear times. As Negri (2003) points out, the *Jetzt-Zeit* of now-time and cyclical, eternal relations (such as that of Benjamin's Angel of History; 1999 [1955]) will not guarantee new intellectual insights or politics (see Agamben [1993], Badiou [2003], and Casarino [2008], who suggest that it will). These representations of time, Negri suggests, can be absorbed into the routinized social rhythms of both administration and production. Each of these depends on irruptive, charismatic innovations within the routine of command as these also render them 'productive'. We would have to look beyond the question of time towards the deeper one of inequality to resolve the dilemmas of labouring in/of time. The papers in this special issue follow Negri's lead in this respect. They focus on the ways in which practices of modern social time form the basis for agency, legitimacy, and politics (Lazar, Mathur, Bear, Nielsen). Our interest in social time is because it is a central site for social conflict and a symptom of the inequalities within capitalism.

With the help of Marxist political philosophy, in this section it has been possible to develop a theoretical framework through which to analyse various representations of social time, their distinct effects, dominance, and interrelationship. We have also been able to trace their connections to multiple, divergent social and non-human rhythms. Now we can begin to explore, as anthropologists, the hierarchy, conflict, and heterochrony characteristic of modern social time.

Anthropology's contribution: mediation and the labour in/of time

Yet what can anthropology contribute to this dialogue with Marxist philosophy, and more generally with other disciplines, about modern social time? The various answers to this question are illustrated in the papers in this volume. Each piece is an experiment in how to approach this topic with anthropological theories and methodologies. Our subject matter extends the sole focus on capitalism in Marxist political philosophy. In these papers, we analyse the social time of bureaucracy and politics as well. Anthropology also offers the analytical insights forged through a long tradition of analysis of ritual and religious temporalities, including recent discussions of conversion and pilgrimage (Coleman 2005; Engelke 2004; Robbins 2010). These can be drawn upon to explore the entailments of long-term representations of time, the practices they generate, and how representations are sustained (Kravel-Tovi & Bilu 2008; Smid 2010). This work, of course, takes us far beyond the reductionist discussions of time-maps as either ideology or discourse. Our analysis draws on this in an emphasis on ethics and agency rather than only on legitimation and resistance (Lazar, Bear, Nielsen, Franklin).

The most significant contribution anthropology can make is to the understanding of an underdeveloped part of Marxist philosophy and other disciplinary traditions. This is a comprehension of the acts of labour through which conflictual social rhythms, representations, and non-human time are mediated. Most analyses of modern social time (especially in Marxist political philosophy) assume routinization or mediation, without examining how this occurs or the contingent effects such action generates. All the papers in this volume illustrate this labour in and of time. The use of the term 'labour' is not intended here as a metaphor for practice or agency. It is meant literally to demarcate our creative, mediating action in the world. With our labour, we have to reconcile disparate social rhythms, multiple representations of time and non-human time. Although our approach builds on Munn's emphasis on temporalizing practices, her concept is refined by our use of the term 'labour'. We argue that the act of working in and on time involves: an encounter with the material world; the limits of the body; multiple tools; and co-ordinations of diverse rhythms and representations. This

Journal of the Royal Anthropological Institute (N.S.), 3-30
© Royal Anthropological Institute 2014

experience of friction, strain, and limits is not conveyed fully enough by Munn's emphasis on human *shaping* of space-time. In contrast to her approach, the term 'labour' draws attention to strenuous mediations. It also suggests that new time-maps might emerge from the pressing back of the non-human material world on human action. Agency would not be a sufficient term either, especially in the manner it is used in Actor Network Theory (ANT). This is because we are interested in the specific qualities of human acts in and with time. To take the ANT route would mean we would have to equalize human and non-human agency. But it is precisely human time-maps that we wish to explore in their relationship with non-human and social rhythms. Consumption or exchange would not be an alternative term either. This is because we wish to retain the sense of labour as a creative act of mediation that is generative of new timespaces. Ultimately, the emphasis on labour allows us to address social time in a materialist rather than idealist frame. Let me now turn to the papers themselves and to how they continue these conversations begun in this introduction.

Economic time: beyond process, becoming, and abstract time

Mediations of economic time are examined in the first three pieces, by Hodges, Ringel, and myself. These essays also centrally address our existing intellectual epistemologies of time, showing how they limit understanding. Hodges opens the volume with a challenge to anthropologists to reflect on and examine their assumptions about time as process. Drawing on Arendt and Deleuze, he argues that process is a dominant chronotope (or time-map) of the social disciplines of capitalism. He traces the unexpected circulation of this modern representation in recent theories of practice in anthropology as well as in market-driven genetic science. His ethnography of the transformation of a French biotechnology project from a research institute aiming to produce self-cloning maize for impoverished farmers into a public-private partnership orientated to profit reveals how process anchored the legitimacy of this transition. It also supported the introduction of new research practices. Old procedures of self-cloning were tightly tied to the unfolding rhythms of cells. New techniques aimed to discipline and control these through genetic engineering so that cells could conform to the market. Here we have an important ethnographic example of dominant time-maps anchoring new social relationships, measures of value and agency. They ran parallel to the social transformations that created new productive scientists and maize that could be profit-making in their teleology. Hodges' paper also examines how farmers in the same region of France activated process to reflect on the 'state of flux' which affects life in their peri-urban village. They use it to represent the existence of newly uncontrollable economic forces in their lives, against which they idealize 'enduring temporalities' of cultural practice. Here the chronotope acts in a different, if problematic, manner. It is the basis for claims against new migrants, denying earlier periods of commercialization and migration. Hodges' central point is that in all these situations, process supports exclusionary reckonings of value and agency that generate inequality. He therefore argues that it should not form the basis for our epistemology of time as it fundamentally excludes the heterogeneity of actually existing social and non-human times. Hodges offers instead an epistemology of immanence, which he suggests is more able to uncover diverse times.

Ringel continues this critical analysis of intellectual epistemologies by questioning the model of time as becoming and as politically productive only when it is a site of new, millennial hopes. From an ethnography of Germany's fastest-shrinking city,

Hoyerswerda, which is subject to the decline produced by privatization and outsourcing, he shows the limits to such approaches. Also developing the themes with which I opened this introduction, he argues that accounts of the evacuation of the near future are over-stated. All of these assumptions about time and neoliberal times run counter to the projects of endurance carried out by the citizens of Hoyerswerda. In these they attempt to render their community permanent. It is the slow, steady work of restoring buildings, gaining support for various civic clubs, and achieving funding from the local city hall that preoccupies them. They improvise new traditions that they attempt to take into the future. Here is a compelling example of the labour with/of time that anthropology can reveal. Civic clubs seek to mediate the social rhythms of the disappearance of the young, the demolition and decay of buildings. Their mediations are material, including the physical renovation of structures. Their civic actions aim to overcome a time-map of an inevitable process of decay that threatens to restrict their agency entirely. Alongside this dominant representation is another of sustainability that is associated with accounting practices that crucially determine whether the local city hall will fund their projects. The clubs have to adopt this time-map in order to survive. Here, where our current theories of becoming, new millennial hope, and neoliberal futures would least anticipate finding it, we have a modern pursuit of permanence and continuity. Ringel suggests that we should not, therefore, dogmatically adopt philosophies as in themselves guarantees of knowledge or forms of liberating politics. This suggestion supports the argument made throughout this introduction that we must make explicit our philosophies of time and reflect on their differences and/or similarities to the concepts of agency and time among our informants. Change in social life is ultimately more likely to come from small practices of endurance that build futures in the material world like those of the citizens of Hoyerswerda. It cannot be guaranteed by prescriptive philosophies of time and politics such as those of Badiou, Agamben, and proponents of an anthropology of becoming.

My paper then turns to the limits of an intellectual epistemology of abstract time as the only important part of capitalist time. The ethnography on which these arguments are based is of the responses to accidents among river pilots on the Hooghly river, on whose labour the global flow of commodities and raw materials depends. By tracing the impact of one accident and the technical solutions that river pilots introduced for it, I reveal the affect and ethics that inform capitalist time. I suggest that if we only focus on the abstract time of capitalism, we cannot understand contemporary circulation time. Instead I argue that in global workplaces time is at once an ethical, affective, and technical problem. The solutions for the contradictions that arise from the use of abstract time as a measure of value are developed from senses of workmanship among managers and workers. These emerge from experiences of acts of labour in which people attempt to reconcile contradictory social rhythms, non-human forces, predictive devices, and representations of time into productive acts. This experience thickens time with layers of meaning and generates an ethics of skill and duty of care between workers. It is from these ethical and affective experiences that technical solutions to contradictions in capitalism develop. This leads to a second critique of approaches to capitalist circulation time in the work of authors such as Harvey and Castree. They analyse 'fixes' in the contradictions of circulation as macro-level processes, such as the advancing of credit. I argue instead that circulation is a contingent result of micro-level ethically informed attempts to 'fix' it according to diverse representations of productivity, agency, and time. Importantly, I also examine the different kinds of effectivity of time-maps, their hierarchical relationships to each other, and their accompanying social relationships at work in the marine department. These include a core chronotope of public deficit reduction, predictive devices tightly tied to the rhythms of the river, and the representations among river pilots of the Hooghly as linked to lineage and divinity. As Negri suggests, here we have an example of time becoming dense with conflicts and meaning because of contradictions in circulation. It would be misleading if we were to focus only on abstract time, time discipline, and large-scale process in our analysis of this (and other forms of) economic time.

Read together, these three papers fundamentally alter our understandings of economic time, revealing three possible epistemological directions as alternatives to those of process, becoming, and abstract time. They also show that the economic time of the present is not radically distinct from that of the past, but is an intensification of the dominant time-maps of process and creative destruction that have always been part of capitalism.

Political time: social movements, heterochrony, and agency

The two papers by Lazar and Franklin move us into the arena of political time, specifically that of social movements. Here they correct the lack of attention to time in the analysis of collective endeavours to bring about social change. They show that it is impossible to understand how citizens construct political agency without attention to their representations of and labour with time. Lazar's ethnography focuses on two public sector unions in Buenos Aires and residents and street vendors' movements in the city of El Alto, Bolivia. She uncovers two hetereogenous time-maps at work in the representations and actions of these movements. These, she suggests, are akin to the temporalizing practices of Munn through which timespaces are given shape and transformed. But unlike Munn, Lazar uncovers a complexity to the content of time in these practices. In these, activists refer to historical time, which is made up of a narrative of continuous political action from a past of exemplary ancestors and into a future of transformation. They explicitly draw on imagery of kinship lineage, of politics as 'in the blood' of protesters. Such a representation allows activists to emplace their daily struggles in a long-term sense of time. Activists also take part in, but do not narrate to the same extent, attritional time. Attritional time is the mundane social discipline of protest and negotiation with no specific origin in the past or endpoint in the future. This mundane time opens out into dramatic manifestations of the movement to itself in demonstrations that overcome the banality of everyday protest.

Lazar uses her anthropological analysis of the labour in/of time in these movements to challenge profoundly theories of radical political change. She critiques both Marxist-influenced philosophers and some practice theorists for their emphasis on the event as a source of radical discontinuity. For example, she detects in Badiou's discussion of political transformation as conversion a problematic emphasis on radical discontinuity. In Sahlins and Das, she finds a similar reliance on the event that disrupts social repetition. Through an analysis of the revolutionary movements in Bolivia from 2000 to 2005, she shows that new politics and new political times do not emerge in a moment of a clean break from the past. Instead in events participants activate routine practices of attritional and historical time, suddenly bringing together time-maps that are usually kept separate. They identify their routines as close to and within history, not as a dramatic rupture from it. A further shaping of the event occurs through a practice of hailing the time as revolutionary not only during the protests, but also, more commonly, retrospectively in the accounts of activists, journalists, and scholars. Lazar's point is that there is nothing in the event itself that produces a radical break in political time. In this way, political revolution and change are profoundly unlike the 'conversions' described by Badiou. In Christian conversion, God appears and manifests His presence in hailing the convert, but in politics it is activists who hail themselves as agents of change in human history. Revolution and social movements are therefore founded on a quite different form of agency and time from that of conversion. It is only from the perspective of a secular analyst such as Badiou that they could be seen as equivalent. Our task as anthropologists is to understand agency and time from the perspective of others, not ourselves. Therefore such prescriptive philosophical models are not helpful to us. Lazar's approach, in contrast, reveals the contours of the political time of social movements and provides us with theoretical tools we can apply elsewhere.

Franklin takes us into the layered representations of time in social movements associated with reproductive politics in the United Kingdom. By tracing the debates that have occurred over thirty years, she is in the unusual position of being able to follow the sequential borrowing of time-maps between opposed sides in a political struggle, Christian Right-to-Life groups and campaigners for new reproductive technologies (NRT). She demonstrates that through these debates both sides unintentionally reconfigure the political time and agency of human life. This has increasingly been emplaced within a mixed chronotope of long-term time projected using both scientific and Christian temporal frames. Such representations displace the logics of lineage and descent that were the basis for the conceptualization of human worth, production, and reproduction in the past. Franklin traces how during the 1980s Christian Right-to-Life groups adopted a secularized defence of human life using the material culture and imagery of science. In the political debates around the Human Fertilization and Embryology (HFE) Act in 1990 in Parliament, politicians and scientists adopted their opponents' sacralized biology to argue for the absolute value of scientific research. Franklin then shows that the consequence of this was an absence of public controversy about an amendment to the HFE bill in 2008 to allow the use of cybrid embryos. The exchanges of the debate have profoundly shifted our public sense of the value of human life. Humans now gain their value and their individual rights because they are part of a sacralized deep time of biology and its 'facts'. In this the beginning of life is determined by the biological, scientific event of the 'primitive streak' (which appears at fourteen weeks) and our agency is emplaced in long-term genetic time. Yet this foregrounded scientific, natural time contains the thickening of Christian religious chronotopes of the transcendent value of humankind. As Franklin points out, this layering of times is a response to an elusive absence at the centre of both of these political movements, which is the meaning of 'biological time'. This meaning has long been problematic since the emergence of natural, biological time in the work of Darwin in the nineteenth century. Its apparently simple linearity and presence has to be constantly witnessed to by cultural production of evidence and debate. Franklin shows that forms of biological citizenship can only be understood by attention to this cultural history, including the micro-history of the Right-to-Life and pro-NRT social movements. The modern forms of time that emerged in the nineteenth century, along with their Christian backgrounding, recur in these debates about the value of human life, the nature of human time, and agency.

Lazar and Franklin reveal the current forms of the modern time of the citizen. As I illustrated with nineteenth-century cartographies of time, citizenship has long been dense with religious, scientific, kinship, and natural times. Most writing on recent social movements ignores this history and the dimension of time in favour of an emphasis on spaces of contestation and exclusion (Chatterjee 2004; Hardt & Negri 2004). The few writings on social movements that examine time understand it as a neutral dimension in which politics unfolds as a process or conjuncture (Castells 1997; Touraine 1981). Read together, these two pieces intervene in these absences, showing the importance of understanding social movements as profoundly shaped by mediations and conflicts between diverse representations, social disciplines, and rhythms of time.

Bureaucratic time: planning, risk, and conflicts in time

Following models of Weberian rationalization and Foucauldian social discipline, we have assumed that bureaucratic time-maps and techniques of time generate predictability and a routinization of social life. Even recent analyses of risk and scenario planning only differ by suggesting that the threats to predictability are more constructed than real. They still continue to argue that these projections produce routines and disciplines. The papers by Abram, Mathur, and Nielsen challenge these lingering assumptions. They explore the sheer variety of representations of time in planning and the conflictual encounters that are generated by bureaucratic routines.

Abram offers a profound critique of suggestions that there has been a retreat of planning and evacuation of the near future in contemporary state practices. She shows that these arguments ignore the fact that in many contexts, such as the planning offices in Norway and Sweden (where she carried out her fieldwork), recent decades have seen a proliferation of planning and greater contacts with the public. She argues that spatial democratic planning has produced a diversification and expansion of debates about the future between officials and citizens. What has occurred is a 'fecund' intensification that continues the modernist project of attempting to discipline the space and time of citizens. Like this older project, the results of these practices are unpredictable and incomplete mediations of various understandings of the past, present, and future. The planning offices themselves are also filled with multiple representations and practices of time, including backcasting and plans with various temporal and spatial scales. The sheer variety of these time-maps and the social rhythms they generate may even bring projects to a halt. This is especially because participatory planning involves contradictory temporal goals and procedures of mediation that refuse to take into account the long-term past of regions and the necessity of taking time to consult with the public. It is the routines and time-maps in these planning offices that generate conflictual, irresolvable outcomes. Abram follows these contradictions in time in the introduction of participative planning by a business consultant to a Norwegian planning office. Here local politicians called in to be 'resources' for the building of a prosperous future stalled the attempts of the consultant because these cut through their already-existing routines of consultation. In this case, bureaucratic rhythms along with the hierarchical nested representations of the future at work in the institution produced a stalemate in the linear, progressive process of planning. In the Swedish case, bureaucratic routine generated a different sort of conflict, in this situation between citizens groups and bureaucrats. Here the building of a new railway was being negotiated through participatory consultation. Abram shows that the dedication to process on the part of bureaucrats generated the exclusion of the opinions of the public that they were supposed to be consulting with. This is because public interests groups' representations of the future were always 'out of time' since they threatened to slow down the teleology of the participatory process itself. Abram suggests that accounts of neoliberal planning or evacuated futures elide these complexities and contradictions in the time-maps of planning. Like this introduction, she calls for an approach that reveals the varying degrees of effectivity of plans; their different scales in time and space; the procedures that plans are inserted in and generate; as well as the multiple, 'layering and folding of presents and futures that persist from modern into neoliberalizing states'.

Mathur develops the issues raised by Abram further, arguing that there has been little attention to everyday bureaucratic routines in anthropology. This means that we have largely assumed the accuracy of general theories about the significance of risk to contemporary institutions. If we have analysed daily practices, it is to suggest that bureaucracies make citizens wait for their attention and refuse to ameliorate their conditions in gestures of indifferent power. Mathur brings these two themes together in an analysis of the responses of local state officials and citizens to the threat of a man-eating tiger in the Himalayan town of Gopeshwar. She tracks the consequences of the dominant time-map of legal conservation regimes that enforce procedures to prevent the risk of the tiger's extinction. These produce a frustrating stalemate for officials and citizens because they make it impossible to act quickly to protect the inhabitants of the town. The social rhythms and routines produced in the bureaucracy by this representation of the tiger's potential extinction become unmanageable. Bureaucrats have to generate paper trails that show they have no choice but to kill the tiger. Citizens have to seek compensation from officials though long-drawn-out procedures of proof. In the duration in which the state fails to act, citizens and bureaucrats generate nostalgic time-maps of a colonial past in which a state could hunt down animals without restraint, thereby protecting its subjects. This enforced waiting for the state to act does not ultimately produce passivity, as our existing theories would predict. Instead the clash of temporalities that prevents the bureaucracy from acting generates political critique and demonstrations imperilling its legitimacy. Mathur reveals the limits of our existing approaches to everyday bureaucratic time. She suggests that we need to rethink bureaucracies as unfolding at the intersection of conflicting social times that officials attempt to mediate with their labour.

The last paper, by Nielsen, returns to concerns about the epistemology of time, closing the circle of the debates first begun in this introduction. His work is a good end-point because he combines a concern with modern time and agency, insights from Gell and Munn, and an engagement with Deleuzian philosophy. He turns this innovative synthesis towards the analysis of the tactics of generating a future among urban squatters in an illegal settlement, Mulwene, in Maputo. In particular he is interested in how they use strategies that deploy non-linear time-maps to enable the materialization of new possible futures. Nielsen concentrates on the case of Alberto, to whom a community leader has promised a plot of land on which to build a house. Alberto starts to build on this plot, inserting a trench into it, in order, Nielsen argues, to collapse the future into the present. He is ultimately unsuccessful because the plot is disputed land, but his tactics draw the attention of the local authorities to him. Ultimately, this act leads to Alberto's recognition as a legitimate citizen by the district administrator, who allocates him a plot. Nielsen suggests that this strategy is a different way of making time present from the linear time-maps of bureaucratic planning. He argues that Alberto uses a logic of durational time. This durational structure also echoes practices of divining the future in Maputo. In these, people seek to know their fate in order to use this information in the present in order to bring a desired virtual future into being. Divination therefore does not presume a linear structure for time, but instead suggests that it is only by knowing your future in the present that you can ensure it will come to pass. Likewise, Nielsen suggests that for Alberto and other inhabitants of Mulwene, planning does not involve a promise of a specific future that will be reached as a goal, but is used as a medium to create a different set of virtual possibilities for the present. Reading this piece in relation to those by Abram and Mathur, which demonstrate that linear time is only characteristic of the documentary representations of bureaucracies, leaves us with the interesting question of whether such strategies are similar to or different from the backcasting described by Abram or if they could be found within Mathur's chaotic, negotiated bureaucracy. Now that we have moved away from our initial epistemological assumptions founded in the debates between philosophy and science about time, we can begin to ask open questions for future research such as these. It might be that we could uncover practices of Bergsonian durational time within the routines of modern bureaucratic time. There are no limits now to the questions we can ask.

Let me end this discussion of modern time where I started, at the Durga Puja *pandal* in Santosh Mitra Square. How might we now understand this spatialization of ruins of the past and vanished futures with the goddess Durga at its centre? Why did this representation draw such large crowds on the day that plans for prosperity in West Bengal collapsed? The journey we have taken in this introduction suggests that the answer will lie not in neoliberal or uncertain futures, but in concepts of productive agency and time. Ostor (1980) describes how every element of worship of Durga serves to enable exchanges of productive force between various kinds of life and domains of human action, emphasizing their interdependence and common essences. Durga returns each year to act as a mediator who brings productivity to the world of the city. The citizens of Kolkata that day found in her presence a confirmation of the permanence of this productivity. She was not from a different millennial time like Benjamin's Angel of History; instead she was within the modern time of the civic and promised its continuation. This introduction and the essays in this volume ultimately seek to make visible such heterochronies within modern time and its layered, and sometimes conflictual, forms.

Acknowledgements

This research has been a co-operative project enriched by everyone who has taken part in the 'Conflicts in Time: Rethinking "Contemporary" Globalization' research network and seminar series (funded by the ESRC from 2008 to 2011). The participants (apart from those in this volume) who generated lively, creative conversations in the five workshops and exhibition included: Catherine Alexander, Nicolas Argenti, Sultan Barakat, Sue Barnes, Andrew Barry, Paul Basu, Richard Baxstrom, Véronique Bénéï, Eeva Berglund, Sid Beynon, Xiang Biao, Rose Biela, Lynn Bingham, Maxim Bolt, Georgina Born, Glen Bowman, Beverley Butler, Sharad Chari, Kimberly Chong, Tony Crook, Jamie Cross, Ferdinand de Jong, Matthew Engelke, Harriet Evans, David Featherstone, Melanie Friend, Neil David Galway, Rafi Greenberg, John Hacker, Casey High, Mette High, Eric Hirsch, Michael Hoffmann, Mekhala Krishnamurthy, Harry Lyons, Penny McCall Howard, Sally MacDonald, Andy Moran, Mary Morris, Rosie O'Driscoll, Luo Pan, Frances Pine, John Plummer, Rebecca Prentice, Annie Rae, Dinah Rajak, Josh Reno, Andrew Sanchez, Michael Scott, Sebina Sivac-Bryant, Eyal Sivan, Cornelia Sorabji, Nicolai Ssorin-Chaikov, Hans Steinmuller, Olivia Swift, Sharika Thiranagama, Helen Walasek, Nick Weekes, David Wengrow, and Gisa Weszkalnys.

Support was also given by the departments of anthropology at Cambridge, Edinburgh, the London School of Economics, and University College London; and by the Hastings Arts Forum. This project had its origins in the inspirational ideas shared by Harriet Evans, Stephan Feuchtwang, Olivia Harris, Michael Lambek, and Mike Rowlands in meetings seized from the term-time routine in 2006-7. This volume is dedicated to Stephan Feuchtwang, whose energy, wisdom, and openness led our way throughout. I'm looking forward to the conversation with him in which he reveals the flaws in this introduction (the faults of which are entirely my own) and takes my arguments in new, unexpected directions.

REFERENCES

ADAM, B. & C. GROVES 2007. *Future matters: action, knowledge, ethics*. Leiden: Brill.

AGAMBEN, G. 1993. Time and history: critique of the instant and the continuum. In *Infancy and history: essays on the destruction of experience*, 89-106. London: Verso.

ALLEN, T. 2008. *A republic in time: temporality and social imagination in nineteenth-century America*. Chapel Hill: University of North Carolina Press.

ALTHUSSER, L. 1970. The object of capital. In *Reading capital* (eds) L. Althusser & É. Balibar, 71-194. London: New Left Books.

BADIOU, A. 2003. *St Paul: the foundation of universalism* (trans. R. Brassier). Stanford: University Press.

BAKHTIN, M. 1981. *The dialogic imagination: four essays* (trans. C. Emerson & M. Holquist). Austin: University of Texas Press.

BEAR, L. 2007. *Lines of the nation: Indian railway workers, bureaucracy, and the intimate historical self*. New York: Columbia University Press.

BECK, U. 1992. *Risk society: towards a new modernity*. London: Sage.

BENJAMIN, W. 1999 [1955]. Theses on the philosophy of history. In *Illuminations*, 245-54. London: Random House.

BESTOR, T. 2001. Supply-side sushi: commodity, market and the global city. *American Anthropologist* **103**, 76-95.

BHATTACHARYA, T. 2007. Tracking the goddess: religion, community, and identity in the Durga Puja ceremonies of nineteenth-century Calcutta. *The Journal of Asian Studies* **66**, 919-62.

CANALES, J. 2005. Einstein, Bergson, and the experiment that failed: intellectual co-operation at the League of Nations. *MLN* **120**, 1168-91.

CANNELL, F. & S. MCKINNON 2013. *Vital relations: the persistent life of kinship*. Santa Fe, N.M.: SAR Press.

CASARINO, C. 2008. Time matters: Marx, Negri, Agamben, and the corporeal. In *In praise of the common* (eds) C. Casarino & A. Negri, 219-45. Minneapolis: University of Minnesota Press.

CASTELLS, M. 1997. *The power of identity: the information age, economy, culture, society*. Oxford: John Wiley & Sons.

CHATTERJEE, P. 2004. *The politics of the governed: reflections on popular politics in most of the world*. New York: Columbia University Press.

COLEMAN, S. 2005. Pilgrimage to 'England's Nazareth': landscapes of myth and memory at Walsingham. In *Intersecting journeys: the anthropology of pilgrimage and tourism* (eds) E. Badone & S. Roseman, 52-67. Urbana: University of Illinois Press.

COMAROFF, J., J. COMAROFF & R.P. WELLER 2001. *Millennial capitalism and the culture of neoliberalism*. Durham, N.C.: Duke University Press.

ENGELKE, M. 2004. Discontinuity and the discourse of conversion. *Journal of Religion in Africa* **34**, 82-109.

FOUCAULT, M. 2012. *Discipline and punish: the birth of the prison* (trans. A. Sheridan). New York: Knopf Doubleday.

GELL, A. 1992. *The anthropology of time*. Oxford: Berg.

GLENNIE, P. 2009. *Shaping the day: a history of timekeeping in England and Wales 1300-1800*. Oxford: University Press.

GOULD, S.J. 1987. *Time's arrow, time's cycle: myth and metaphor in the discovery of geological time*. Cambridge, Mass.: Harvard University Press.

GREENHOUSE, C. 1996. *A moment's notice: time politics across cultures*. Ithaca, N.Y.: Cornell University Press.

GUYER, J. 2007. Prophecy and the near future: thoughts on macroeconomic, evangelical, and punctuated time. *American Ethnologist* **34**, 409-21.

HAN, C. 2011. Symptoms of another life: time, possibility and domestic relations in Chile's credit economy. *Cultural Anthropology* **26**, 7-32.

———— 2012. *Life in debt: times of care and violence in neo-liberal Chile*. Berkeley: University of California Press.

HARDT, M. & A. NEGRI 2004. *Multitude: war and democracy in the age of empire*. New York: Penguin.

HARMS, E. 2011. *Saigon's edge: on the margins of Ho Chi Min City*. Minneapolis: University of Minnesota Press.

HARRIS, O. 2004. Braudel: historical time and the horror of discontinuity. *History Workshop Journal* **57**, 161-74.

———— 2006. The eternal return of conversion: Christianity as a contested domain in Highland Bolivia. In *The anthropology of Christianity* (ed.) F. Cannell, 51-76. Durham, N.C.: Duke University Press.

HARVEY, D. 1989. *The condition of postmodernity*. Oxford: Blackwell.

HELL, J. & A. SCHONLE 2010. *Ruins of modernity*. Durham, N.C.: Duke University Press.

HO, K. 2009. *Liquidated: an ethnography of Wall Street*. Durham, N.C.: Duke University Press.

HOPE, W. 2006. Global capitalism and the critique of real time. *Time and Society* **15**, 275-302.

INGOLD, T. 1995. Work, time and industry. *Time and Society* **4**, 1-28.

INNIS, H. 2004. *Changing concepts of time*. Lanham, Md: Rowman & Littlefield.

JAMES, D. 2012. Money-go-round: personal economies of wealth, aspiration and indebtedness. *Africa* **82**, 20-40.

JAMES, W. & D. MILLS 2005. *The qualities of time: anthropological approaches*. Oxford: Berg.

JAMESON, F. 2003. The end of temporality. *Critical Inquiry* **29**, 695-718.

JOHNSON-HANKS, J. 2005. When the future decides: uncertainty and intentional action in contemporary Cameroon. *Current Anthropology* **46**, 363-85.

KAPLAN, D. 2009. The songs of the siren: engineering national time on Israeli radio. *Cultural Anthropology* **24**, 313-45.

KRAVEL-TOVI, M. & Y. BILU 2008. The work of the present: constructing messianic temporality in the wake of failed prophecy among Chabad Hasidim. *American Ethnologist* **35**, 64-80.

LAKOFF, A. 2006. Preparing for the next emergency. *Public Culture* **19**, 247-71.

LANDES, D. 2000. *Revolution in time: clocks and the making of the modern world*. Cambridge, Mass.: Belknap Press of Harvard University Press.

LATOUR, B. 1993. *We have never been modern* (trans. C. Porter). Cambridge, Mass.: Harvard University Press.

LAW, J. 2004. And if the global were small and noncoherent? Method, complexity and the Baroque. *Environment and Planning D: Society and Space* **22**, 13-26.

LUHMANN, N. 1993. *Risk: a sociological theory*. Berlin: Walter de Gruyter.

McDERMOTT, R. 2011. *Revelry, rivalry and longing for the goddesses of Bengal: the fortunes of Hindu festivals in Bengal*. New York: Columbia University Press.

MACKENZIE, A. 2001. The technicity of time: from 1.00 oscillations/sec to 9,192,631,770 Hz. *Time and Society* **10**, 235-57.

MAINS, D. 2007. Neoliberal times: progress, boredom, and shame among young men in urban Ethiopia. *American Ethnologist* **34**, 659-73.

MARX, K. 1992 [1885]. *Capital*, vol. 2 (trans. D. Fernbach). London: Penguin.

MASSEY, D. 2005. *For space*. London: Sage.

MAY, J. & N. THRIFT 2001. *Timespace: geographies of temporality*. London: Routledge.

MIYAZAKI, H. 2003. The temporalities of the market. *American Anthropologist* **105**, 255-65.

MUNN, N. 1986. *The fame of gawa*. Chicago: University Press.

———— 1992. The cultural anthropology of time: a critical essay. *Annual Review of Anthropology* **21**, 93-123.

NEGRI, A. 2003. *Time for revolution*. London: Continuum.

ONG, A. & S. COLLIER 2004. *Global assemblages: technology, politics and ethics as anthropological problems*. Oxford: Blackwell.

OSBORNE, P. 1995. *The politics of time: modernity and avant-garde*. London: Verso.

OSTOR, A. 1980. *The play of the gods: locality, ideology, structure and time in the festivals of a Bengali town*. Chicago: University Press.

PANDIAN, A. 2012. The time of anthropology: notes from a field of experience. *Cultural Anthropology* **27**, 547-71.

PARRY, J. 1999. Lords of labour: working and shirking in Bhilai. *Contributions to Indian Sociology* (N.S.) **33**, 107-40.

PICKERING, A. 1995. *The mangle of practice: time, agency and science*. Chicago: University Press.

———— & K. GUZIK 2008. *The mangle in practice: science, society and becoming*. Durham, N.C.: Duke University Press.

PIOT, C. 2010. *Nostalgia for the future: West Africa after the Cold War*. Chicago: University Press.

POSTONE, M. 1993. *Time, labour and social domination*. Cambridge: University Press.

REITH, G. 2004. Uncertain times: the notion of 'risk' and the development of modernity. *Time & Society* **13**, 383-402.

RICOEUR, P. 1980. Narrative time. *Critical Inquiry* **7**, 169-90.

RILES, A. 2004. Real time: unwinding technocratic and anthropological knowledge. *American Ethnologist* **31**, 392-405.

ROBBINS, J. 2010. Anthropology, Pentecostalism and the new Paul. *South Atlantic Quarterly* **109**, 623-52.

ROSENBERG, D. & A. GRAFTON 2009. *Cartographies of time*. New York: Princeton Architectural Press.

——— & S. HARDING 2005. *Histories of the future*. Durham, N.C.: Duke University Press.

SHOVE, E., F. TRENTMANN & R. WILK 2009. *Time, consumption and everyday life: practice, materiality and culture*. Oxford: Berg.

SMID, K. 2010. Resting at creation and afterlife: distant times in the ordinary strategies of Muslim women in the rural Fouta Djallon, Guinea. *American Ethnologist* **37**, 36-52.

SSORIN-CHAIKOV, N. 2006. On heterochrony: birthday gifts to Stalin, 1949. *Journal of the Royal Anthropological Institute* (N.S.) **12**, 355-75.

STOLER, A. 1995. *Race and the education of desire*. Durham, N.C.: Duke University Press.

STRATHERN, M. 1992. *Reproducing the future: anthropology, kinship and the new reproductive technologies*. Manchester: University Press.

THOMPSON, E.P. 1967. Time, work-discipline and industrial capitalism. *Past and Present* **38**, 56-97.

TOMLINSON, J. 2007. *The culture of speed: the coming of immediacy*. London: Sage.

TOURAINE, A. 1981. *The voice and the eye: an analysis of social movements* (trans. A. Duff). Cambridge: University Press.

WALLMAN, S. 1992. *Contemporary futures: perspectives from social anthropology*. London: Routledge.

WEBER, M. 2008 [1922]. *Economy and society* (eds G. Roth & C. Wittich). London: Taylor & Francis.

ZALOOM, C. 2009. How to read the future: the yield curve, affect, and financial prediction. *Public Culture* **21**, 245-68.

Doute, conflit, médiation : l'anthropologie du temps moderne

Résumé

Dans son introduction, l'auteure affirme qu'en dépit des récentes discussions sur notre époque globalisée et néolibérale, l'anthropologie du temps moderne reste sous-explorée. Il faut entendre ici le temps moderne comme un produit historique complexe, centré sur la perception abstraite du temps du capitalisme, qui fait fonction de mesure universelle de la valeur mais entre toujours en conflit avec l'expérience concrète du temps. Ses disciplines sociales sont issues de la pratique chrétienne, mais leur éthique s'affiche comme séculière et universelle. Sa politique se fonde sur des représentations des liens naturels entre communautés, dans un temps historique homogène. Sa science et sa technologie associent étroitement le temps social ou humain aux rythmes externes, non humains. Il est important que les anthropologues réfléchissent au temps modernes, parce que notre discipline a été profondément influencée par la découverte de sa profondeur, de sa sécularité et de sa relativité. Les controverses nées des révolutions darwinienne et einsteinienne constituent encore le cadre de beaucoup de nos théories, notamment celles qui ont trait à la philosophie phénoménologique. Dans cette introduction, l'auteure avance que le moyen principal de pallier cette importante lacune en anthropologie résiderait dans un rapprochement entre l'épistémologie du temps d'Alfred Gell et les approches des philosophes politiques marxistes. Cette combinaison, alliée à l'accent mis sur le travail dans le temps/du temps, soulève de nouvelles questions et révèle de nouveaux aspects du temps moderne dans le présent.

Economic times

1

Immanent anthropology: a comparative study of 'process' in contemporary France

MATT HODGES *University of Kent*

This paper presents a comparative critique of the 'processual temporalities' which infuse both social-scientific theorizing and selected Western cultural practices. Through study of a public-private partnership which emerged from a biotechnology project devised for producing 'self-cloning' maize for resource-poor farmers, I analyse how processual temporalities were central to re-gearing knowledge practices towards market-orientated solutions. In a study of characterizations of the 'state of flux' which affects life in a French peri-urban village, I explore how processualism is identified as a component of a metropolitan hegemony which villagers 'resist' through idealizing 'enduring temporalities' of cultural practice. Drawing on Arendt and Deleuze, I analyse processualism as a dominant contemporary chronotope, mediating and disciplining conflictive temporalities and practices, underwriting economic projects of deterritorialization and restructuring – whose idiom is also prominent in social-scientific paradigms. I substitute an 'immanent anthropology', which advocates a non-transcendental ontology of cultural practice and analysis – displacing anthropological analysis onto a polychronic temporal foundation.

It is increasingly apparent that since the 1980s, 'process' has emerged as a central and governing trope in the Western social-scientific imaginary.[1] While theoretical arguments for why this should be so have been widely voiced (e.g. Giddens 1979; Smith 1982; Wolf 1982), the social context for this intellectual transformation is less transparent, nor has the conceptual meaning of this influential trope been extensively debated (Hodges 2008: 400-3; Lyman 2007). Following Michael Herzfeld's observation that one of the potential contributions of an anthropology of Western societies is its ability to analyse 'where "our" [anthropological] ideas come from' (Asad *et al.* 1997: 713), in this paper I explore correspondences between social-scientific invocations of 'process' and 'processual temporalities' prevalent in selected Western cultural practices. The hegemony of 'process' as a dominant analytical trope is also linked to an epochal revolution in the temporality of anthropological analysis, involving a shift from static, a-temporal analytical frames to approaches grounded in the ontological assumption that social life exists in 'time', 'flow', or 'flux'.[2] This inquiry therefore takes the form of a comparative ethnographic study informed by the anthropology of time. In the context

Journal of the Royal Anthropological Institute (N.S.), 33-51
© Royal Anthropological Institute 2014

of this special issue, I explore how processual temporalities in their multiple forms both are ethnographically emblematic of 'modern time' and operate as a core trope of contemporary social science, and I analyse this correspondence.[3]

The impetus for this inquiry comes from research on how 'processualism' is manifested in Western European and scientific cultural practices. This primarily concerns ethnographic contexts in which processual temporalities are conspicuous and discursively enabling (Hodges 2010; 2012), and where they may be entangled with what can be termed processual or disciplinary 'regimes of truth' (Foucault 1980). A parallel focus, however, targets the temporal idioms of anthropological discourse, in which the concept of process, in the contemporary era, has acted as a core concept (Hodges 2008). Over twenty years ago, Munn argued that 'when time is a focus [for anthropologists], it may be subject to oversimplified, single-stranded descriptions or typifications, rather than to a theoretical examination of basic sociocultural processes through which temporality is constructed' (1992: 93). Arguably, the dominant notion of timespace that underwrites contemporary anthropology is couched in the processual idiom, which Munn invokes. While this idiom is not necessarily oversimplified, it operates, in Osborne's definition, 'insofar as all such totalizations abstract from the concrete multiplicity of differential times co-existing in the global "now" a single differential ... through which to mark the time of the present' (1995: 28). In this sense, it anchors anthropological analysis in a potentially monological temporal outlook that can obscure as well as enlighten.

'Process', it can be proposed, has become such an integral cog in the doxa of social science that it is easy to forget that it is a socio-historical *concept*, a cultural figure with which to frame action and conjure 'time' (Arendt 1958: 230-6). In its common, shorthand analytical form, it is used by anthropologists to construct the transcendent temporal unity of cultural practices, bounded or open-ended 'processes' often incorporating change but which exhibit a coherent, systematic set of linkages 'over time', which are documented ethnographically and require elucidation.[4] Simultaneously, it can invoke a diachronic, spatialized temporal foundation for study that, in the words of White, views cultural practice as 'a stream flowing down through time [comprising a] process' (1959: 16-17). These words underpin White's evolutionary approach, but they inhabit the same conceptual neighbourhood as influential contemporary formulations. One of White's students provides a familiar image, with the notion that 'the world of humankind constitutes a manifold, a totality of interconnected processes' (Wolf 1982: 3) – itself echoed in a range of canonical texts with distinct genealogies and analytical foci that nevertheless concur on the processual character of social life and its rootedness in the 'flow of time' (e.g. Bourdieu 1977; Fabian 1983; Giddens 1979). Yet, notably, such works rarely define or clarify this constitutive processual ontology.[5]

Such uses of the concept are not necessarily teleological and can acknowledge emergence. And processes are sometimes said to coexist and operate at different tempos, as the *Annales* historians notably argued (e.g. Braudel 1994). But it is uncontroversial to assert that these assumptions underwrite an increasing majority of ethnographic and analytical practices. 'Process' is used to construct a relation in which past-present-future are conjoined in a structured epochal moment, usually for the purposes of achieving a future goal – as in Wolf's (1982) concept of 'historical processes'; or Bourdieu's (1977) notion of the gift as a temporal process of deferred reciprocity; or, in a precedent, Turner's (1969) concept of the 'ritual process'. It is also used, often simultaneously, to invoke the soul of 'time', a spatialized, riverine 'flow' or

Journal of the Royal Anthropological Institute (N.S.), 33-51
© Royal Anthropological Institute 2014

'flux' in and through which processes unfold – that cousin to 'linear' or 'homogeneous empty time' (see Bourdieu 1977: 8; Giddens 1979: 55; cf. Agamben 1993: 90-105; Hodges 2008: 399-400). Processual transit towards future goals can thereby be conceived in terms of spatial direction. In this regard, 'process' is to the temporality of anthropological analysis what 'place' was to anthropological studies of community (Gupta & Ferguson 1997): it operates as a foundational core concept, furnishing a constructed epochal moment or temporal 'clearing' that serves (largely unquestioned) as a frame for study.

This correspondence between manifestations of processual temporalities in Western cultural practices and the centrality of the processual idiom within the social sciences invites closer examination. Could it be a case of anthropology's doxic Euro-American cultural foundations emerging in theoretical paradigms (Asad *et al.* 1997)? According to Arendt, one genealogy of processual time has played an influential role in the development of industrial societies, in a multiplicity of ways. Most significantly, this processualism concerns the subjection of raw materials and people to *procedures* of production. Such procedures instrumentalize social relations and 'things' into means which are subsumed into end-products and their correlates in profit (Arendt 1958, cf. Thompson 1967). In this sense, it is a key template for modern social organization – yet this materialist manifestation is paralleled in the increasing visibility of processual idioms in Western scientific, political, and historical discourses from the eighteenth century onwards (Arendt 1968). Arendt opposes this instrumental processualism with the disruptive character of human action, capable of initiating new processes, of which the emblematic symbol is birth ('natality'), suggesting that the value of processualism is ambivalent – a point to which I return (Arendt 1958: 305-9; Passerin d'Entrèves 1994: 53-8).

Another key processual idiom in Western discourse can arguably be traced to the pre-Socratics, notably Heraclitus (cf. Barnes 1987), and comprises that temporalized philosophical discourse which in its twentieth-century incarnation has been highly influential in shaping the social sciences, chiefly through phenomenological philosophy (Heidegger 1993; Merleau-Ponty 1962; Schutz 1967).[6] In this respect, social life and time itself are viewed as inherently processual and the moment is subordinated to temporal flow, in the context of which it achieves its intelligibility. The prominence of this tradition since the early twentieth century should be viewed alongside the emergence of other processual idioms that Arendt identifies.

The heterogeneity of such idioms and cultural templates therefore suggests that processualism is a *polythetic* category of cultural practices, with both academic and wider variants. Nevertheless, for Arendt (1958: 232-3; 1968: 62), these varieties of processualism are complexly related, as they appear to be in anthropological discourse – although it is unclear to what extent anthropological reliance on such idioms is related to wider socio-economic developments in Western societies, as this correspondence has gone largely unremarked in the literature. Jameson offers a more assertive outlook, suggesting that the hegemony of processualism

> may be open to all kinds of other doubts and suspicions, particularly in a society whose current economic rhythms perpetuate and thrive on permanent change: capital accumulation, investment and realization, the dissolution of stable firms and jobs into a flux of new and provisional entities, awash in structural unemployment, its cultural infrastructure committed to permanent revolution in fashion and to the imperative to generate new kinds of commodities, [or] in deeper crises ... wholly new production technologies (1998: 169-70).

Just as postmodernism is arguably the 'cultural logic' of late capitalism (and structural-functionalism that of the colonial era), one can infer that, for Jameson, the hegemony of processualism is symptomatic of contemporary historical circumstances, and, in particular, neoliberal political economic practices (cf. Blackwell & Seabrook 1993; Jameson 1991). This view is echoed in Koselleck's (1985) analysis of the temporality of 'modernity', which is marked, he argues, by the ideology that history and time are an incessant movement or process to which every historical object and actor is subordinated, and by a hegemonic processualism operating at the level of social organization. In Koselleck's conceptualization, the increasing disjunction between contemporary 'horizons of expectation' and 'spaces of experience' ultimately enforces this triumph of the processual (1985: 255-75).

Such correspondences are intriguing, if counter-intuitive, and suggest that some processual approaches may be marked by temporal obfuscation, and even ethnocentrism. It is also clear that the monological character of processual idioms can obscure those 'conflicts' in timespace that would become apparent with use of a differential, non-spatialized temporal idiom (e.g. Adam 1998; Gurvitch 1964). How can this correspondence between social-scientific and Western temporalities be posed as an anthropological problem? The route adopted here is to undertake a comparative, exploratory 'anthropology of process' – in contrast to a 'processual anthropology'. This approach presents an ethnographic perspective on contemporary, processual, at times disciplinary regimes of truth, and includes anthropology within its scope. I proceed with two comparative ethnographic cases – of a multinational public-private partnership in agricultural biotechnology research based chiefly in Marseille, France; and of local conceptualizations of history and process among the conflictive population of a rural *commune*, in coastal Languedoc. Rather than taking 'processes' as an object and temporal frame for study, I focus on their temporal and epochal construction, discursive agency, and analytical manifestation. Discussion then moves to consider anthropological temporalities. Drawing on an analytical frame that can be characterized as temporally 'immanent' rather than 'processual' in orientation (Agamben 2000; Deleuze & Guattari 1994), and focused on how processes are 'achieved' rather than taking their 'transcendental coherence' as given (cf. Whitehead 1979: 208-18), I query the hegemony of this modern temporal figure, and explore the implications.[7]

Processual regimes: the molecularization of plants

On the outskirts of Marseille, among the umbrella pines and dusty industrial parks, stands the futuristic oval building – *la caprice des Dieux*, to its staff – housing the headquarters of Agromonde International.[8] In the summer of 2009, as part of an ESRC-funded investigation into the influence of seed corporations over development of agricultural biotechnology for resource-poor farmers, I am on one of several visits there to speak with a distinguished French geneticist and plant breeder, Dr Jean Marceau.

For many years, Marceau was at CILLOT,[9] the Mexican agricultural station which helped produce the short-stemmed wheat and rice varieties that drove the Green Revolution. He was director of a French-funded 'Apomixis Project' to transfer 'apomixis' into crop plants such as maize and wheat. Apomixis is the ability found in some wild plants to *self-clone* through producing seeds which contain copies of maternal DNA. It is said to have a revolutionary potential for plant breeding that has been recognized since at least the 1960s, when it was the subject of secret Soviet research programmes. The introduction of apomixis into a commercial crop would have many repercussions. It could enable farmers to clone hybrid seed, freeing them from the need to buy it annually from the seed industry. It could serve as a breeding tool for the resource-poor, enabling them to fix local hybrids for niche microclimates and improve food security. But it would also permit seed corporations to increase profits significantly, through resulting economies in hybrid seed production. Such claims are contested, yet they are taken seriously by major players in the seed industry, which have run confidential 'apomixis projects' for many years. It is also possible that some corporations have actively sought to undermine public sector research that has the production of open-source apomixis technologies as its goal, in an attempt to head off an open-source apomixis technology that could undermine profits.

Which returns us to Marseille, where Marceau is explaining how he lost control of his project to a team of postdocs and a syndicate of transnational seed corporations. The project, which he spent twenty years developing, aimed to produce the world's first commercial apomictic maize, in an open-source form. Marceau was a leading expert on apomixis, and the research was at the forefront of the field. Results, he claims, could have been just around the corner. So what happened?

One of the things it came down to, he explains, was the new genomics. Marceau trained as a plant breeder and classical geneticist. His project was characterized by a heteroculture of approaches (cf. Richards 2004), including conventional plant breeding, classical genetics, molecular genetics, and genomics technoscience, with a flexible research timeline and agenda. In Marceau's view, apomixis is triggered by a gene cluster that intervenes during the plant's reproductive cycle to divert conventional sexual reproduction into asexual cloning. During the late 1990s, however, molecular biologists working primarily in laboratories argued that new genomics-based approaches showed that apomixis results from a 'deregulation of the sexual developmental program in space and time, leading to putative cell fate changes and the omission of critical steps in the sexual process' (Koltunow & Grossniklaus 2003: 556), triggered in turn by epigenetic processes. This 'molecular turn' in apomixis research – which is characterized by an idiom that insists on the processual character of apomictic reproduction as opposed to the interventionist idiom of Marceau's classical genetics – was accompanied by wider political economic changes of a processual character (cf. Jameson 1998: 169-70). As in other fields, technoscientific practices were giving rise to genomic approaches to plant breeding that were rapidly displacing established practices. At the same time, public sector plant breeding institutes were being privatized, and private sector influence was extending via new public-private assemblages focused on the production of biocapital. In this regard, the other key mitigating factor was the entry of Marceau's team into a public-private partnership, the 'Apomixis Syndicate', where there were strict procedural constraints on future research trajectories, enforced by legal contracts. I now review the technical and wider shift provoked by this processualist rupture.[10]

Let us commence with the CIILOT breeding programme, which was a focus for CILLOT research and development (R&D). Interspecific or 'wide' hybridization, also termed 'wide crossing', involves cross-fertilizing two plants of distinct but related genera. The objective is 'introgression' of a target trait from one genus to the other, which in this case concerned transferring apomixis from *Tripsacum dactyloides* (Gamagrass) to *Zea mays* (Maize). The technique involves undertaking multiple experimental crosses with the goal of creating a hybrid containing the target trait. The practice is also enabled by plant breeding technologies. Once a suitable hybrid plant is identified – in this case with apomictic capability – this is 'backcrossed' with a plant from the target genus to excise unwanted hybrid features, which usually takes at least four generations. Interspecific hybridization is based on a 'natural' evolutionary model – wide hybridization events have been central to the development of a number of key human crops in the past.[11]

From a temporal perspective, wide crossing is a breeding practice where temporal emergence is 'thematized' methodologically (cf. Pickering 1995: 9-27): in this sense, 'unruly' mixing of distinct genomes during 'meiosis' underpins the technique, generating novelty. The temporality of R&D therefore demands an open-ended, flexible funding arrangement and timeline. An apomictic maize created via wide crossing would thus constitute a new species, which could *not* be easily 'switched' on and off via a 'Genetic Use Restriction Technology', for example. It would be resistant to intellectual property rights, although some control over production and distribution could be exerted via patenting and plant breeders' rights.[12] As the time needed to achieve success is an unknown variable, the practice may also clash with the calendar for deliverables enshrined in a public-private partnership contract.

The breeding technique can thus be said to comprise a relational, self-conscious 'dance of agency' (Pickering 1995: 21-2) between technology, human actors, and the creative agency of plant species, with the objective of producing hybrid apomictic maize. Its ethos is one of 'revealing' (*aletheia*) rather than 'enframing' (*Gestell*) (Heidegger 1993). Enframing is symptomatic of an instrumentality associated with procedures of commodification central to producing biocapital; revealing is, to an extent, temporally subversive of such goals through its valorizing of emergence (Feenberg 2005; Pickering 2008). Additionally, the end result would be a species of plant whose genomic and reproductive identity was resistant to commodification. It would be challenging to control 'unauthorized' recycling of cloned seeds via existing regulatory means. A resistance to transformation into biocapital thus remains at the level of both the relation of the final product to control by intellectual property rights, and in terms of research and development practices. Ultimately, this form of apomictic maize would exhibit those classic subversive qualities associated with an apomixis technology: that is, a capacity for seed saving, and for crossing with commercial hybrids, thus rendering them apomictic and undercutting corporate markets. This breeding practice was embedded in a flexible research programme where structured procedures were subordinated to emergent wide hybridization results, under the control of Marceau as principal investigator.

Molecular genetics was initially utilized within the CILLOT Project in association with 'flow cytometry', a technology for accelerating screening of wide hybrids for apomictic capability. This facilitated a modest level of technical instrumentalization, although it had a minor role. Within the Apomixis Syndicate, by contrast, a selection of genomic technologies were implemented, financed by corporate members (e.g. AFLP-PCR, RFLP analysis; see Leblanc *et al.* 2009: 594). These could facilitate technical manipulation of the enduring temporality of plant reproduction and so render apomixis functional to commodification (Grimanelli, Perotti, Ramirez & Leblanc 2005). As Helmreich proposes: '[C]ontemporary biological science has become expert at stopping, starting, suspending and accelerating cellular processes, wedging these dynamics into processes that look like a molecular version of industrial agribusiness' (2007: 294). The objective, arguably, is subordination to disciplinary procedures (Foucault 1977). Scientific arguments were made within the public-private partnership for the greater efficiency and instrumentality of such technical practices, which lent weight to the argument that the project would stand a greater chance of succeeding if the objective was creation of a genetically modified (GM) apomict (Grimanelli, Tohme & González-León 2001). Corporate partners thought that GM techniques would also facilitate control of apomictic maize via intellectual property rights and technical means (Marceau, pers. comm., 2008).

The project's 'molecular turn' is comparable to what Rose (2007) has termed 'molecularization'. As Rose writes: '[M]olecularization strips tissues, proteins, molecules ... of their specific affinities – to a disease, to an organ, to an individual – and enables them to be regarded, in many respects, as manipulable, and transferable elements or units, which can be delocalized' (2007: 36). This disciplinary programme also has an inherently temporal quality. Landecker (2005) comments:

> These powerful techniques themselves belong to a genre of experimentation directed at *making cells live differently in time*, in order to harness their productive or reproductive capacities ... [L]ong-standing genres of intervention in cellular plasticity and temporality are now moving from the background into the foreground of biochemistry and molecular biology, disciplines previously focused on knowledge of gene sequences and molecules in a more disembodied, atemporal fashion (original emphasis).[13]

As a consequence of molecularization, plant DNA was instrumentally functionalized ('enframed') by Apomixis Syndicate scientists utilizing new biotechnological techniques, with contingent processual aims which correlated with the creation of biocapital. This 'techno-cellular' processual temporality of deterritorialization and re-embedding to enable future utility bears resemblance to that of 'time in advance of itself, where ... the future becomes present. This time [is] predominant in competitive capitalism' (Gurvitch 1964: 33). 'Natural processes' were thereby reassembled into instrumentalized processual constructions. For corporate partners, these biotechnologies also promised to create GM products which could be patented, hence enabling production of biocapital.

In sum, then, the shift to a processual scientific idiom and practices of disciplinary deterritorialization and re-embedding was accompanied by a structural engineering of procedures, timeframes, and futures. This was mediated by legal contracts. The principal sideshadows[14] of this monoculture were the alternative technologies and alternative futures that wide hybridization and the Marceau heteroculture of idioms and techniques might impel. While processual idioms and templates were not absent from Marceau's heteroculture, they did not play a disciplining role, given greater flexibility in research practices and a related valorizing of emergence – which arguably comprised an Arendtian 'ethic of the interval' (Braun 2007). By contrast, the procedures engineered by Apomixis Syndicate contracts and timescales ensured that processual ideologies of genomic understandings of apomixis remained dominant in a timescape comprising multiple trajectories, temporal modalities, and tempos. Process, for the Apomixis Syndicate, acted as a means of disciplining and controlling knowledge practices, enabling 'molecularization' whose goal is to render apomixis manipulable. It was embedded in turn in a wider configuration of political-economic relations – that of the corporate stranglehold on the global seed industry. It is an illustration of how processual knowledge and organizational practices operate together, as Arendt (1958: 232-3; 1968: 62) proposes. In this way, 'process' was discursively employed to weld a conflictive field of force and emergence into a disciplined transit through time towards a specific goal – a commodifiable apomixis technology, or nothing. It is a goal, one should add, that remains virtual owing to the unruly actions of plants, which, to date, have resisted such instrumental disciplining.

Resisting process: *le changement continuel* in contemporary Languedoc

During fieldwork in a peri-urban commune in Languedoc, processualism took a markedly different form. While there were many processes of an Arendtian nature that structured everyday life in the village of Villeneuve – from the production processes associated with commercialized wine growing to those procedures which individuals encountered in a wide range of working practices in service and light industries in the nearby city of Narbonne – among the most conspicuous examples of processualism was its invocation to characterize the contemporary epoch. A vivid example was supplied by a fisherman, Raymond Cabart. Cabart came from a family of fishermen who had worked the lagoon of Villeneuve for many generations. Indeed, his own name first made an appearance in the village archives in 1698, when a forebear called Raymond Cabart signed as a member of the village council. On first appearances, his life was emblematic of such symbolic continuity and enduring temporalities. Yet in conversation, it emerged that, for Cabart, life around him was anything but enduring. His characterization of modern times was neatly captured in the expression he often repeated, *tout a changé* – everything in local life had changed.

Monsieur Cabart was the first of many informants to speak of an epoch of *changement continuel* – incessant change – which had apparently gripped life in Villeneuve since the 1960s. This characterization cropped up frequently as I conducted research on historical consciousness in the locality, and is a more open-ended, flexible processual idiom than was encountered in the previous case. When I informed new acquaintances that I was keen to learn about life in Villeneuve, I was often referred to *le changement continuel* that now dominated everyday life. Indeed, I would normally be told that *tout a changé* – 'everything has changed' – which would be followed by selection of empirical contrasts between the changeability of life today and the enduring quality of life in the 'old days' to make the point. This portrait of contemporary history as comprised of contrasting historical epochs, adjacent intervals in the 'flow of time' (*le temps qui coule*) divided by a major rupture in Villeneuvois life that took place (I was told) in the 1960s, was not just on show for outsiders such as myself. It was frequently conjured as a temporal and historical frame of reference for interpreting everyday events, and comprised a moral and temporalizing resource which *les Villeneuvois* used to decipher the contingencies of everyday existence and, at times, symbolically invoke their collective identity. Contemporary Villeneuve was said to exist in a flux of incessant changes, but this processual epoch was offset by an *enduring* idiom of how life was lived in the past, a collective portrait of a time prior to the 1960s when life was stable and unchanging that subverted the processual present.[15] Let us now explore the context for, and saliency of, this processual motif.

Villeneuve is a village of some 600 permanent inhabitants, and lies on a brackish lagoon bordering the Mediterranean Sea, some 10 kilometres from the city of Narbonne in southern France. The lagoon supports one of the two economic activities for which the village is locally renowned: it is still fished by a handful of artisanal fishermen for eels. As for the other, much of Villeneuve's arid, stony earth is planted with vines whose grapes produce the local variety of Corbières wine. The population, however, is far from comprising an integrated community living off fishing and agriculture. While 55 per cent of permanent residents claim to be from the village, the other 45 per cent are recent immigrants, and 30 per cent of the housing belongs to second-home owners, of predominantly urban, northern European origin.[16] These social distinctions as perceived by the anthropologist are viewed as such by local people as well. Any sense of community is thus fragmented, and ongoing tensions exist between Villeneuvois and other inhabitants – whom many Villeneuvois view as 'colonizing' the village in a pejorative sense, contributing to their marginalization and dispersal as a social group, and driving up house prices to an unaffordable degree. Agriculture and fishing are also no longer the dominant sources of employment: only 13 per cent of the village live exclusively off viticulture and fishing, as opposed to 75 per cent in 1946, and those who grow grapes do so to supplement an income derived from other jobs. More than 60 per cent of the active population work in the shops, service industries, and factories of nearby Narbonne.[17] The village council is also largely comprised of incomers; and the 'intangible cultural heritage' (UNESCO 2003), as we might term it, of indigenous Villeneuvois is increasingly appropriated for the heritage tourism projects of incomers.

If the preceding description comprises a contemporary snapshot of the village, during the 1960s life was significantly otherwise. To begin with, the population, 367 in 1968, stood at less than half its current number, and over 50 per cent of the village's working adults still laboured within the *commune*, chiefly in viticulture and fishing. Only a third of women worked, as opposed to two-thirds at the turn of the twenty-first century. Notably, second-home owners possessed a fifth of the available housing, and there were few incomers. The village still 'belonged', then, to the Villeneuvois. The chief ritual events of the year also revolved about established local industries: the *fête de la vendange* ('harvest fête') in October and the *fête des pêcheurs* ('fishermen's fête') in July were the mainstays of the year's festivities. They would disappear or pale in significance by the late 1970s, to be replaced by festivals that were increasingly orientated towards tourism by the early twenty-first century.

Villeneuve was rocked by the unstable political economy of viticultural capitalism throughout the late nineteenth and twentieth centuries, and is no stranger to change. But at a general level, many cultural features of everyday life in the 1960s also pertained to the 'deep' or 'enduring time'[18] of long-term traditional practices – from the cooking and eating of homegrown or locally hunted food, to the widespread playing of ritualized practical jokes, to the communal evening *veillées*.[19] Such everyday practices, which comprised core emblems of Villeneuvois belonging, had been consolidated in their current forms during the long nineteenth century of viticultural expansion, with the emergence of a Languedocian working class rooted in pre-capitalist 'peasant' living traditions (Fabre & Lacroix 1973). Ultimately, then, this enduring social time, if fractured and rent by the periodic convulsions of viticultural capitalism, still retained its potential for symbolization as the cusp of an epoch of long-term temporal continuity, in relation to the duration of a life being lived. This rendered the lived experience of the 1960s qualitatively different from life at the turn of the twenty-first century.

The 1970s, however, would bring the consolidation of ruptures in living traditions that were already in progress: the decline of viticulture and contraction of the agricultural workforce; new work in industries such as the Narbonne tile factory or supermarkets; the spread of car ownership and 'technologies of comfort' such as the washing machine; and a shift in the authority of living traditions symptomatic of the times. In sum, enduring time was being substituted by more *erratic* forms of social timespace.[20] Significantly, there was also a broadening of cultural horizons and conceptions of identity, as the mass media rendered Villeneuvois more conscious of a world beyond the immediately tangible. This encouraged local identification with regional, French, and European imagined communities (Anderson 1983). It also precipitated a rupture in the local temporal fabric,[21] as the past loosened its ties to the cultural media of communal oral history, to be invoked more frequently via the mass media of televised history, the local papers, the *lieu de mémoire*, on an expanded spatio-temporal scale (cf. Le Goff 1992: 90-7; Nora 1997). These historical transitions provided the foundation for contemporary conceptions of process and stasis, which I now address.

I have written at length elsewhere about how the manner in which Villeneuvois invoke a past of enduring social traditions is not validated by the historical record (Hodges 2010). Rather, it is more directly concerned with the positing of group belonging in relationship to a shared past. The contrast drawn by Villeneuvois between a processual present and a static past was thus partly an historical mythologization, exaggerating those enduring qualities of a communal past and the changeability of the present. Villeneuvois had in fact authored a myth of origin to satisfy the needs of the present – which had conspicuous precedents. Most significantly, this mythologization portrays the diverse population of the pre-1960s, comprised to a significant degree of migrants who had arrived to work in viticultural capitalism, as a small community dominated by relatives of contemporary indigenous residents. Such a portrait clearly strengthened indigenous claims to the locality at a time when their dominance was under threat by a new generation of incomers and economic developers.

If mythologization of the past was therefore a way of addressing present needs, when the contemporary epoch was invoked, it was done with greater ambivalence and complexity. Bringing into focus our interest in the processual, what is characteristic about the *contemporary* Villeneuvois epoch is thus its metaphorical grounding in *changement continuel*. In part, it was invoked and constituted in binary opposition to the previous epoch, to characterize a fluid present or runaway world; in part it made reference to a vague, open-ended, and unpredictable future of uncertainty and change. And the future itself was not usually given a secure character beyond this notional evocation of difference, although at times it might become a more empirical, nuanced set of possibilities, if queried. There is a clear parallel with radical modernist periodizations, of course. A past epoch of enduring time and organic community is set off against a contemporary era of disillusion, and *erratic time* – and imagined in local terms. Extending this parallel, the notion that contemporary societies subsist in a globalized panorama of continual change is a truism for modern social theory; as is the echo in anthropological theory that all human life is fluid, processual, and in a state of becoming beneath the multiplex cultural practices of global human diversity (Hodges 2008: 399-403). Putting aside evident differences, it is clear that such invocations – rural French, academic, anthropological – are *processual* at a foundational discursive level.[22]

Villeneuvois invocations of *changement continuel*, then, invoke wider processual tropes which are scaled to local contexts of cultural meaning and practice. In turn, the *time of the interval* in Villeneuve, this mythologized, communal past, furnishes a resource in the globalized, uncertain, processual timescapes of modern France, creating an 'interval' in local and wider hegemonic narratives of *changement continuel* to house enduring values and invoke collectivity. This invocation of an enduring idiom and past epoch also embodies the subversive alternative of a *non-processual* temporality; and implies that such a time of enduring social traditions might one day emerge. In

Villeneuve, then, processualism is rhetorically invoked as a shorthand for an encroach-
ing modernity and its local agents, and takes its place in a figurative and conceptual
scheme for local identity politics and resistance to such developments.

In sum, the Villeneuvois processual idiom invoked French-language tropes of
change, flow, and flux that conjured that 'integrated series of connected developments'
which Rescher (2000: 22) views as characteristic of processualism, with an ineliminable
temporal dimension. Yet it was focused on an open-ended, uncertain future, and
change, contingency, and emergence were thus viewed as endemic to it. While this
appears less structured than the processual biological idiom and legally sanctioned,
disciplinary processualism of the Apomixis Syndicate, it concords with contemporary
anthropological formulations of social life as flux-like, processual, and in a state of
becoming in a foundational sense. It is in this sense, then, that processualism can be
viewed as a polythetic category of cultural practice. Making 'process' visible as a
temporalizing practice, and placing it *within* the frame of social critique, enables
ethnographic purchase on this complexity. To achieve this, certain temporal assumptions latent in anthropological analysis must be set aside. How might the temporal
modalities of analysis be reconfigured to render this explicit?

Towards an immanent anthropology

Where should an 'anthropology of process' turn for critical precedents, in an academic
and wider world where the discourse of 'process' is dominant? Let us begin by extending our commentary on Arendt, before drawing out insights from the preceding examples and discussion. Arendt's critique of processualism is interwoven in a complex
fashion with her guiding theory of 'natality', and is recognized as a precursor of
Foucault's work on 'biopower' (Agamben 1998). She viewed the processual idiom and
processual temporalities as operating on multiple levels in society – some positive,
many negative. Processualism, she argues, gained ground with the growing hegemony
of scientific outlooks and the influence of historiography on Western historical consciousness, but was simultaneously embedded in the expansion of capitalist economic
organization, in which working activity is subordinated to end products and profit
(Arendt 1958). It took on instrumental roles in the operation of power within the
totalitarian regimes of the twentieth century (Arendt 1951), and is also a key feature of
so-called 'disciplinary societies' in the early twenty-first century (Hardt & Negri 2000).

Processualism is also central to Arendt's concept of natality. 'For Arendt', writes
Passerin d'Entrèves, 'the modern worldview is characterized by its emphasis on the idea
of process, on the "how" of phenomena, be they natural or historical, and by the
corresponding loss of the idea of Being' (1994: 53). The natality concept, by contrast,
highlights the human capacity to bring novelty into the world, thus disrupting the
automatism of processes (and the temporal continuum) and initiating emergent acts
and processes. The ontological fact of birth underwrites, for Arendt, this human
freedom, and is invoked each time an individual introduces some new action into the
world. Natality is central to Arendt's critique of the hegemonic processual temporalities
that, in her view, adversely fashioned key domains of twentieth-century cultural practice. It allowed her to argue for the value of the 'time interval between birth and death'
that could act as an existential frame with which to structure the span of a meaningful
human life (Arendt 1958: 97; cf. Braun 2007: 19-21). Ultimately, it enabled her to produce
a philosophical outlook that displaced 'process' from its symbolic and conceptual
throne and conjure a world in which alternative idioms and practices might crowd into

view, and 'time' itself take a differential form. Arendt's approach is thus multi-layered, granting recognition of the value of the process concept and the insights it permits – while enabling critique of its cultural hegemony and use as a totalizing frame.

Arendt provides a critical, socio-historical purchase on processual idioms and regimes that can inform ethnographic critique. The process concept is a dynamic temporal bridge between past and future that enables multiplex conceptual invention and co-ordinated action, in historically contingent forms (Rescher 2000). Processual idioms, often grounded in synoptic and organizational models of processual time, thereby serve foundational roles in processualist cultural practices, and processual regimes of truth in a range of contexts. The social-scientific processual idiom, in a comparable fashion, identifies 'time' as a foundational frame, and imagines it as a flow or flux that enables processual study – and, indeed, the continuities and transformations of real-world processes (Smith 1982). In this way, the world is conceptualized as a processual realm, and action and event are framed and subordinated to selected pasts and futures. To what extent, then, might this 'temporal ontology' obscure conflictive fields of temporal practice, social complexity, and related virtual sideshadows?[23] What does processual time render invisible that an immanent, differential temporal idiom could induce? And to what extent is its prominence in anthropological theory reflective of the hegemony of processualism, in its many forms, in contemporary societies, particularly as it pertains to neoliberal globalization?

Anthropology, as Bourdieu (1990) put it, is 'fieldwork in philosophy', and in this case, philosophical writings on temporal immanence offer a pathway to clarifying this anthropological problem. An 'immanent anthropology', substituted for a processual anthropology, does not imply a wholesale rejection of the 'processual turn'.[24] Rather, it demands nuanced recognition of the temporally constructed nature of processes – and other genres of continuity, rupture, and transformation, analytical and ethnographic – and an exploration of the consequences of such insights for anthropology. It finds an origin and foundation in a genealogy of thought that adheres to and informs the writings of philosophers of immanence such as Spinoza, Deleuze, Foucault, Bergson, or Nietzsche. The principal insight of such philosophers is an exclusion from conceptual schemes of any taken-for-granted assumptions of a transcendence of Being. All that exists of timespace resides and differentiates 'within' the living present. This might be conceptualized in terms of a Spinozan principle of 'immanent cause' which produces by remaining in itself, for example, or, for some philosophers, as a 'plane of immanence' (Deleuze & Guattari 1994). As Agamben writes: 'Immanence flows forth ... [y]et this springing forth, far from leaving itself, remains incessantly and vertiginously within itself' (2000: 226). In this sense, any event belonging to a 'process', conceived immanently, is a form of birth, with no transcendent or procedural frame (Whitehead 1979).[25]

Nevertheless, as Agamben points out, an aspiration to or invocation of transcendence cannot be wholly excluded from philosophical or social theories which adhere to the principles of immanence:

> [I]mmanence is not merely threatened by [the] illusion of transcendence, in which it is made to leave itself and to give birth to the transcendent. This illusion is, rather, something like a necessary illusion in Kant's sense, which immanence produces on its own and to which every philosopher falls prey even as he tries to adhere as closely as possible to the plane of immanence (Agamben 2000: 227).

In this regard, the illusion of transcendence is the corollary of any form of intelligible discourse, and Husserl (1966) provides one well-known, if problematic, model for how human consciousness subverts the immanence of being in time with his theory of 'internal time consciousness'. In temporal terms, then, a principal tenet of an immanent anthropology must be that discursive aspiration to temporal transcendence should be rendered *self-aware* – and, where appropriate, subverted. This operation would require a deconstruction of assumptions of transcendence inherent in social-scientific usages of process, and the substitution of a reflexive analytical frame ontologically grounded in temporal immanence that can accommodate the multiplicity of timespace.

This philosophical discourse of temporal immanence must now be reframed for anthropological practice. Let us draw on our ethnographies of 'process' as a starting-point. I have illustrated how a major shift in trajectory within frontier research in ag-biotech development was enabled by a foregrounding of processual idioms in knowledge practices, and processual agreements for public-private partnerships – a will-to-power that mediates the conflictive timescapes of research via legal sanction and a range of disciplinary procedures, thereby excluding undesirable sideshadows. I have examined how processual idioms operate quite distinctly in rural Languedoc, enabling discursive identification of an oppressive contemporary 'other' which enables resistance and subversion of cultural and economic hegemonies by local people. By utilizing an *immanent temporal frame*, it is possible to analyse how such processualism attains social form, and assess its efficacy, rather than taking process for granted as a foundational feature of social life. In the case of the Apomixis Syndicate, this informed a critical perspective on how processualism was a key element of transitional, disciplinary practices engineered to produce biocapital. In the case of Villeneuve, it enabled the identification and analysis of a processual idiom as a temporal critique of contemporary hegemonies, and facilitated a temporally nuanced interpretation of local identity politics. Both exploratory cases, taken comparatively, reveal the cultural embeddedness of processual idioms and temporalities, and the anthropological implications of analysing this cultural figure and organizational practice in its socio-historical context.

It would be an error to directly correlate how process operates in these contexts with social-scientific usages, which themselves are embedded and contingent. It should also be noted that philosophies of immanence have Western European origins.[26] Without doubt, an extended ethnographic study of links between metaphors of fluidity, change, process, and the social context of anthropological practice and writing would reveal much about processual practice among Western anthropologists. But it is clear from the theoretical literature cited above that discursive and organizational processualism enable temporal relations of continuity of action and an at times unreflexive analytical frame that are central to contemporary anthropological discourse, and would benefit from such analysis. In sum, 'processes' permit what is at stake in the rhythmic tension of the moment to be mediated by a transcendent linkage of past and future. Processualism is a key conceptual tool and action framework for willing pasts and futures into procedural alignment, whether at the level of wider cultural practice, or academic anthropological discourse. Let us conclude by critically assessing selected manifestations of timespace implicit in such practices, alongside conceptions afforded by an immanent perspective and tradition.[27]

Under the processual regime, time thus becomes the spatial flow which we colonize, rather than this differential, conflictive field of force which we conjure through our practices. In this sense, 'real time' exists in the same way for all social actors, just as reality is said to exist and we project our representations onto it – a temporal incarnation of the scheme-content distinction (cf. Davidson 1973; Henare, Hobraad & Wastell

2007: 12-14). Used as a doxic analytical frame, likewise, process 'cools' the tensions of becoming. It obscures the virtual 'fullness of time' (Morson 1994) through its monological focus on constructing interconnections between successive actualizations 'over time'. By contrast, the task of an anthropology of immanence is to render visible this act of mediation – while acknowledging that immanence itself, as 'reality in the making', must ultimately elude anthropological practices of conceptualization and representation (cf. de Beistegui 2010: 192). The actualization of an event is immanent in time – time is not the transcendent measurement of the event. 'Past and future', Turetzky writes, 'and consequently all time, arise in the moment. This moment is not in time as one moment among many in a container, it is time' (1998: 109). Time is likewise not a flowing or flux-like backdrop for anthropological analysis, but an emergent property of events. It is a differential multiplicity, materialistic, multi-vectorial, complex, aleatory (Deleuze 2004; Hodges 2008). Such images enable us to think process from Arendt's standpoint: as a contingent figure for configuring 'time' that both enables and disables; and as a concept that must be displaced from a totalizing discursive role, which often marks seminal social-scientific usages of 'process' (e.g. Bourdieu 1977; Smith 1982; Wolf 1982), if we are to detect the temporalizing practices and reterritorializations integral to how 'processes' are constructed.

'Processual practice' therefore operates to disembed and reincorporate intensities into pathways of actualization. We can recall that, when integrated with disciplinary programmes, this is a key dimension of practices of instrumentalization and rationalization (Feenberg 2004), as suggested by the first of our cases, above. One overlap between this wider processualism and totalizing invocations of process where they occur in social-scientific discourses lies in how the social sciences themselves can constitute disciplinary activities (see Hodges 2011). To be processed, to be disciplined, is to enter into procedure. All such disciplinary programmes arguably operate through making life available for re-embedding in processual cultural practices – that is to say, practices intended to create an ordered course of action or complex linkage between pasts and futures. Many are grounded in corresponding images of fluid time. Processualism, conceived polythetically, is perhaps the dominant temporality of the disciplinary society, in its many forms.[28] To create an interval in process, therefore, is an act of freedom in Arendt's sense: the time of the interval. Such intervals exist as perpetual sideshadows that many procedures may be said to work continuously to exclude (de Certeau 1984; Pickering 1995).

In this respect, it is important to displace these fluid idioms – to speak, at times, of the *pulse* of timespace, an immanent, differential pulsation which contracts and conflicts and in which everything is at stake;[29] or employ shifting metaphors, as appropriate, that reflect the topological qualities of timespace (e.g. Serres & Latour 1997); or view the eternal renewal of metaphors as a method for combating the transcendental impulse and engaging with immanence itself (de Beistegui 2010; Deleuze & Guattari 1988).[30] In this sense, the quest for an anthropology of immanence compels an 'immanent anthropology'. Concepts no longer constitute empty forms awaiting content, or different representations of the same social reality, but are actively produced in analytical and ethnographic practice. If this is comparable in some respects to the position advanced in the 'ontological turn' in anthropology, one notable omission from such debates is temporal nuance (cf. Hodges 2008). An immanent anthropology acknowledges the 'radical constructivism' endorsed by other anthropologists (e.g. Henare *et al.* 2007; Latour 2007; Viveiros de Castro 2002). Yet it engages with temporal immanence to reframe the radical construction of processes, for example, as socio-material temporalizing practices – concerned with the creation of epochal moments – rather than transcendent frames for analysis. Social life is no longer posited as existing within the 'flow of time', but as *generated in an immanent field*. 'Process' is an illuminating tool for analytical thought, but it should not dominate our theories of cultural practice. Conjuring such modalities of time might, ultimately, enable more effective anthropological purchase on conflictive, multiplex 'timespace in the making'; and inspire a complementary, radically constructivist anthropology of contingent temporal actualization – human and non-human – within time's plasticity.

NOTES

An earlier version of this paper was presented at 'Making Time Present', the final seminar of the ESRC seminar series 'Conflicts in Time: Rethinking "Contemporary" Globalization', convened by Laura Bear and Stephan Feuchtwang. I am very grateful to the convenors for providing such rewarding opportunities for discussion of the anthropology of time. My thanks also to colleagues at the seminar for their incisive feedback, and, in particular, to Michael Scott for his illuminating comments, and to Laura Bear for encouragement and inspiration.

[1] *The Concise Oxford Dictionary of English Etymology* defines process in this way: 'fact of going on or being carried on XIV; proceedings at law; outgrowth XVI; continuous operation XVII. (O)F. *procès* L. *prōcessus*, f.pp. stem of *prōcēdere* proceed'. See: *http://www.oxfordreference.com/views/ENTRY.%20html?subview=Main &entry=t27.e11947* (accessed 7 January 2014). Compare:

> **process** (n.): early 14C., 'fact of being carried on' (e.g. 'in process'), from O.Fr. *proces* 'journey' (13C.), from L. *processus* 'process, advance, progress,' from pp. stem of *procedere* 'go forward'. Meaning 'course or method of action' is from mid-14C.; sense of 'continuous series of actions meant to accomplish some result' (the main modern sense) is from 1620s (Dictionary.com, *http://dictionary.reference.com/browse/process*, accessed 7 January 2014).

[2] Fabian writes:

> As soon as a culture is no longer primarily conceived as a set of rules to be enacted by individual members of distinct groups, but as the specific way in which actors create and produce beliefs, values, and other means of social life, it has to be recognized that Time is a constitutive dimension of social reality (1983: 24).

[3] Lyman (2007: 220-4) reviews anthropological usages of process prior to the 1980s, illustrating how the trope did not occupy the foundational place it does today. In opening my paper with a contextualization of social-scientific usages of 'process' in relation to, and as implicitly emergent from, 'historical processes', I illustrate how the invocation and analytical construction of such processes is perhaps a 'necessary' and illuminating moment of contemporary anthropological framing. But as I argue in the final section of the paper, from an immanent perspective, it must be recognized as a conceptual *construction* and invocation, rather than an objectivist assertion (cf. Agamben 2000: 227).

[4] For Rescher:

> A process is an actual or possible occurrence that consists of an integrated series of connected developments ... that are systematically linked to one another either causally or functionally ... Processes develop over time: any particular ... process combines existence in the present with tentacles that reach into the past and future (2000: 22).

He identifies three key characteristics:

> 1. A process is a complex of occurrences – a unity of distinct stages or phases ... 2. This complex of occurrences has a certain temporal coherence and integrity, and processes accordingly have an ineliminably temporal dimension. 3. A process has a structure, a formal generic patterning of occurrence, through which its temporal phases exhibit a fixed format (2000: 24).

[5] See Bourdieu (2000: 206-45) for clarification of these issues, towards the end of his career.

[6] Consider also 'process philosophy'. Some process philosophers propose a transcendent concept of process comparable with contemporary social-scientific discourse. Others, such as Whitehead (1979), argue for a

radical conceptualization of 'process', closer to the immanent philosophy of Spinoza and Deleuze, asserting that any occasion belonging to a 'process' is an incidence ('concrescence') of novelty or form of 'birth' with no transcendent frame.

[7] See Hodges (2008: 408-17) for analysis of one possible foundation for the temporal ontology that underpins this approach.

[8] Agromonde is a French state-funded organization focused on research and consultancy in the fields of agriculture, biodiversity, and the environment, chiefly for the developing world. Pseudonyms are used for companies and individuals mentioned here, and some inconsequential details have been changed for legal and confidential reasons.

[9] 'International Rice and Wheat Improvement Centre'.

[10] Hodges (2012) provides a study of Marceau's project and its transformation into the 'Apomixis Syndicate'.

[11] For example, *Triticum aestivum* (common bread wheat).

[12] T-GURT is a 'genetic use restriction technology' that allows seed saving, but any genetic enhancements require activation by a spray. V-GURT controls GM plants by ensuring that second-generation seeds are not fertile. These are known as 'terminator-technologies' and are currently subject to a UN moratorium.

[13] Landecker views this as part of a wide-ranging temporal transformation: 'The operationalization of biological time is a dominant characteristic of the interactions of humans and cells in technical environments over the last fifty years. In short, living matter is now assumed to be stuff that can be stopped and started at will' (2007: 232-3).

[14] 'Sideshadowing relies on a concept of time as a *field of possibilities*. Each moment has a set of possible events (though by no means every conceivable event) that could take place in it. From this field a single event emerges ... Sideshadowing restores the field and thereby recreates the *fullness of time* as it was ... we do not see contradictory actualities, but one possibility that was actualized and, at the same moment, another that could have been but was not' (Morson 1994: 118, 120-1). Sideshadows can be of ephemeral or durable consequence. Their potential for actualization can be tied to a contingent historical context or endure. Timespace can thus be grasped as emergent, differential, and dialogical, incorporating the actual *and* its virtual sideshadows (Hodges 2012: 26-7; cf. Deleuze 2004). Giving processual 'direction' to cultural practice requires obviating selected sideshadows, and actualizing others.

[15] I analyse this periodization in Hodges (2010), providing more detail than is possible here.

[16] This overview masks differentiation within these social groupings.

[17] Censuses of 1946 and 1999.

[18] For Gurvitch, *enduring time* is where

> the past is projected in the present and in the future. This is the most continuous of the social times despite its retention of some proportion of the qualitative and the contingent penetrated with multiple meanings ... Among the social classes it is the peasant class, and among the global societies the patriarchal structures which appear to actualize this time (1964: 31).

[19] In rural France, a *veillée* was a 'vigil' (*veille*) or gathering of villagers during the evening, to work alongside each other while telling stories, for example. These have now largely disappeared. In Villeneuve, they were known as '*les clubs*'.

[20] *Erratic time* is that

> enigmatic series of intervals and moments placed within duration. This is a time of uncertainty par excellence where contingency is accentuated, while the qualitative element and discontinuity become prominent eventually. The present appears to prevail over the past and the future, with which it sometimes finds it difficult to enter into relations ... This is the time of global societies in transition, as our society of today so often is (Gurvitch 1964: 32-3).

[21] Those cultural media used for the evocation and co-ordination of time and activities, and time's dimensions (past-present-future). These might include calendars, clocks, and so on, involved in 'time-reckoning'; but also other symbolic media such as language with its complex temporal markers or narrative genres (cf. Gell 1992: 118-26).

[22] Berger expresses this worldview succinctly when he writes: 'History ... no longer speaks of the changeless but, rather, of the laws of change which spare nothing' (1984: 12). Arendt is more pithy: 'In the place of the concept of Being we now find the concept of Process' (1958: 296-7).

[23] See note 14.

Journal of the Royal Anthropological Institute (N.S.), 33-51
© Royal Anthropological Institute 2014

[24] An 'immanent anthropology' should be distinguished from influential forms of 'immanent critique' associated with the Frankfurt School, although this is not to say that they are incompatible. Likewise, no theological association is intended.

[25] Deleuze writes: '[W]e have no other continuities apart from those of our thousands of component habits', yet '[h]abit draws something new from repetition – namely difference' (2004: 94-5).

[26] Immanence is also a feature of philosophical systems from other parts of the world, for example Zen Buddhism.

[27] An allowance should be made for the limited number of social-scientific approaches grounded in Whitehead (1979) and comparable process philosophers. See note 6.

[28] Hardt and Negri gloss:

> The disciplinary society is ... constructed through a diffuse network of ... apparatuses that produce and regulate customs, habits, and productive practices ... [D]isciplinary institutions (the prison, the factory, the asylum, the hospital, the university, the school, and so forth) ... structure the social terrain and present logics adequate to the 'reason' of discipline. Disciplinary power rules in effect by structuring the parameters and limits of thought and practice (2000: 23).

[29] Turetzky writes of Nietzsche's philosophy of time: 'Time is not a flow, but a pulsation. If time merely flowed it would lack tension and no differentiation would occur. The whole of time is at stake in the rhythmic tension of the moment' (1998: 109).

[30] As de Beistegui writes:

> [I]mmanence always remains to be made, that is, conceptualized. This, however, does not amount to turning immanence into a concept ... [T]he plane of immanence is never given as such, or fully intuited; it needs to be drawn through the creation of concepts. In a sense, such a task is never-ending ... (2010: 24).

REFERENCES

ADAM, B. 1998. *Timescapes of modernity: the environment and invisible hazards.* London: Routledge.

AGAMBEN, G. 1993. Time and history: critique of the instant and the continuum. In *Infancy and history: essays on the destruction of experience*, 89-106. London: Verso.

――― 1998. *Homo sacer: sovereign power and bare life.* Stanford: University Press.

――― 2000. Absolute immanence. In *Potentialities: collected essays in philosophy*, 220-39. Stanford: University Press.

ANDERSON, B. 1983. *Imagined communities: reflections on the origin and spread of nationalism.* London: Verso.

ARENDT, H. 1951. *The origins of totalitarianism.* New York: Harcourt, Brace.

――― 1958. *The human condition.* Chicago: University Press.

――― 1968. The concept of history. In *Between past and future*, 41-90. New York: Viking.

ASAD, T., J. FERNANDEZ, M. HERZFELD, A. LASS, S.R. ROGERS, J. SCHNEIDER & K. VERDERY 1997. Provocations of European ethnology. *American Anthropologist* **99**, 713-30.

BARNES, J. 1987. *Early Greek philosophy.* London: Penguin.

BERGER, J. 1984. *And our faces, my heart, brief as photos.* London: Writers and Readers.

BLACKWELL, T. & J. SEABROOK 1993. *The revolt against change: towards a conserving radicalism.* London: Vintage.

BOURDIEU, P. 1977. *Outline of a theory of practice.* Cambridge: University Press.

――― 1990. *The logic of practice.* Cambridge: Polity.

――― 2000. *Pascalian meditations.* Cambridge: Polity.

BRAUDEL, F. 1994. *The identity of France*, vol. 1: *History and environment.* London: Fontana.

BRAUN, K. 2007. Biopolitics and temporality in Arendt and Foucault. *Time and Society* **16**: 5, 5-23.

DAVIDSON, D. 1973. On the very idea of a conceptual scheme. *Proceedings and Addresses of the American Philosophical Association* **47**, 5-20.

DE BEISTEGUI, M. 2010. *Immanence: Deleuze and philosophy.* Edinburgh: University Press.

DE CERTEAU, M. 1984. *The practice of everyday life.* Berkeley: University of California Press.

DELEUZE, G. 2004. *Difference and repetition.* London: Continuum.

――― & F. GUATTARI 1988. *A thousand plateaus: capitalism and schizophrenia.* London: Athlone.

――― & ――― 1994. *What is philosophy?* London: Verso.

FABIAN, J. 1983. *Time and the other: how anthropology makes its object.* New York: Columbia University Press.

FABRE, D. & J. LACROIX 1973. *La vie quotidienne des paysans du Languedoc au XIXe siècle.* Paris: Hachette.

Feenberg, A. 2004. Modernity theory and technology studies: reflections on bridging the gap. In *Modernity and technology* (eds) T.J. Misa, P. Bray & A. Feenberg, 73-104. Cambridge, Mass.: MIT Press.

——— 2005. *Heidegger and Marcuse: the catastrophe and redemption of history*. New York: Routledge.

Foucault, M. 1977. *Discipline and punish: the birth of the prison*. London: Allen Lane.

——— 1980. *Power/knowledge*. London: Harvester Wheatsheaf.

Gell, A. 1992. *The anthropology of time: cultural constructions of temporal maps and images*. Oxford: Berg.

Giddens, A. 1979. *Central problems in social theory*. London: Macmillan.

Grimanelli, D., E. Perotti, J. Ramirez & O. Leblanc 2005. Timing of the maternal-to-zygotic transition during early seed development in maize. *Plant Cell* **17**, 1061-72.

———, J. Tohme & D. González-León 2001. Applications of molecular genetics in apomixis research. In *The flowering of apomixis* (eds) Y. Savidan, J.G. Carman & T. Dresselhaus, 83-94. Mexico DF: CIMMYT.

Gupta, A. & J. Ferguson 1997. *Culture, power, place: explorations in critical anthropology*. Durham, N.C.: Duke University Press.

Gurvitch, G. 1964. *The spectrum of social time*. Dordrecht: D. Reidel.

Hardt, M. & A. Negri 2000. *Empire*. Cambridge, Mass.: Harvard University Press.

Heidegger, M. 1993. The question concerning technology. In *Basic writings*, 307-42. London: Routledge.

Helmreich, S. 2007. Blue-green capital, biotechnological circulation and an oceanic imaginary: a critique of biopolitical economy. *BioSocieties* **2**, 287-302.

Henare, A., M. Holbraad & S. Wastell 2007. Introduction: thinking through things. In *Thinking through things: theorising artefacts ethnographically*, 1-32. London: Routledge.

Hodges, M. 2008. Rethinking time's arrow: Bergson, Deleuze and the anthropology of time. *Anthropological Theory* **8**, 399-429.

——— 2010. The time of the interval: historicity, modernity, and epoch in rural France. *American Ethnologist* **37**, 115-31.

——— 2011. Disciplinary anthropology? Amateur ethnography and the production of 'heritage' in rural France. *Ethnos* **73**, 348-74.

——— 2012. The politics of emergence: public-private partnerships and the conflictive timescapes of apomixis technology development. *BioSocieties* **7**, 23-49.

Husserl, E. 1966. *The phenomenology of internal time-consciousness*. Bloomington: Indiana University Press.

Jameson, F. 1991. *Postmodernism, or, the cultural logic of late capitalism*. Durham, N.C.: Duke University Press.

——— 1998. *Brecht and method*. London: Verso.

Koltunow, A. & U. Grossniklaus 2003. Apomixis: a developmental perspective. *Annual Review of Plant Biology* **54**, 547-74.

Koselleck, R. 1985. *Futures past: on the semantics of historical time*. Cambridge, Mass.: MIT Press.

Landecker, H. 2005. Living differently in time: plasticity, temporality and cellular biotechnologies. *Culture Machine* **7** (e-journal available on-line: *http://www.culturemachine.net/index.php/cm/article/viewArticle/26/33*, accessed 7 January 2014).

——— 2007. *Culturing life: how cells became technologies*. Cambridge, Mass.: Harvard University Press.

Latour, B. 2007. *Reassembling the social: an introduction to actor-network theory*. Oxford: University Press.

Leblanc, O., D. Grimanelli, M. Hernández-Rodriguez, P.A. Galindo, A.M. Soriano-Martinez & E. Perotti 2009. Seed development and inheritance studies in apomictic maize-*tripsacum* hybrids reveal barriers for the transfer of apomixis into sexual crops. *International Journal of Developmental Biology* **53**, 585-96.

Le Goff, J. 1992. *History and memory*. New York: Columbia University Press.

Lyman, R.L. 2007. What is the 'process' in cultural process and in processual archaeology? *Anthropological Theory* **7**, 217-50.

Merleau-Ponty, M. 1962. *The phenomenology of perception*. London: Routledge.

Morson, G.S. 1994. *Narrative and freedom: the shadows of time*. New Haven: Yale University Press.

Munn, N. 1992. The cultural anthropology of time: a critical essay. *Annual Review of Anthropology* **21**, 93-123.

Nora, P. 1997. *Les lieux de mémoire* (3 vols). Paris: Gallimard.

Osborne, P. 1995. *The politics of time: modernity and the avant-garde*. London: Verso.

Passerin d'Entrèves, M. 1994. *The political philosophy of Hannah Arendt*. London: Routledge.

Pickering, A. 1995. *The mangle of practice: time, agency and science*. Chicago: University Press.

——— 2008. New ontologies. In *The mangle in practice: science, society, and becoming* (eds) A. Pickering & K. Guzik, 1-14. Durham, N.C.: Duke University Press.

Rescher, N. 2000. *Process philosophy*. Pittsburgh: University Press.

RICHARDS, P. 2004. Private versus public? Agenda-setting in international agro-technologies. In *Agribusiness and society: corporate response to environmentalism, market opportunities and public regulation* (eds) K. Jansen & S. Vellema, 261-88. London: Zed Books.

ROSE, N. 2007. *The politics of life itself: biomedicine, power, and subjectivity in the twenty-first century.* Princeton: University Press.

SCHUTZ, A. 1967. *The phenomenology of the social world.* Evanston, Ill.: Northwestern University Press.

SERRES, M. & B. LATOUR 1997. *Conversations on science, culture, and time.* Ann Arbor: University of Michigan Press.

SMITH, M.E. 1982. The process of sociocultural continuity. *Current Anthropology* **23**, 127-42.

THOMPSON, E.P. 1967. Time, work-discipline, and industrial capitalism. *Past and Present* **38**, 56-97.

TURETZKY, P. 1998. *Time.* London: Routledge.

TURNER, V. 1969. *The ritual process: structure and anti-structure.* Ithaca, N.Y.: Cornell University Press.

UNESCO 2003. Convention for the safeguarding of the intangible cultural heritage (available on-line: *http://www.unesco.org/culture/ich/index.php?pg=00006*, accessed 7 January 2014).

VIVEIROS DE CASTRO, E. 2002. O nativo relativo. *Mana* **8**, 113-48.

WHITE, L.A. 1959. *The evolution of culture.* New York: McGraw-Hill.

WHITEHEAD, A.N. 1979. *Process and reality.* New York: Free Press.

WOLF, E. 1982. *Europe and the people without history.* Berkeley: University of California Press.

L'anthropologie immanente : étude comparative du « processus » dans la France contemporaine

Résumé

Le présent article présente une critique comparative des « temporalités processuelles » qui sous-tendent les théories socioscientifiques aussi bien que certaines pratiques culturelles occidentales. À travers l'étude d'un partenariat public-privé, dans le cadre d'un projet de biotechnologie destiné à produire du maïs « auto-clonant » pour les agriculteurs à faible niveau de ressources, j'analyse la manière dont les temporalités processuelles sont essentielles pour réorienter les pratiques de savoir vers des solutions orientées vers le marché. En étudiant les caractérisation de « l'état de flux » qui affecte la vie d'un village périurbain français, j'explore la manière dont le processualisme est identifié comme une composante de l'hégémonie métropolitaine, à laquelle les villageois « résistent » au travers de « temporalités durables » de la pratique culturelle. En m'inspirant d'Arendt et de Deleuze, j'analyse le processualisme comme un chronotope contemporain dominant, qui médie et discipline des temporalités et des pratiques en conflit et sous-tend les projets économiques de déterritorialisation et de restructuration, dont le langage domine aussi les paradigmes socioscientifiques. Je lui substitue une « anthropologie immanente », favorable à une ontologie non transcendantale de la pratique et de l'analyse culturelle, en déplaçant l'analyse anthropologique vers une base temporelle polychrone.

2

Post-industrial times and the unexpected: endurance and sustainability in Germany's fastest-shrinking city

FELIX RINGEL *University of Vienna*

This paper investigates the impact of recent politico-economic changes on contemporary experiences of time from the perspective of the future. By discussing endurance, permanence, and sustainability in Germany's fastest-shrinking city, I present a set of future-orientated practices which are post-industrial, but unexpectedly so: namely, hopeful and not subject to the widely attested phenomenon of 'enforced presentism'. I subsequently position the temporal logics of endurance and sustainability against current academic responses to accelerated change, captured in the misleading uses of the Deleuzian concepts of emergence and becoming. My informants' epistemic investments in the future allow for a different understanding of what I describe as post-industrial temporal agency and the conflictive politics that shape these otherwise unexpected temporal relations.

> No matter what is given to see, we persist in seeing alternatives – often very possible ones that are implicit in the forms we see as dominant.
> But why can't we be realists and demand impossible hopes – in different times?
>
> Maurer 2005[1]

The closing lines of Bill Maurer's 2005 conference paper on 'Chronotypes of the alternative' might seem out of place in an introduction to a paper on permanence and endurance in Hoyerswerda, Germany's fastest-shrinking city. Maurer's general urge for alternatives is a very common trope among contemporary social scientists, including some of the currently most prominent anthropologists (cf. Ringel 2012); it is part of our own academic imaginaries and personal hopes in times that many refer to as 'postmodern', 'neoliberal', or – as I do in reference to my fieldsite – 'post-industrial'. However, Maurer gives this common source of relevance for contemporary anthropology an interesting twist by claiming that we should be realists and demand *impossible* alternatives. Accordingly, being realistic means striving *against* what is dominantly expected rather than towards what is *not-yet* expected. It entails a different form of temporal agency – an unforeseen relationship to *other* times and *other* futures.

This impossible hope for the non-appearance of the expectable (to rephrase) can only be realistic if the locally dominant form of knowledge in time – the one of post-industrial decline, in relation to which this hope is positioned – turns out to be unrealistic, out-of-date, or inaccurate in its predictions of the future. Although clearly

Journal of the Royal Anthropological Institute (N.S.), 52-70
© Royal Anthropological Institute 2014

faced with a predictably worse future, many Hoyerswerdians continuously fight for the survival of the forms of their social, relational, material, and economic environment – rather than, as would be expected, hope for something new to emerge. In times of post-reunification shrinkage and decline, when half of the city's population has left their hometown and a third of the cityscape has subsequently been demolished, this fight often seems unrealistic; yet, still, people in my field strive for permanence in a context otherwise increasingly and often literally deteriorating. They practically and concretely appropriate, indeed shape and structure, their own 'near future'. This near future, in turn, appears in our times to be 'evacuated' worldwide, according to Jane Guyer's seminal article on 'temporal reasoning': that is, on the different ways of 'implicating oneself in the ongoing life of the social and material world' (2007: 409). This should apply even more forcefully in a settlement once built for the socialist future as the GDR's second model city.

Plans for Hoyerswerda's New City (subsequently: Neustadt) in the mid-1950s included the erection of seven living complexes along a grand *Magistrale*. As the nearby lignite industrial complex demanded increasingly more workers, its settlement quickly extended by three further districts, accommodating a population that was skyrocketing from the Old City's initial 7,000 to over 80,000 inhabitants. Socialist life in a proper modernist setting flourished towards a thoroughly planned communist future: schools, sport clubs, and cultural associations emerged everywhere. Neighbourhoods or single staircases (*Aufgänge*) of the increasingly taller socialist apartment houses held their Saturday voluntary work sessions (*Subbotniks*) or organized house parties in their fondly decorated basement club rooms (*Klubräume*). The city's social life was structured by the three work-shifts in the surrounding mines, factories, and power stations – for which countless buses would leave and return from the city's main terminal.

These buses stopped running with the rapid modernization of the East German coal industry in the early 1990s. A vast majority of jobs were made redundant. Hoyerswerda suddenly experienced a decline that, as many informants underlined, was – in peacetime – unprecedented in human history. Younger people, especially, left in their thousands each year. Neustadt's population shrank back to today's meagre 21,000 inhabitants; and with the end of the twentieth century Hoyerswerdians saw their first apartment houses being demolished – only a few decades after their completion. However, this socio-economic shrinkage does not only affect the legacies of socialism. Even post-socialist buildings such as small shopping centres on Hoyerswerda's outskirts stand abandoned since most of their former users have left the city. Furthermore, this sudden de-industrialization also severely affects the city's once tightly knit social fabric. Without exception, all social, cultural, political, and economic institutions face persistent hardship – if not their actual redundancy and closure. The generation who once built this city materially and socially now witness not only Hoyerswerda's physical deconstruction, but also the demolition and closure of former bars and restaurants, doctors' practices, sports grounds, youth clubs, kindergartens, schools, and other parts of the city's social infrastructure.

However, stemming from a certain hopeful and anticipatory, but at the same time pragmatic and conservative, form of 'temporal reasoning', my informants maintain in their representations of the future what seems to be threatened by such dystopian representations of Hoyerswerda's certainly difficult present. They thereby exercise a very specific form of temporal agency in their many practices targeting their local

Journal of the Royal Anthropological Institute (N.S.), 52-70
© Royal Anthropological Institute 2014

futures. I take this agency to be indicative of the role that the future plays in human life and experience in contemporary post-industrial times. Consequently, I argue against a whole variety of other presumably dominant and expected relations to – and conceptualizations and experiences of – time and the future in such fieldsites: the temporal regimes of post-socialist transition and failure; the temporal order of post-industrial decline off the beaten track of a neoliberally orchestrated globalization; and, importantly, the epistemic proposition of hope imposed by the currently dominant anthropological modes of temporal reasoning captured in particular authors' use of such terms as 'becoming' and 'emergence'. Beyond a surprising heterogeneity of different forms of temporal reasoning and the many local socio-political clashes resulting from them (Ringel 2013), it is an unexpected return to surprisingly 'conservative' modernist and – at the same time – counter-intuitively progressive understandings of time and the future. I focus on that understanding through the lens of my ethnographic material with Maurer's twist in mind.

This paper looks at several different practices of endurance. It starts with some more general observations and then explores in more depth one communal example of the practical re-appropriation of the (near) future. This example concerns the fight over the reconstruction and future use of one of Hoyerswerda's most prestigious buildings. I focus on both the continuous work my informants put into rescuing this building from a very probable future of decay and collapse (or its sale to private investors), and the all-pervasive use of (post-industrial) tropes and figures of sustainability instead of progress and growth (or the latters' variant of decline). These tropes dominate local discourses and involve a different imaginary of the future, which actively targets and reclaims the previously evacuated near future. My informants refer to this continuous process as *die Zukunft gestalten*: giving gestalt, a certain form or shape, to the future. This is a slightly different conceptualization of the future than the modernist idea of linear progress or the postmodern reduction of the future to continuous emergence. Despite Hegel's description of the future as 'formless' (cited in Bloch 1986 [1959]: 883), I emphasize how people in 'inchoate' circumstances (Carrithers 2007) – which are characteristic of the era of post-socialism – engage in the maintenance of established forms and structures in their lives and practices.

In the last part of this paper, I will engage critically with three analytical tools that exemplify how anthropology came to approach issues of time and accelerated change: emergence, becoming, and assemblage. Instead of debunking these terms, I want to link them strongly to my informants' experiences of time and pose the question of how such presumably emergent and continuously becoming forms are made to endure. This focus on the aftermath of emergence analytically underlines the efficacy of human practice, investigating the topic of (temporal) agency without denying aspects of contingency and indeterminacy. I claim that by giving particular material objects, forms of practice – communal or otherwise – and social institutions a direction to the future, my informants maintain a sense of vigilant anticipation of the future, which is linked to a hard-won hope in their own efficacy rather than a distribution of agency away from them. This sense of agency is not simply a matter of survival or a (typically post-socialist) pragmatic approach to life in reaction to the impossibility of knowing the future of an 'everlasting present' (Baxstrom 2012) – or of Guyer's 'enforced presentism' (2007). Instead, the citizens of Hoyerswerda are invoking a form of agency that, in Maurer's words, demands the impossible: it transcends the present by striving to make this very present practically endure against all odds.

New traditions and practices of permanence

I begin with a simple observation: during my fieldwork in 2008/9, I often heard people proudly referring to a recurrent event as a 'new tradition' (*neue Tradition*). At most anniversary celebrations of the many post-1989-founded clubs and associations, the Lord Mayor or his deputy stressed the 'by now traditional character' of these social institutions in their congratulatory speeches. At more recent celebrations, they repeatedly expressed the hope of more of these events to come by underlining 'how wonderful and important this new tradition for the city is' and 'how much it is already an essential part of local socio-cultural life'. But even beyond official addresses, people in private celebrations expressed their joy about a recurrent occasion and called it their 'own little new tradition'. The notion of 'new tradition' also recurrently appeared in the local newspaper, most interestingly in a local journalist's critical response to the County District Administrator's opening speech at the *Second* (!) Lusation Lake District Fair.[2] Whilst praising the fair and wishing it good luck for the future, the Administrator had declared that presently 'everything from three times onward is a tradition' ('Alles ab drei Mal ist Tradition'). In his article, the journalist asks acrimoniously which jubilee should constitute something as 'traditional' – one hundred, fifty, or twenty years? He favours a minimum of ten years, but feels obliged to resign subserviently to the new official verdict. Despite such irony, the logic of 'new traditions' widely prevailed and expressed a certain hope for – and appreciation of – endurance of valued social forms of the present irrespective of their past.

As a remark on an – itself – traditional anthropological topic, the somewhat paradoxical phrase draws attention to traditions' own 'inventedness' (Hobsbawm & Ranger 1983), but turns their predictable temporal claims on the past upside-down. Instead of linking a recurrent event in the present to its apparent predecessors in the past, many of my informants did the opposite: they linked a recurrent event in the present to its anticipated, desired, or intended recurring successors. They hence gave relevance and meaning to an event in the present by granting it the quality of endurance. For a city with a dramatically fractured relationship to its still delegitimized vanguard, at times glorious, socialist past – its Neustadt proudly constituted the first city in the world to be erected solely by industrially pre-fabricated concrete units – an epistemic evacuation of the socialist past seems expectable. In fact, neither the infamous East German variant of nostalgia, *Ostalgie* (cf. Berdahl 2009; Boyer 2006), nor an in-depth evaluation of the GDR era beyond its ideological delegitimization in local politics of the past was a common phenomenon. The notion of 'new traditions' is more a response to a loss of the *post-socialist* future as well as the contemporarily visible and omnisciently tangible material demolition of one's everyday environment. But Hoyerswerdians are thereby not only giving their present a (near) future against Guyer's observation and in support of Crapanzano's subsequent urge for considering a greater variety of temporal practices (both 2007). Rather, they are giving these social forms a tradition with regards to the future; their future, not their present, has pre-emptively been given a past. By looking at the present not as an endpoint or outcome of a tradition (which was previously seen to constitute its capacity to endure further), they reverse the temporal order in looking at a specific event as the starting-point of a new tradition. However, is claiming a new tradition an expression of an 'anticipatory consciousness', in Blochian terms (1986 [1959])? Is the hope for something to endure the same as the hope for the 'not-yet-become': that is, the emergent, virtual, and potential, which Bloch and his recent Deleuzian discussants so strongly favour?

For a city like Hoyerswerda, endurance in time is, indeed, a pressing, but hopeful, since improbable, concern. Having lived through the peaceful revolution of 1989/90 and the following years of dramatic change, my informants' understanding of traditions is less fixed to the past. In contrast to the rural revival of local Sorbic traditions,[3] which fits more easily within common definitions of traditions, the urban invocation of 'new traditions' dwells on a strong relationship to the future. Following Olivia Harris's (1996; 2004) interventions, we should take investments in traditions seriously, and in turn question our own discipline's currently fashionable focus on events, emergence, potentiality, and new alternatives. As Harris pointed out, people are not ideologically dominated when they subscribe to notions of tradition and continuity – even more so, I argue, if these traditions refer to the future. The experience of decline, in fact, alters the meaning of 'conservative' usually attached to a past-orientated notion of tradition. Such practices can be understood as acts of agency along the lines of Mahmood's influential study of ethics and agency amongst a women's pious movement in Egypt (2001; 2005), Berlant's 'lateral' reformulation of agency as an 'activity of maintenance, not making' (2007: 759), or Povinelli's (2011) sophisticated account of 'perseverance' and 'endurance' in late liberalism. I here approach them through the epistemic *and* practical difference they make *vis-à-vis* a variety of dominant regimes of (non-) futurity. Despite their conservative undertones, new traditions can be seen as hopeful practices of the future, which exhibit actual transformative effects and help to secure and shape my informants' impossible futures.

For instance, the many archiving and documenting practices by Hoyerswerdian clubs and associations seem conservative or past-orientated at first sight. However, they subscribe to the same temporal logic as new traditions in their own striving for future endurance. Especially in the socio-cultural milieu, so heavily dependent on state funding, a whole year's projects and activities are carefully documented: firstly, in order to preserve the memories and accounts of things accomplished, and, secondly, for procuring the club's survival in the future. Such documentations are used for proving (as much to oneself as) to local authorities or potential sponsors one's worth, right, and ability for continuous existence, emphasizing one's eligibility for external funding. They are therefore, in a double sense, techniques to create a future: imaginarily as a commemorative trace of the past present that is made to last (again, giving these presents a form and a future) and actually as the promise of – and basis for – continuity in time. I have seen countless folders with pictures, collections of leaflets, and posters; internet archives of photos, short movies, and collections of media coverage.[4] Whereas some clubs passionately decorate their collections of photographs of the preceding year's events with coloured pens, others excel in producing little videos that are posted, stored, and rendered accessible on the club's website. Such documentation entails a general promise of endurance in the future. Similar concerns with the future are prevalent in most clubs, associations, schools, or private companies. Coverage in local and regional media, especially, is seen as a highly valued currency to gain public reputation and support for one's future survival. Documenting practices are thus seen as efficacious investments in the endurance of one's institution. For most Hoyerswerdians, this practical construction of a new tradition is one of the many constant investments in the forms that make up their life. It requires considerable time, money, and personal commitment. Against better knowledge and bleak prospects, many citizens – whether organized in social organizations or not – maintain these forms with a perspective set on the future, not the past. Or to be more precise: after severe and existential struggles throughout the post-socialist era, they came to be able to deploy this alternative temporal logic by freeing themselves from the epistemic limits imposed by the idea of shrinkage and 'no future'. In the next part, I will concentrate on the work invested in the survival of one particular building and introduce the notion of sustainability in order to elaborate on its temporal and hopeful logic.

However, that the post-industrial notion of sustainability can itself gain so much currency in Hoyerswerda is a new phenomenon. It indicates a general shift in the civic space since an invocation of a sustainable future forcefully claims that the city itself and particular social institutions, practices, and relations in it do have – after all – a future. Whereas this seems commonly to be expected in areas of growth and prosperity, and particularly in institutional settings, it is far from obvious in a city which has seen so much outmigration, closure, and unforeseen deconstruction. The social personnel we are to encounter below are therefore not just the average members of a civic organi-zation who strive for their own professional survival or expresses the elsewhere pre-dictable logic of institutional endurance. The opposite is true: whilst attempting to convince others as much as themselves of a potential endurance in the future, all of the people involved in the struggles described in the succeeding section have to counter what they have been convinced by on a daily basis and throughout recent decades: the impossibility of planning the local future; the fragility of Hoyerswerda's social and institutional infrastructure; and the survival of the city as a whole. It is therefore even more surprising that in the public sphere of Germany's fastest-shrinking city a civic claim to endurance can convincingly take place; indeed, that the citizenry (and all of the club representatives mentioned below are from – and continue to live in – Hoyerswerda) can re-constitute itself along such lines.

The following ethnographic example thus entails only one of the many concrete occasions of the re-appropriation of the city's near future, whose driving logic can be characterized as one of a hope for endurance (as change) rather than for change (as change). It brings together three different (and competing) clubs *vis-à-vis* the city government, whose official evacuation of the near future they oppose through their claims to sustainability and endurance. These clubs are only three prominent examples of a surprisingly vibrant civic sphere, in which both the few remaining clubs from socialist times and the many associations newly founded after German reunification continue to search for the right strategies, tools, and arguments to secure the city's and their clubs' survival. In 2008/9, the logics of endurance and sustainability gained centre-stage in these struggles. Although seemingly dominant in many (post-industrial) parts of the world, they entail a novel relationship to the process of shrink-age, which so easily predicts and takes for granted the demise and closure of Hoyerswerda's social infrastructure.

Claiming sustainability: the future of Braugasse 1

Some of the many endangered houses in Hoyerswerda carry a higher symbolic value in an ever-disappearing architectural environment. The building Braugasse Nr 1 (1 Brewing Alley) is one of them. Owing to its severe state of dilapidation, it was closed by the city in 2000. Since then the building's disrepair has made it look very much out of place, a ruin more than a house so heavily invested with hopes, dreams, and futures. Many people are awaiting its renovation and reopening. It is one of Hoyerswerda's most central and popular buildings, located at the Old City's market square. Since its construction more than a century ago, it has already functioned as a ballroom, a

Journal of the Royal Anthropological Institute (N.S.), 52-70
© Royal Anthropological Institute 2014

grammar school, and a youth club. The city council as much as the local government had repeatedly declared their full commitment to trying to acquire the external funding needed for its reconstruction. However, these wishes were continuously disappointed over the last decade. In response, a new club – the 'Braugasse 1 e.V.' – was founded by a politically diverse range of committed citizens in March 2006. One of their interventions aiming at promoting this building's renovation was initiated by the head of the socio-cultural club Cultural Factory (KuFa e.V.), the building's last user. This intervention, as he informed us one Sunday morning at a cultural brunch in the 'Temporary Occupancy' (*Zwischenbelegung*), the KuFa's 'interim' exile after evacuating Braugasse 1, was an idea copied from a Tibetan tradition.

In Tibet, we were told, people who go on long journeys or start other major endeavours attach wishing scarves to holy trees or erected monuments. On these scarves, they write their wishes, and hope that the supernatural force related to the place of worship will help them make this wish come true. Accordingly, all supporters of a renovation of Braugasse 1 were invited to take pieces of old linen, tear them into strips, write their wishes for the building on them, and attach them to the house's fences. The idea was enthusiastically received and many of the approximately seventy attendants at the brunch soon pursued it. The strips of linen bore wishes, dreams, and hopes referring to the building's future. Some simply read 'Children's laughter', 'Creativity, pleasure, stimulation', or 'A place for our grandchildren, our children, and us. A place for everybody'. Others critically demanded 'Some reason in the Mayor's Hall and the City Council'. Hundreds of strips decorated the fences over the course of several months, creating a colourful expression of hope and resistance. Even after rain and sunshine had faded their colours, they still reminded passers-by of the hope directed to the future that endured here visibly and in material form. In a crucial municipal council meeting, the Braugasse 1 club distributed to all councillors a blank strip of cloth attached to a sheet of paper supporting the proposed amendments, thereby drawing the councillors into this mode of both wishful thinking (concerning the renovation) and concrete anticipation (with regard to what is to follow that renovation). The amendments, in turn, were the outcome of the city's working group (*Arbeitsgruppe*) on 'Braugasse 1', which was concerned with the practicalities of this building's future that the club members so passionately fought for. It is the success of a newly and specifically founded civic organization or movement, consisting of diverse and previously unconnected members, to have secured the building's already lost or abandoned future against its expectable demolition. Whereas deconstruction is normally endured without any form of protest, the club's continuous struggle and its interferences in the city's public sphere explicate a new epistemic and affective relation to the future, a hope for an unexpected endurance of specific forms or aspects of the precarious present.

Subsequently, by searching for the places where Hoyerswerda's, and this building's, future are actually made, one might end up in the city council – or at a rather dull, but no less intense meeting in Hoyerswerda's guild hall. This is where the public imaginary expects binding future decisions to be made. The meeting discussed here concerns the (re-)utilization plan for the not-yet renovated building Braugasse 1. The main quest for all attending is not the question of whether the house will be renovated or not, but, once it is renovated (which at that point was still undetermined), who will be using it – in fact, rather, who will be *able* to do so.

In his introductory remarks, the Deputy Mayor recurrently underlines that all assembled potential users face severe problems in the near future, as does any other club in Hoyerswerda; fewer finances, fewer members, fewer audiences are his undeniable predictions. He pre-emptively evacuates the future with a rather discouraging claim: 'Nobody can predict what each club's developments will look like in the future'. He insinuates that those running the clubs will grow older and, owing to the demographic changes, there will be an increasingly smaller clientele in the future. More serious are the financial concerns he alludes to: Will the city, district, or state continue to fund these clubs? Are the clubs' own finances sound enough to guarantee that they will be able to run the building and pay the maintenance costs, which the city no longer wants to be burdened with? The quest is, in that sense, not about the emergence of something new and hoped for: the renovation. Of concern is how this hoped-for future moment can be made to endure – thereby securing a guaranteed maintenance in a future that is predictably like the present: full of insecurities, financial scarcity, and potentially paralysing hopelessness. The house's maintenance is the very practical question that is posed in the face of this undeniable unpredictability.

Contrary to its instrumental character, the debate's subtext is tense. Assembled are the local government's main personal, including the Lord Mayor and his deputy, the commissioned architect, and representatives of three of the clubs, which, following the last council's resolution, are understood to be moving into the renovated building. As potential occupants, they shall discuss the usage of the yet only planned and still virtual new building. The stakes are high. It was only by bringing these three clubs together that the city council reached a majority approval for renovating the building – too many other projects, clubs, and institutions demanded a secure home and financial provision. Although this had been decided already a decade earlier, the city had run increasingly out of money, being unable to provide the so-called *Eigenanteil*, its financial equity ratio, which German communes have to pay in order to acquire state funding. As the last decade of deferred renovation promises shows, the future might turn out very differently, despite official proclamations. The performance of planning in such meetings could be simply yet another attempt to mediate between different parties' mutually exclusive interests in a shrinking city. However, the main trope and logic used is one of sustainability with all its promises of secured permanence. It seems to be the sole reference-point and evaluation criterion, covering all other fissures and conflicts. I will shortly introduce the three clubs' representatives and their stakes in this meeting.[5]

Frau Nagel, the executive head of the NATZ club, the 'Natural Science and Technology Centre' (NAturwissenschaftlich-Technisches Zentrum), seems to feel quite uncomfortable in this setting. A former coal engineer who had experienced a period of unemployment after reunification, she appears blunt rather than articulate and diplomatic. Her job of leading the NATZ is not easy. The NATZ is a typical GDR institution. Founded in the late 1960s in the by then expanding socialist New City, it was to educate Hoyerswerda's children and youth in their free time about scientific and technological issues. Pupils could pay a visit after school and build their own miniature racing tracks, do experiments in physics, help care for all sorts of pets and animals, or construct robots. Since it was at first sight not ideologically charged, the NATZ survived the turmoil of the early 1990s and remained financially sustained by the city. However, during Frau Nagel's time as CEO, the club ran into serious spatial and thus future problems. In the mid-2000s, whilst still being housed in living complex WK 4, its building was hit by an exceptional storm, which led to a prompt evacuation and the club's move to a former school in the younger district WK 9, one of the living complexes most severely affected by shrinkage and deconstruction. Relocated on the outskirts of the New City, the NATZ faced difficulties attracting its main clientele. For some children (or their parents), WK 9 was just too far from the city centre. Furthermore, the place the NATZ now occupied was soon to be demolished as part of further deconstructions. Facing future cuts in public funding, a further decline in the already small number of children, and existential housing issues, the club, despite its excellent reputation, encountered crucial problems. Moving into the to-be-renovated Braugasse would solve these issues and, it is hoped, grant access to a more secure future – with fewer maintenance costs, more children, and a better standing in the city. Although the least experienced of those attending the meeting, Frau Nagel firmly believes that the NATZ's natural science and technology education programme is essential for the city's youth in its preparation for the future. With this logic of endurance in mind, she hopes to secure a future for her club and its five employees – simply by being allowed to continue their successful work under conditions permitting permanence.

Uwe, the long-term executive from the KuFa, is also not very comfortable at such meetings. He is a quiet and arduous worker, not a loud and flamboyant strategist. However, he has been employed in the socio-cultural milieu since the mid-1980s and has much experience of such negotiations. Also, it was his club which most actively and progressively shaped alternative local discourses on the future – successfully directing claims for the club's and Hoyerswerda's future towards city officials, the city council, and the wider public. None the less, his stake in this is essential as well. His club had run the Children's and Youth Centre in Braugasse 1 until its closure. Having moved to the Old City's outskirts, the KuFa also struggled in attracting its clientele. More importantly, the new location made its formerly very successful café unprofitable, thus decreasing the KuFa's income. It is the general perception that the club depends on the renovation of this building for its survival. As was commonly agreed in most of the club's board meetings during this time, there is an economic necessity to relocate from the outskirts to the centre. The club's main clientele are children and youth, but increasingly also older people, who might be attracted in higher numbers to a central domicile. The restoration would make the reopening of a café lucrative and hence guarantee financial income independent of public funding.

But the KuFa's return to Braugasse 1 after years of intense conflict, endless fights, and severe public denunciation is for its supporters linked in yet another way to an issue of the future, indeed, of survival: this time the survival of the whole city. As several people claimed, without the KuFa's admirable work, 'nothing would keep them in the city' ('dann würde mich nichts mehr hier halten'). Supporters argue in the name of the public good that the KuFa's return and the establishment of a vibrant community centre would strengthen the Old City. Conflicts arise: adjacent residents fear the respective noise, whereas nearby shop-owners for obvious reasons appreciate the 're-vitalization' (*Wiederbelebung*) of their quarter. Some of those running the KuFa fear the loss of their jobs (there are six employees and almost seventy voluntary club members) if no future solution with the city is found. Others know that the KuFa's current building, too, will have to be closed soon according to building laws. Instead of a nomadic future of having to move from one dilapidating house to another, they hope for a secure future in an enduring abode. Moreover, the maintenance costs of their 'Temporary Occupancy' are so high that, once privatized – which is part of the negotiations with the local government and yet another municipal attempt at out-sourcing – they will not be affordable for long.

The third club is the Computer Forum Konrad Zuse, founded in 2002 in memory of the famous inventor of computers, who had taken his A-levels in the early 1920s in the Braugasse 1 building, then a progressive grammar school. Its CEO, the retired former leftist Lord Mayor Horst-Dieter Brähmig, also has much at stake and he thus brings into the debates all his post-1989 political experience in order to convince his immediate conservative successor. Currently, the Forum's 'Computer Museum' is housed inadequately in a mediocre office building on the northern outskirts in the former industrial area, where it occupies several large rooms exhibiting an impressive collection of Zuse's and other antique computers. The Forum also owns a rare collection of items from the then emerging GDR computer industry. The exhibition needs a proper makeover – an interactive multimedia-based exhibition, comprehensive and well-designed explanations, a sound pedagogic concept. At present, its attendance numbers are underwhelming. Indeed, despite the city using Zuse's name and trying to marketize his greatly influential invention, this museum is not an attraction. Plans to rescue its survival by relocating it have been put forward time and again. A move to the spacious 'Energy Factory', the Saxon museum for the land's industrial history and culture, finally failed. Braugasse 1, moreover, soon turned out to be structurally unable to harbour the heavy machines of the computer collection. The construction of a new building adjacent to it could have been a sustainable future solution, but the city cannot raise enough money for such a project. Dreams of some wealthy benefactor or some illustrious friend of Zuse or Bill Gates were only half-seriously entertained. Finally, the Computer Forum executives had demanded to be at least included in the plans for the Braugasse 1 community centre, which shall carry Zuse's name. A room of more than 120 square metres has been granted to them in recent plans – not for a museum, but for a 'commemorational room' (*Gedenkzimmer*). In the future, visitors could be directed from there to the museum, wherever it would then be located. Because they intended to equip the room with posters, photos, and smaller artefacts in memory of Zuse, competitors for the same space reproached the whole idea as a horribly old-fashioned 'pennant room' (*Wimpelzimmer*), indicative of the club not having any contribution to make to the community centre's, and thus the city's, sustainable future. To bring Zuse back to the heart of the city, none the less, remained the Forum's aim, claiming that with his name to the fore the city in the long run would benefit, regain identity, attract external investors, and thus secure its own survival.

As shown, all three clubs – like all of the city's voluntary associations – are similarly affected by Hoyerswerda's socio-economic and demographic changes, and subsequent crucial spatial repercussions. All of them are forced to operate strategically to secure their future. To do so in this meeting, they have to prove their ability to survive (in an almost Darwinian sense) and to endure in the future. In order to be found worthy of state funding, they have to confirm their capacity for sustainability. Demographics become bound up with spatial and temporal strategies of survival. All three clubs suffer from decreasing external support and the dwindling reliability of their own ranks: what Germans call 'offspring-problems' (*Nachwuchsprobleme*), the result of an inevitably ageing and diminishing cohort of members in a city that in only four decades turned from Germany's youngest to its oldest city, demographically speaking. To overcome these problems, they try to adapt to the complicated present with various strategies, one of them being the attraction of constant media attention to publicize their compassionate work. All of them invest the renovation of Braugasse 1 with high hopes to overcome many of the aforementioned problems with their relocation into it. To this

Journal of the Royal Anthropological Institute (N.S.), 52-70
© Royal Anthropological Institute 2014

end, throughout the intense debates with the local administrative elite and other representatives, each club representative continuously underlined his or her own club's power to endure in the future. The discourse in this professional meeting, however, only replicates more general claims these clubs repeatedly make in the public sphere – and that enable them to sustain their committed practices. Again, the future has a high currency in Hoyerswerda's civic space when effectively and epistemically countering the threat to – or the city government's forceful denial of – the possibility of continuity in times of shrinkage.

After fierce quarrels about the practical details of who gets how much space (hence the presence of the architect to update the construction plans), it was finally agreed that the only club able to run the centre was the KuFa. The KuFa is seen to have better professional skills and, over the long run, more resources to sustain the house and its management. The other proposed forms of collaboratively organizing the maintenance of the building were withdrawn. However, it was also agreed that only by co-operation among the three clubs would it be possible to get the city council's approval. Once approved by the council, the concluded outcome of the meeting will endure until the virtual plan has been realized: that is, the house has been renovated and the clubs have moved in. As all participants, despite enduring conflicts and competitive tensions, indicated their support, this agreement will only be amended in minor details. However, all clubs also underlined after that meeting that they still need to see what the future will actually be like. Perhaps the NATZ will need less space than required – or it will no longer exist. Similarly, the Zuse Forum might be busy enough occupying its future domicile. Or the KuFa members might have, as viciously predicted, 'grown too old to bother anymore'. Despite such bleak speculations, the KuFa members distinctively concentrate on the practical re-appropriation of the future's future. With a grant from the Federal Foundation for Culture they have started a project called 'Training Activity Braugasse 1' ('Trainingsmaßnahme Braugasse 1'). This project involves probing the co-operation among the three clubs before the move-in. It also allows for a practising of the elsewhere already outdated idea of a community centre with Hoyerswerda's citizens. Several projects have already been conducted in order to secure a smooth running of the centre once it has been built in the future. As these examples underline, concerns with and practices of permanence, continuity, and maintenance can in a context of shrinkage be seen as reinforcements of agency and a form of re-appropriating the (near) future.[6] I am now going to compare the very distinct notion of the hope of endurance to the hope that many academics invest in the promises of change, most currently expressed in the analytical terms 'emergence' and 'becoming'.

Imagining change: from emergence and becoming to maintenance and permanence

The possible, the new, and the emergent have long held some promise for change. Bourdieu's hope for expanding the limits of 'the possible' (cf. Gell 1992: 266-7) was persuasive for many scholars, who thereby deployed a very particular notion of change, freedom, and the efficacy of human practice. The logic is usually the same: change the virtual limits of the possible in order to affect the actual world. At first, a new idea emerges, then follows its actualization in practice. Utopian writing, for instance, accordingly serves as an 'imperative to imagine' 'radical alternatives' (Jameson 2005: 416); and 'imagination as social practice' becomes a 'collective tool for the transformation of the real, for the creation of multiple horizons of possibility' (Appadurai 2002:

34). The hoped-for outcome of these imaginary, virtual, or utopian practices in the scholarly imagination is usually the emergence of the alternative or the new – posed against any notion of predetermination. Such practices rightly add to the sense of 'multiplicity of possible worlds' in our own temporal maps (Gell 1992: 239). But what if the predetermination of the future, not the past, becomes the main focus of local practices?

In this section, I scrutinize such imaginaries of change, especially the more current tropes of 'emergence' and 'becoming'. I want to contrast the academic urge for the emergent (cf., e.g., Rabinow 2003; 2007; Rabinow, Marcus, Faubion & Rees 2008) with my informants' concern with the maintenance of the threatened forms that make up their life. For them, hope is not located in awaiting the new as an anticipation of something becoming – Bloch's 'not-yet-become'. Their promises rather lie in the tedious maintenance of things they hold dearly in the present. This is not an instance of 'enforced presentism' (Guyer 2007). Rather, there is hope in the continuous work that members of the aforementioned clubs invest their practices with. For example, in the Braugasse 1 Club the hope of influencing the local administration to support the renovation of the building involved hundreds of working group meetings, and endless badges, stickers, raffle tickets, and mulled wine sold at dozens of promotional public events, which recurrently have to be organized and attended. But it also involved the constant reminder that what one is doing is worth it despite the dire prospects for success. The KuFa and the Braugasse 1 Club both went through phases when they believed they were unable to maintain their efforts and public interventions. In a counter-intuitive logic, change for them consists of the old *not* disappearing (as predicted); their practices of maintenance were driven, amongst other things, by an improbable vision of an 'alternative' future paradoxically similar to the present. This does not re-deploy the modernist notion of progress. Rather, it indicates a relation to the future (unexpectedly) characteristic of post-industrial times.

Waiting for something to become or emerge, whether as an anthropologist or a Hoyerswerdian, has a certain millennial, messianic flavour. It is also passive, despite its often radical political gesture in academic imaginaries. Although constant becoming obviously involves continuous human practice, it lacks form and structure. This can be celebrated for good reasons as a form of liberation. My informants, however, miss the security and predictability that the times before shrinkage used to provide them with. The efficacy of hope as the anticipation of the 'not-yet-become', according to Bloch's determinist-Marxist theory, consists only of the direction and stimulation of practice: '[T]he "anticipatory consciousness"... prepares the way for the Not-Yet-Become, the realized material reality of the future which however cannot yet be described, only hoped-for and willed-for. This "Not-Yet"... is ... "a directing act of a cognitive kind" ' (Bloch 1986 [1959]: 561). That said, hope has this capacity only as long as its content is actually anticipating the future and not just contemplative. In Bloch's theory, this truth-value is judged not by its efficacy, but by whether it correctly predicts the 'yet-to-become', provoking a serious epistemic and directional dilemma for those acting. If correct, the content of a particular hope turns into a 'real fragment' or 'pre-appearance' of the future (Bloch 1986 [1959]: 210, 217-19; cf. also 108-9). Otherwise it fails to 'notice the real tendencies' (Bloch 1986 [1959]: 479).

However, as Bloch puts it in a rare *non*-pre-deterministic statement, 'everything real passes over into the possible at its processual Front, and possible is everything that is only partially conditioned, that has not yet been fully or conclusively determined' (1986

[1959]: 196). The present is open to change 'as long as reality has not become a completely determined one, as long as it possesses still enclosed possibilities' (1986 [1959]: 197). Generally, Bloch's philosophy none the less continuously caters to a particular fashion in current theories of affect, hope, and the future. In such perspectives, hope, as an affective force, activates people and functions like a catalyst, keeping people tuned to the future. It is the guarantor of change, although there is much to be said about Bloch not living up to academically prevalent concerns about indeterminacy and contingency. Despite differing from postmodernist scholars' 'performative understanding of moments of hope' (Kraftl 2007: 126), his take on hope still promises the emergence and becoming of the new – in his eyes the predetermined communist future.

Ben Anderson's article 'Becoming and being hopeful' (2006) offers a good example of how emergence is in such terms approached with academic hopes. As a post-representational geographer, he argues that hope 'heralds the affect and emotive as always "not-yet-become"' and thus 'discloses the creation of potentiality and becoming' (Anderson 2006: 733). Its affective impact, as in Bloch's thinking, directs action and stimulates the emergence of something new by opening up the present to change. Hope and other affects are seen as the motor of change and against determination since they facilitate emergence and becoming through their affective anticipations. They remain inherently underdetermined. Becoming in Anderson's sense does not anticipate something doomed to come. It has an open, not a predetermined, idea of the future and is directed against theories of predetermination. For Anderson, affects seem to produce change to a large extent at random. Change results less from intentional practice. The efficacy of the practices I am concerned about certainly does not translate flawlessly into the future, as indeterminacy and contingency make us aware (cf. note 6). Some acts, however, are successful in their intentional, even if hopeful, performance. Moreover, there are areas of life over which people claim efficacy, as shown above. Is there, then, a false hope in the academic imagination of a postmodern utopia of 'enduring indeterminacy' (Bloch in Anderson 2006: 749)?

The endurance of hope in Hoyerswerda stems only partially from a belief in the emergence of something new. It also emerges out of the partial efficacy of continuous practices. How does that relate to the idea that 'hope enacts the future as open to difference and reminds us that the here and now are "uncentered, dispersed, plural and partial"' (Anderson 2006: 733)? Anderson uses Massumi's theory of affect as the basis for establishing his take on hope, becoming, and emergence. Accordingly, affect is always on the 'edge of the virtual, where it leaks into the actual' (Massumi in Anderson 2006: 737), and hope, more specifically, is an overspill of the virtual into the actual. The virtual thus produces change in the actual: much like in Bloch's reasoning, it is the immaterial that creates real material changes. Put differently, and much to the contrary of what my informants hope for: 'The eruptive overspill of affect therefore enables an ingression that "ruptures" or "disturbs" that which is "actually existing"' (Anderson 2006: 738). However, the hope for change for my informants does not stem from an abstract affective dimension, but is strongly related to particular, material, and actual forms of life and practice, and remains continuously directed towards their own and their city's future. In contrast, affects such as hope in Massumi's opinion (following a more Agambian take on Deleuze) emerge 'out of the groundless ground of the virtual' (in Anderson 2006: 737). Accordingly, Anderson presents the ideas of space-time as a 'sphere of plentitude' and of the actual 'being haunted by possibility' (Anderson 2006: 739). For him, hope is not an 'intentional act directed towards the future' (Anderson

Journal of the Royal Anthropological Institute (N.S.), 52-70
© Royal Anthropological Institute 2014

2006: 741), and becoming hopeful is 'not an act of transcendence to a good elsewhere and elsewhen', but 'an act of establishing new relations that disclose a point of contingency within a present space-time' (Anderson 2006: 743). In his view, change depends on disclosing this contingency. However, hope for permanence, as expressed by my informants, counters both such a point of contingency and the need for its disclosure. Hope in Anderson's perspective can indeed be cherished as a much-needed response to hopelessness and 'absolute impossibility' (2006: 746). However, any virtual idea which is given form in the actual still needs to be maintained and thus in its own aftermath depends on the efficacy of practices targeted at its endurance – even if this endurance is rightly perceived as being itself contingent.

Similarly, 'becoming' in Biehl and Locke's paper 'Deleuze and the anthropology of becoming' results from a 'transformative potential' in 'immanent fields of action and significance', which are 'leaking out on all sides' (2010: 317). It is again affect that initiates that leaking and possibility for change (still unintentional). In Biehl and Locke's eyes, 'desire can break free open alternative pathways' towards 'unexpected futures', especially in contexts like their fieldsites, where people are 'moving through broken institutions and infrastructures in the making' and 'when life chances are foreclosed' (2010: 318). Whilst celebrating potentiality, Biehl and Locke claim that their informants in contexts of decline and threatened survival (similar to Hoyerswerda) make this passively given possibility a 'crucial dimension of what is/was' (2010: 323). In contrast, my informants have very practical concerns and would be opposed to this idea of fluidity as a source for hope. Rather, they make endurance crucial to their lives, and are critical with the present's character of becoming, its 'element of flight that escapes its own formalization' and its refusal to 'attai[n] a form' (Deleuze in Biehl & Locke 2010: 326). They precisely want things to have a form as a basis for their endurance. Similarly, Locke's informant Maja concentrates on practices 'of small hopes and aspirations, of better maths grades and prowess in snow-boarding' (Biehl & Locke 2010: 333). This is concrete and productive. Why not include Locke's informants' 'much more specific expectations' of the political elite 'to again provide the kind of social protections and safety nets they recall from the communist era' (Biehl & Locke 2010: 332) as one way of understanding how these informants 'endure and try to escape constraints and articulate new systems of perception and action' (2010: 336)? It might elicit new aspects of the 'abiding of intolerable present circumstances' of 'a new kind of day-to-day survival' and of a temporality of 'in between, in flux and transition' (Biehl & Locke 2010: 336). What else is their 'key to anticipating ... the future' (Biehl & Locke 2010: 337)? In contrast, the authors conclude that 'a crucial element of this immanence is the day-to-day anticipation or envisionings of alternative forms of existence' (Biehl & Locke 2010: 348).

Biehl and Locke position possibility and emergence against the contemporarily 'anxious uncertainty and open-endedness of life' and 'routinized urgency and crisis' (2010: 336), thus verging on a distorted critique and simultaneous celebration of neoliberal ideologies of possibility. Does it help my analysis to perceive my informants as showing 'a passion for the possible' (Biehl & Locke 2010: 319), for the new and emergent? By prescribing openness, Biehl and Locke end up accusing others of a 'straitjacketing of the future' (Hirschmann in Biehl & Locke 2010: 319). However, in the sense of Maurer's quote at the beginning of this article, it might actually be these practices aiming at straitjacketing the future in which we find 'a little more allowance for the unexpected – and a little less wishful thinking' (Hirschmann in Biehl & Locke 2010: 319). Hope in its anticipatory and wishful capacity can therefore be found in the improbable continuity of particular forms of life (cf. Miyazaki 2004), still functioning as a progressive drive of human action. Such thought might make us appreciate our informants' many creative ways of dealing with the problems they face and their own forms of 'mobilization and flight into indeterminate futures' (Biehl & Locke 2010: 323). I follow the guidelines for judging the future laid out by my informants in the prior section – shifting their own temporal reasoning away from progress and constant innovation to the logic of sustainability when maintaining their club's, association's, school's, or kindergarten's existence in time. Instead of waiting for emergent new ideas, many Hoyerswerdians are busy trying to keep things alive. If they did not make the effort, these forms would cease to exist. And some forms do indeed cease existing when the strength and motivation to maintain them perish. As I have shown above, this motivation for – or incentive to – action does not simply derive from the notion or ethics of becoming and potentiality, but stems from a different temporal logic, the one of endurance, which has been too easily lost sight of in current academic debates.

Another, though rather different, version of this analytical preference comes from Rabinow's concern with the emergent in his development of Foucault's history of the present into an anthropology of the contemporary. Rabinow starts with the simple question 'what difference does today make with respect to yesterday – and to tomorrow?' (Rabinow *et al.* 2008: 67) and focuses on 'concepts to make visible what is emerging' (2008: 64). As Rees summarizes: 'For Rabinow, "today"... is a logical and conceptual challenge. The present is a historical, open moment in which what is or has been is, at least potentially, changing. His aim as an "anthropologist of the contemporary" ... is to identify, trace, and name such changes' (in Rabinow *et al.* 2008: 9) by focusing 'on events and actualizations that take place in a particular field' (in Rabinow *et al.* 2008: 78). In the same volume, Marcus criticizes Rabinow's focus on the present for a lack of historical consideration, detecting a familiarity to neoliberal ideology and enforced presentism, preached and practised by 'consultants' and 'advisers of policy makers' (Rabinow *et al.* 2008: 56). However, as Rabinow admirably explains, a focus on the contemporary, inherent in our presentist methodology, is not about forgetting the past, but it is also about analytically opening up the present for the future. He quotes Blumenberg saying we should remain 'open to the present, against narratives of decline, disaster, and other forms of closure' (in Rabinow 2007: 13). For Rabinow, the question is, 'as Nietzsche saw long ago, whether historical conditions are everything. And I believe strongly that they are not. There is a great deal of contingency and underdetermination in most situations' (Rabinow *et al.* 2008: 56). Although I support his emphasis on the contingent character of the present, I feel there is more to be said about human agency and the role the future plays in the present he wants to open up against predetermining narratives. In my ethnographic material, an active stance against contingency reveals how the continuous can be – and should be approached as – one form of emergence.

One of the critiques of theories of emergence has been voiced by Miyazaki and Riles (2005: 327-8). They compare its analytical logic to the response of Japanese finance experts to what they perceive as 'failures of knowledge'. The authors claim that for

> the anthropologist of the contemporary, the failure at issue is a failure in the ability to 'know' the ethnographic subject. In response to such failures of knowing, the focus on 'emergence', 'complexity', and 'assemblage' implicitly resigns itself to the fact that little can be known about the world except for the fact of complexity, indeterminacy, and open-endedness, since reality, in this view, is always emergent, indeterminate, and complex (Miyazaki & Riles 2005: 327).

Rather unconvincingly, Miyazaki and Riles fear that 'anthropology becomes "a chronicle of emergent assemblages" ' (2005: 327), and offer in response the strategy to stabilize (i.e. to know) such failures as endpoints (of knowledge) and transform them into new beginning-points. However, my informants' hopes propose yet another logic by attempting not to abandon the forms they care about, but to – yet again – give them a future (thus creating neither just endpoints, nor only beginnings). What both approaches share is the concern for concrete (knowledge) practices. Rabinow remains particularly attuned to the emergent, meanwhile, shaping and sculpting new forms and norms of practice for our analytical toolkits. For him, the contemporary is where 'older and newer elements are given form and worked together' (Rabinow 2007: 3) – and, I add, where some of these forms are made to endure.

These last remarks on form have much to say about a potential imaginary of endurance. Yet another fashionable trope – assemblage – seems to entail both aspects: the one of impermanence found in the only temporary, constantly changing, and shifting constellation of different elements, and the propensity to endure inherent in its formal character (cf. Collier & Ong 2005). The work on the persistence of particular assemblages, as shown in this paper, could be seen as one way of giving shape to the future. As Rabinow puts it, after Dewey: '[T]he giving of form (whether discursive, logical, artistic, scientific, political, and the like) is a primary task in living in general as well as in specific practices themselves conditioned by traditions and habits' (Rabinow 2007: 9). As shown in regard to my ethnographic material, giving particular forms a future (and thus the future a form) can be seen as the next and crucially important step. Performing the future (i.e. having per- or transformative effects on future presents) means very specifically attempting to give form to the future.[7] Formal features, in turn, allow a higher probability of enduring in time, which does not deny the contingency and indeterminacy of practices of endurance. These practices can target the renovation of a house as much as the general epistemic make-up of a shrinking city's local economy of knowledge.

As I have shown in this section, the relationship to such forms (social, communal, or material) can be a hopeful one. Their maintenance in times of change thereby offers the promise of an actual, concrete near future – more so than the waiting for something new to emerge or to become. Such reasoning does not part from notions of indeterminacy, but links theories of the future, practice, forms, and change in order to explain the hope stemming from practices of maintenance and endurance. It offers a new take on modern, postmodern, and post-industrial experiences of time, and on rather unexpected forms of temporal reasoning.

Conclusion

In this paper, I have presented a take on the unpredictability and heterogeneity of temporal experiences in modern times that is based on a perspective of the future. One phenomenon I tracked was the re-emergence of the improbable belief in the efficacy of human practice in times of rapid change. Although I have situated such hopeful practices in a context shaped by the impact of so-called 'neoliberal' policies of outsourcing and the demise of state regulation, I focused on local citizens' somewhat dire and conservative – but none the less progressive and hopeful – responses to decline and accelerated change. I was able to show with the help of a concrete example that their epistemic and practical reaction to this inchoate context is not – as academically expected – the evacuation of the near future with a messianic belief in the new or emergent, but a proper, agentive investment in the endurance, maintenance, and sustainability of the social and material forms that make up their lives. This investment surprisingly accesses different temporal resources (of bureaucracy, local governance, the national welfare state, as much as local social, cultural, and economic capitals) – despite their own demises – and targets particular material objects and social forms in very concrete long-term practices, with their own repetitive tempi and rhythms, and their own constantly renewed and reconsidered forms of 'temporalization' (Munn 1992). The future – as well as change *and* continuity, for that matter – is thereby *concretely* and *materially* crafted, enabled, and actively reclaimed rather than *passively* expected or *idealistically* awaited in some Agambian or Blochian messianic manner. For Hoyerswerda's civic sphere, this position and temporal logic had to be (re)gained in long and hard-fought political as much as epistemic struggles.

Subsequently, I have contrasted the logic of permanence and its corresponding notion of temporal agency – both exhibited in my informants' temporal concerns, logics, and practices – to some of the (hopeful) imaginaries used in the discipline of anthropology to describe and conceptualize change. Especially recent and – in my understanding – limited and limiting uses of Deleuze's work cater to an obscure notion of hope that shall enable, but simultaneously pre-empts, human agency. However, instead of deconstructing the fashionable notions of emergence, possibility, the virtual, and becoming, I see them as one possible imagination of hope and change – the wishing ribbons at the Braugasse 1 building being an expression of such 'wishful' thinking. Beyond the anthropology of becoming's idealist hope, which by and large remains itself virtual in its anticipation, I urge us to consider the temporal period that follows the moment of emergence: the actual, very material, and concrete time of endurance. Corresponding practices contain some of our informants' most important concerns: for the stability and maintenance (or even survival) of given forms of life – a particular building, a set of social practices, one's socio-cultural club or association. They do not entail less hope, or less critical potential. Rather, concerns for permanence, endurance, and continuity even support notions of indeterminacy and contingency. They are neither less future-orientated nor simply embedded in the past, but are an essential part of the epistemic, social, and political context of human responses to situations of change. In fact, they in their own ways and with a very different temporal logic demand *impossible* alternatives as much as their practical upkeep in a context characterized by post-industrial decline, shrinkage, and discontinuity. Practices of endurance are part of the variety of relations to time that people worldwide currently exhibit – and seem curiously modern in their unforeseen hopeful and practical takes on the future.

NOTES

Research for this paper has benefited from generous support by the ESCR, Sidney Sussex College, Cambridge, and the Division of Social Anthropology at the University of Cambridge. I would specifically like to thank my former Ph.D. supervisor, Nikolai Ssorin-Chaikov, for all his help, the citizens of Hoyerswerda for their openness and general hospitability, and Emily Thomas for her enduring patience and linguistic assistance. Finally, many thanks to Laura Bear, who has put so much effort into organizing the workshops on 'Conflicts in Time' and putting this special issue together.

[1] Quoted by kind permission of the author.

[2] The Lusatian Lake District is the world's biggest artificial lake district. Currently emerging, it is the outcome of the many open-pit mines of the regional coal industry, for whose socialist expansion Hoyerswerda was built as the 'City of Miners and Energy Workers' throughout the 1950s until the fall of the Iron Curtain. It promises new jobs in tourism and thus a deceleration of shrinkage.

[3] The Sorbs are the officially acknowledged Slavic minority in the region of Lusatia ('Lausitz'), which surrounds Hoyerswerda.

[4] Cf. *http://www.kufa-hoyerswerda.de*, *http://www.kunstverein-hoyerswerda.de*, and *http://www.stadtzukunft -hy.de* for some particularly interesting examples.

[5] I should mention that I approach the club representatives as exemplary members of Hoyerswerda's public sphere. As indicated above, they are ultimately aware of the fact that their own personal and professional as much as their clubs' futures are intimately linked with the city's future survival. In their self-understanding, it is this survival that all of them are working for in their personal and professional efforts.

[6] Elsewhere (Ringel 2012), I have detected the same temporal logic in practices of self-formation by following research on ethics in religious contexts. Although Zigon's 'ethics of hope' underlines ethical practices' 'creative participation in the possibilities of becoming' (2006: 75) and thus speaks to a Deleuze-inspired understanding of hope as criticized in the last section of this paper, I have here in mind what he calls 'little projects' (2006: 72), in which, through experience (*melete*) and training in real situations (*gymnasia*) (cf. Zigon 2006), *askesis* is practised and particular *teloi* are pursued. This take on the process of ethical practice with its long-term efficacy via repetition allows for the configuration of hope as a matter of a concrete 'temporal orientation of intentional and ethical action' (Zigon 2009: 267). Yet the idea of a simple linear application of moral codes has rightly been challenged by notions of moral multiplicity and failure (Simon 2009), moral breakdown (Zigon 2007), and moral ambivalence, fragmentation, and incoherence (Schielke 2009).

[7] This may include 'practices of regularization and situational adjustment' (cf. the discussion of Moore's work in Turner 1987). For Moore, for instance, writing in the heyday of the struggle between processual and structural approaches in anthropology, such an approach is 'a declaration against indeterminacy' (in Turner 1987: 30). Regarding her informants' legal and religious rituals, she claims that through 'form and formality they celebrate man-made meaning, the culturally determinate, the regulated, the named, and the explained ... Indeed there is no doubt that any analysis of social life must take account of the dynamic relation between the formed and "the indeterminate" ' (in Turner 1987: 30).

REFERENCES

ANDERSON, B. 2006. Becoming and being hopeful: towards a theory of affect. *Environment and Planning D: Society and Space* **24**, 733-52.
APPADURAI, A. 2002. The right to participate in the work of the imagination (interview by Arjun Molder). In *TransUrbanism*, A. Appadurai *et al.*, 32-47. Rotterdam: V2 Publishing.
BAXSTROM, R. 2012. Living on the horizon of the everlasting present: power, planning and the emergence of baroque forms of life. In *Southeast Asian perspectives on power* (eds) L. Chua, J. Cook, N. Long & L. Wilson, 135-50. London: Routledge.
BERDAHL, D. 2009. *On the social life of postsocialism: memory, consumption, Germany*. Bloomington: University of Indiana Press.
BERLANT, L. 2007. Slow death (sovereignty, obesity, lateral agency). *Critical Inquiry* **33**, 754-80.
BIEHL, J. & P. LOCKE 2010. Deleuze and the anthropology of becoming. *Current Anthropology* **51**, 317-51.
BLOCH, E. 1986 [1959]. *The principle of hope*, vols 1-3. Oxford: Blackwell.
BOYER, D. 2006. *Ostalgie* and the politics of the future in Eastern Germany. *Public Culture* **18**, 361-81.
CARRITHERS, M. 2007. Story seeds and the inchoate. *Durham Anthropology Journal* **14**, 1-20.
COLLIER, S. & A. ONG 2005. Global assemblages, anthropological problems. In *Global assemblages: technology, politics, and ethics as anthropological problems* (eds) A. Ong & S. Collier, 3-21. Oxford: Blackwell.
CRAPANZANO, V. 2007. Co-futures (commentary). *American Ethnologist* **34**, 422-5.
GELL, A. 1992. *The anthropology of time*. Oxford: Berg.
GUYER, J. 2007. Prophecy and the near future: thoughts on macroeconomic, evangelical, and punctuated time. *American Ethnologist* **34**, 409-21.
HARRIS, O. 1996. The Temporalities of tradition: reflection on a changing anthropology. In *Grasping the changing world: anthropological concepts in the postmodern era* (ed.) V. Hubinger, 1-16. London: Routledge.
——— 2004. Braudel: historical time and the horror of discontinuity. *History Workshop Journal* **57**, 161-74.
HOBSBAWM, E. & T. RANGER (eds) 1983. *The invention of tradition*. Cambridge: University Press.
JAMESON, F. 2005. *Archaeologies of the rupture: the desire called utopia and other science fictions*. London: Verso.
KRAFTL, P. 2007. Utopia, performativity, and the unhomely. *Environment and Planning D: Society and Space* **25**, 120-43.
MAHMOOD, S. 2001. Feminist theory, embodiment, and the docile agent: some reflections on the Egyptian Islamic revival. *Cultural Anthropology* **16**, 202-35.

———— 2005. *Politics of piety: the Islamic revival and the feminist subject*. Princeton: University Press.

MAURER, B. 2005. Chronotypes of the alternative: hope for the new economy. Paper given at the conference 'Hope in the New Economy', Cornell University.

MIYAZAKI, H. 2004. *The method of hope: anthropology, philosophy, and Fijian knowledge*. Stanford: University Press.

———— & A. RILES 2005. Failure as endpoint. In *Global assemblages: technology, politics, and ethics as anthropological problems* (eds) A. Ong & S. Collier, 320-31. Oxford: Blackwell.

MUNN, N. 1992. The cultural anthropology of time: a critical essay. *Annual Review of Anthropology* **21**, 93-123.

POVINELLI, E. 2011. *Economies of abandonment: social belonging and endurance in late liberalism*. Durham, N.C.: Duke University Press.

RABINOW, P. 2003. *Anthropos today*. Princeton: University Press.

———— 2007. *Marking time: on the anthropology of the contemporary*. Princeton: University Press.

————, G. MARCUS, J. FAUBION & T. REES 2008. *Designs for an anthropology of the contemporary*. Durham, N.C.: Duke University Press.

RINGEL, F. 2012. Towards anarchist futures? Creative presentism, vanguard practices, and anthropological hopes. *Critique of Anthropology* **32**, 173-88.

———— 2013. Differences in temporal reasoning: temporal complexity and generational clashes in an East German city. *Focaal – Journal of Global and Historical Anthropology* **66**, 25-35.

SCHIELKE, S. 2009. Being good in Ramadan: ambivalence, fragmentation, and the moral self in the lives of young Egyptians. *Journal of the Royal Anthropological Institute* (N.S.) Special Issue: Islam, politics, anthropology (eds) F. Osella & B. Soares, S24-S40.

SIMON, G.M. 2009. The soul freed of cares? Islamic prayer, subjectivity, and the contradictions of moral selfhood in Minangkabau, Indonesia. *American Ethnologist* **36**, 258-75.

TURNER, V. 1987. *The anthropology of performance*. New York: PAJ Books.

ZIGON, J. 2006. An ethics of hope: working on the self in contemporary Moscow. *The Anthropology of East Europe Review* **24**, 71-80.

———— 2007. Moral breakdown and ethical demand: a theoretical framework for an anthropology of moralities. *Anthropological Theory* **7**, 131-50.

———— 2009. Within a range of possibilities: morality and ethics in social life. *Ethnos* **74**, 251-76.

Les temps postindustriels et l'inattendu : endurance et durabilité dans la ville d'Allemagne qui rapetisse le plus vite

Résumé

Le présent article étudie l'impact des changements politico-économiques récents sur l'expérience contemporaine du temps, du point de vue du futur. En discutant de l'endurance, de la permanence et de la durabilité dans la ville d'Allemagne qui rapetisse le plus vite, l'auteur présente un ensemble de pratiques orientées vers le futur qui s'avèrent postindustrielles d'une façon inattendue : pleines d'espoir et ne participant pas du phénomène largement attesté de « présentéisme forcé ». Il situe ensuite la logique temporelle d'endurance et de durabilité à l'opposé des réponses académiques actuelles aux changements accélérés, telles qu'elles sont révélées dans l'usage trompeur des concepts deleuziens d'émergence et de devenir. Les investissements épistémiques de ses informateurs dans le futur jettent un éclairage différent sur ce qu'il décrit comme une agencéité temporelle postindustrielle et sur les politiques conflictuelles qui donnent formes à ces relations temporelles inattendues.

3

For labour: Ajeet's accident and the ethics of technological fixes in time

LAURA BEAR *London School of Economics and Political Science*

This paper uses an ethnography of river pilots who navigate container ships on the Hooghly to argue for a focus on labour as an act of mediation in the timespaces of global workplaces. A new approach to capitalist time is developed that seeks to combine recent emphasis on knowledge practices with an older Marxist emphasis on the mediating role of labour. Bureaucrats driven by the rhythms of repayment of public deficit have taken on an extractive role on the Hooghly, producing a declining infrastructure. Moreover, the contradictions produced by government policies are making it increasingly difficult to navigate the river, climaxing in frequent accidents. River pilots 'fix' these through technological interventions shaped by the ethics or 'senses of workmanship' that emerge from their acts of labour in specific timespaces. Capital on the Hooghly continues to circulate through these small, piecemeal moves in which time is an ethical, affective, and technical problem rather than through the large-scale temporal fixes described by Harvey and Castree. Therefore, we need radically to rethink our approaches to time in capitalism, moving beyond existing accounts of it as an abstract measure of value or source of time-discipline. Capitalist time is heterochronic and provokes attempts to reconcile diverse, recalcitrant rhythms and representations through our ethical and physical labour.

I begin this paper with the account of an accident, an unusual but important site from which to analyse contemporary capitalism. Four months into my year of fieldwork on the Hooghly, a container ship had raced out of control, sliced through a jetty, and become beached in the bank, precariously balanced on its keel at a place called Hooghly Point. Suddenly all conversations with river pilots and marine officers converged towards this event. Mishaps were not rare on the river – most men had been involved in dangerous situations and some had permanent injuries from accidents. Navigating down the river meant regular encounters with wrecks from as far back as the eighteenth century that had to be avoided. Yet this new event was controversial, provoked debate, and led to creative technological solutions for the mounting dangers on the river.

It was when Tapan, a 30-year-old pilot, took me to see his friend, Ajeet, who had been steering the ship when it ran aground, that the full significance of this event began to emerge.[1] Ajeet had been ordered to revert to harbour work. The stigma of this and his involvement in three accidents in one year, Tapan said, had meant that Ajeet had become 'mentally destroyed and his immune system has collapsed. The whole of his arms have frozen up'. Inside his flat, Ajeet moved like an old man, slowly lowering himself into one of the armchairs. Straight away he launched into the stories of his three accidents. His account portrayed the events as a piling up of an unstoppable sequence of mishaps. 'Nature and everything worked against me', he insisted. 'My job is one that tests every person's limits. That is the kind of work it is'. Tapan began to comfort Ajeet by saying, 'If we had electronic charts with laptops, then it would help in difficult situations like this ... This would save your time in situations where any time delay would create a greater problem'. In the months that followed, Tapan and the Pilots' Association worked together to design and introduce electronic charts for navigation on the river in a collective response to the accident.

In this paper, I explore the origins of this accident and its solutions in a particular timespace of labour. By taking this route, I seek to build on the analyses of capitalist time that have moved beyond E.P. Thompson's (1967) influential arguments about time-discipline (e.g. Postone 1993). Yet I also extend them, by arguing that they have so far underestimated the significance of the act of labour in their accounts. As Tapan and Ajeet's wide-ranging conversations indicate, we need to analyse capitalist time as a simultaneously ethical, affective, and technical problem. Its contradictions are solved through piecemeal, diverse interventions that seek to make work productive. These solutions are sought not solely to produce profit, but according to particular senses of workmanship. These are ethical understandings that emerge from specific timespaces of labour. This approach, as I will show in my conclusion, allows us to interrogate critically the claims about time in contemporary global capitalism made in some of the most influential sociological theories, such as those of Harvey (1982; 1989) and Castree (2009). At the centre of this discussion of capitalist time will be a theoretical emphasis on the act of labour as a mediation of conflicting rhythms, representations, and technologies of time. This mediation does not only produce value, as is suggested in Marxist approaches to labour and abstract time (Postone 1993). Nor is it only an interaction with the material world and other workers that creates useful knowledge and skill (Bloch 1977; Ingold 1993; Marchand 2010). It also generates affective experiences and ethical reflections that profoundly shape the rhythms of capital circulation.

The first wave of ethnographic studies of global capitalism focused on sites of production and the intensifications of Taylorist time-discipline and space-time compression deployed in them (Aneesh 2006; Biao 2006; Freeman 2000). Later work grounded in an analysis of finance capital has taken a different theoretical approach. This research has emphasized the technologies and knowledge practices that create acts of speculation in marketplaces. Pioneering work emphasized the abstractions of systems of risk analysis and calculation in predictive devices (Langley 2008; Li Puma & Lee 2005; D. Mackenzie 2006). Ethnographic work with traders and bureaucrats showed that both time and markets were problems for knowledge that could not be easily resolved because of the contradictions inherent in technical architectures (Miyazaki 2003; Riles 2004). Yet although the categories of agency and knowledge are central to these accounts, the sources of these concepts in the experiences of acts of work are not explored. In addition, generating income in markets is analysed as a technical problem of knowledge rather than as a visceral experience of labour. It is as if the hierarchical distinction between mental and manual labour that emerged through the late nineteenth and twentieth centuries and intensified in the 1980s with the growth of 'the knowledge economy' has been maintained within contemporary academic debates (Massey, Quintas & Weld 1992). The sphere of global production is a site of labour and time-discipline analysis, while that of finance capital is a domain of knowledge and representation. This paper is an attempt to contribute to these important debates by moving beyond this split. It does this by arguing for a return to a focus on labour as an act of mediation in both markets and places of production. Building on the analyses by Upadhyay (2009) and Zaloom (2006; 2009) of the quotidian experience of new technologies and temporal representations, it restores the significance of the sensory affects and ethics that emerge in the act of work. In particular, it will show the importance of focusing on both markets and places of production as complex timescapes that generate contingent affects and effects. We need to push beyond our previous sole emphasis on time-discipline or abstract representations of time in order to capture the reality of contemporary capitalism.

The concept of a timescape is not new. Building on Harvey, in 2001, May and Thrift developed this term into a critique of E.P. Thompson's seminal 1967 essay on work-discipline. They showed that industrial capitalism had not produced a radical reordering of space and time according to the routines of the factory. Instead this transition was historically uneven, countered by other representations of time, both political and religious, and was perennially incomplete. Providing historical evidence for this point, they argued that 'the picture that emerges is less that of a singular or uniform social time stretching over a uniform space, than of various (and uneven) networks of time stretching in different and divergent directions across an uneven social field' (May & Thrift 2001: 10). Moving beyond analyses of abstract time and work discipline, they suggested a focus on four key aspects of time and how they intersect in experience: representations, technologies, social disciplines, and rhythms in time. Yet even over a decade later there have been few attempts to realize this model either in the analysis of markets or in that of production (for an exception, see Bestor 2001). In both of these settings, labour takes place in a complex timescape in which various, often conflicting, temporalizing practices intersect (Munn 1992). The act of work is not simply governed by abstract measures of time and work discipline. It does not occur in time, nor is it simply measured by abstract time. It has to mediate diverse temporal rhythms, representations, and technologies in an orchestration of human action towards their temporary reconciliation. This is not always possible, and the argument in this paper will be that it is becoming less achievable in contemporary global capitalism. This last claim reveals why it is important to move beyond the current split and partial forms of analysis of time in the workplace. We are at risk of missing an important social change that has occurred during the past twenty years. To focus solely on social discipline or representations or technologies of time would provide an incomplete picture of how uncertain the process of capital accumulation has become. It would be to extract one network of time from a specific workplace without tracing how it conflicted or intersected with another element. It also would not allow us to examine the many small acts of labour and their accompanying ethics that undermine or secure the fate of forms of accumulation. But to move into this terrain we have to supplement current approaches to timescapes with an emphasis on how ethics and affects emerge in relation to work within them.

There has been a recent turn towards the analysis of economies of affect that grows out of a Foucauldian model of self-discipline. But the approach proposed here extends this perspective by moving beyond its claim that ethics and emotion, including religious practices, act to 'facilitate neoliberal transformation' (Richard & Rudnyckyj 2009;

Rose 1999). Instead I argue that what I will call a sense of workmanship (i.e. the ethics and affects of work) emerges in relation to and out of the act of labour within a specific timescape (Bear 2012). It may or may not support neoliberal forms of accumulation, because it is a domain of experience emergent from but not containable within its forms of representation and discipline (Bear 2013a; 2013b). It is generated from the act of attempting to reconcile various technological devices, temporal rhythms, and representations into a productive act of work. It reflects the ways in which technological devices open people up to non-human pressures and forces (A. Mackenzie 2001; Pickering 1995; 2008). It often exceeds explicit representations of time and predictive devices. It can also generate a duty of care to fellow-workers, technologies, and the world. It is important to focus on a domain of a sense of workmanship because otherwise we are at risk of reducing the ethics and affects of work to serving the needs of capital or resisting it, whereas this is a rich domain of speculation and action that aims to solve the problem of how human practice makes the world productive. Technologies are often deployed or rejected in relation to solving this problem. Our concepts of economic knowledge practices and discourses need to be supplemented by a point made long ago in a more Marxist framing of representations of time. This is that ideologies are not the same as knowledge used to act on the world, and that labour generates understandings of the world that are not constrained by ideology (Bloch 1977).

Accidents are ideal ground for examining these theoretical issues. As a failed act of labour, they potentially reveal to us and to our informants the limits of attempts to suture together incommensurable temporal rhythms and workplace demands. They also invite extensive explicit ethical reflection on rights and responsibilities. In addition, they push workers to relate acts of work to a universe of productive powers. They provoke speculation on the relationships and boundaries between the human and non-human. As sudden unpredicted irruptions into work routines, they stimulate reflection on representations of time and predictive technologies. Therefore it is striking that the academic analysis of accidents has not considered them from this perspective – their everyday life as part of the ethics and practices of workplaces. Instead they have been analysed as spectacular signs in the public sphere of the fascinating absences in ideologies or of the collapse of capitalism or that complex systems will always fail (Law & Mol 2002; Schivelbusch 1987; Žižek 1999). When they have been considered in relation to work processes, the assumption has been that explicit moral debates take place outside of the workplace and that normal practice involves an embedded implicit balancing of ethical aims. Both Law and Mol (2002) and Graham and Thrift (2007) argue that, unlike accident inquiries, the workplace involves an implicit everyday 'tinkering towards the good' (Law & Mol 2002: 85) that makes urban systems work. Absent from this discussion are the work processes out of which accidents emerge and the ethical debates that follow them within workplaces. Perrow's approach to accidents has addressed the work processes on sea-going ships, showing that a combination of commercial pressures, authoritarian command structures, weak enforcement of insurance laws, multiple commercial ownership, and decentralized agencies of enforcement of legal sanctions inevitably produces what he calls 'normal accidents' (Perrow 1984). But he has not examined the senses of workmanship that contribute both to the production of accidents and to their subsequent normalization. More importantly, once we start to trace the everyday life of accidents in workplaces, it is possible to discern their centrality to contemporary practices of capitalism. Away from dramatic publicized events, accidents have become accepted as inherent in the work process. As I will show in this paper, among river pilots, even as spectacular an accident as Ajeet's led to vibrant debate, but ultimately it became normalized as the exciting cost of productivity and as creative of new technologies and knowledge.

At a more general level, the analysis of accidents allows us to address the important question of how the utility of market devices and predictive technologies is recuperated and/or altered given the mounting contradictions in timescapes of labour and the frequent failures of these modes of framing circulation and production. We can no longer assume the resilience of these forms of incomplete knowledge, but have to explain how and why people remain committed to their partial representations. How do debates and ethical attributions within workplaces maintain their utility? How is consideration of their inability to predict the future and their generation of contradiction deferred from consideration? Finally, this paper will show that it is through small, piecemeal rules of thumb and senses of workmanship that 'fixes' to contemporary unstable capitalism occur. It is through these everyday ethical practices rather than solely the large-scale 'processual' spatio-temporal fixes that Harvey and Castree outline that the contradictory reality of capitalism persists (see Hodges, this volume, for a critique of process). To explore these issues, this paper will now turn to an exploration of Ajeet's accident – or, more precisely, it will turn to an account of the timescape of labour that generated this event and contributed to the senses of workmanship through which it was recuperated and given a technological 'fix'.

Circulation time, public deficit, and the timescape of shipping

Various analysts have argued that shipping underwent an intensification of speed through containerization and informalization during the same period that global capitalism emerged (Levinson 2006; Sampson & Wu 2003). This work focuses on the pressures of commercial private enterprise on the practices of shipping companies. Yet to do this is to forget the emplacement of shipping in a much wider system. It was Marx (1992 [1885]) who first suggested that shipping should be seen as part of larger circuits of capital circulation. He traced the metamorphoses of capital and argued that the movement of commodity back to money was limited by circulation time. He suggested therefore that the drive to speed was central to capitalism and that the labour of transport added surplus value to commodities. Similarly, the long-term investment of capital in infrastructures reaped a return in the form of greater speed of circulation. Marx also argued that credit notes, or finance capitalism, first emerged in relation to long-distance trade, with the length of time for which credit was advanced varying according to the limits of the transport cycle itself. In this model, finance markets have their origin in and are related to the cycles of realization of profit from commodities in timespaces of transport labour.

Marx's model looks optimistic in comparison with present-day infrastructures and rhythms of transport and finance capitalism. There is certainly a well-documented push to speed up circulation time. Yet credit now does not only contribute to investment in fixed capital or the covering of short-term costs. Instead it has taken on a different role in relation to infrastructures through the conversions of public deficit. Credit has been advanced from private banks, investors, and international organizations to governments. Repayments are made through the privatization and dismantling of infrastructure and extraction from the labour of circulation. Production and circulation are not simply supported by the advancing of over-accumulated capital as credit in a temporal fix, as Harvey (1982; 1989) and Castree (2009), following Marx's model, suggest. Instead, credit-advancing institutions are placed in extractive relationships to the infrastructures of circulation. This is what has occurred via the bureaucracy of the state-run Kolkata Port Trust on the Hooghly.

The adoption of government liberalization policies in India from 1980 to 1991 was driven by a series of balance-of-payment crises and pressure from political and business sectors for neoliberal policy responses to them. This led to the emergence of an extractive central state that sought to capitalize public resources, divest itself of permanent labour forces, and draw back revenue to the central government in order to meet its obligations on the repayment of international loans. This process began in 1981 with the acceptance of an IMF loan, and some limited liberalization measures by Indira Gandhi in order to stabilize the economy and gain a wider vote-bank among the business classes. In the second half of the 1980s, under Rajiv Gandhi, the central government faced a regular balance-of-payment crisis caused by the reduction of taxes on the middle classes and business, a spike in oil prices owing to the first Gulf War, and the collapse of the Soviet Union, India's main trading partner. In 1991, under Narasimha Rao, the central government accepted an IMF loan for US$1.2 billion in return for the adoption of economic reforms that would open up the economy to external investors, lessen state control of the market, and end public monopolies. This was followed by further reforms that solidified the political response as one in which private business and trading interests were given priority over social investment (Corbridge & Harris 2000; Dev & Mooij 2002). The changes in the private sector and practices of consumption that occurred as a result of these reforms are a well-known story. The history of the Kolkata Port Trust reveals an entirely different and equally significant process, a movement away from long-term social investment towards the short-term extraction of revenue from public sector labour and infrastructures in order to repay international loans. The loan from the IMF in 1981 was successfully repaid by 1985, but only at the expense of public investment and through the extraction of resources from state industries such as the Port Trust. This tendency escalated through the second half of the 1980s, culminating in the period of 1990-1, when the new reforming Finance Minister, Mammohan Singh, and his Secretary, the former World Bank economist Montek Ahluwalia, placed their allies at the top of ministries. All of them had extensive World Bank or IMF experience, and would ensure fiscal stringency and the repayment of loans. This shift away from policies of social investment to the extractive repayment of debts led to a profound restructuring of working-class employment and capitalization or disinvestment in infrastructure in the public sector. These changes are visible in the recent history of the Kolkata Port Trust.

Crucial to the 'liberalization' process was the new agency given to public deficit, as exemplified by the actions of the Ministry of Surface Transport (MOST). Beginning in 1982, MOST annually reduced its subsidies to the Kolkata Port, with the sudden justification that it owed repayments on costs incurred for infrastructure projects on the river in the 1960s and 1970s. From 1994, it plunged the port into fiscal crisis by demanding repayment on loans that had previously been in permanent moratorium. In addition, further loans to the port became decentralized and profit-driven: they were supplied at commercial interest rates by other ports or foreign banks. It is these extractive debt relationships that have led to successive financial crises in the port. Each accounting year shows that the traffic in goods consistently made a profit or broke even, with the cost of labour on the river easily covered.[2] Levels of trade have remained high:

for example, in 2008-9 the absolute volume of cargo moving along the Hooghly was the third highest among Indian ports. The accounts were consistently thrown into the red, however, by the cost of repayment to an extractive state that now gave priority to its own fiscal obligations to international capital and the interests of business classes at home and abroad.

This shift has affected all aspects of bureaucracy, trade, and infrastructure on the river (Bear 2011). In the Marine Department, the decrepit and insufficient infrastructure in the docks and declining river depths owing to lack of government subsidy for dredging in the river have been most crucial. The physical waterscape has also changed profoundly, making navigation up and down the river increasingly dangerous. The office and river labour of the Marine Department now has to attempt to bring into relation the incommensurable temporal rhythms of the river tides, varying weekly levels of silting, and international trade using a decrepit infrastructure produced by another conflicting rhythm of deficit repayment. The uncertainties of this process are intense, from minor daily negotiations over the use of tugs to take ships with low-powered engines downriver on strong tides to the frequent shutting down of the docks in Kidderpore owing to the failure of the lock gates or accidents such as that at Hooghly Point. Although the situation of the Marine Department is acute, it represents the difficulties many public workplaces in India now have in mediating between disparate rhythms and the instabilities in capital accumulation that emerge from this. As the example of the Port Trust shows, this instability exists both for the public sector agency (the port) and for the national and international capital that is part of its networks (national and international shippers). The dilemmas of my informants ultimately reflect the uncertainties and conflicts in time that are produced when public resources and infrastructure are dominated by the temporal rhythms of credit repayment. Although, as Harvey and Castree suggest, credit provides an interim temporal fix for crises of over-accumulation through recirculating capital, this is a limited description of its present forms. These, especially forms of public deficit, undermine processes of circulation and production, creating multiple uncertainties, frictions, and blockages in the realization of profits and maintenance of livelihoods. Credit can now produce barriers to the further realization of capitalist value and can contribute to its rising uncertainties. Harvey and Castree are correct that the temporal fix of finance credit is a 'huge gamble' and a 'risky claim by current capitalists and financiers on their (and the societies') medium to long-term future' (Castree 2009: 47). But they did not predict its contribution to the rising uncertainty of accumulation when it is activated as part of new debt reduction and austerity policies of the public sector. When governments such as the Indian administration since the mid-1980s and bureaucracies such as the Kolkata Port Trust no longer act as agents of long-term redistributive social investment, this role for credit disappears. It acts to create the rapid extraction of income towards centralized agents of accumulation. In this role, it adds to the problem of over-accumulation rather than 'fixing' it.

At the centre of this deficit reduction politics of the public sector is a dual, mixed representation of time in capitalism. Most general accounts of capitalist time emphasize that it is represented as an abstract container and is a disciplinary unit of measure for human labour (Castree 2009; Postone 1993; Thompson 1967). This abstract time allows us to envisage an accumulative but repetitive social process of time passing and being productive. It generates a processual chronotope that is central to social disciplines that spatialize time by organizing movement (Arendt 1958; Hodges, this volume).

However, writings on globalized time have emphasized another aspect of capitalist time: the drive for speed and/or real time (Harvey 1989; Hope 2006). Behind this drive for speed lies a negative representation of time. In this it is represented as an unrenewable, finite, external force that has to be overcome and/or controlled. Time does not provide a medium for construction and accumulation; it is instead a limit-point to these processes and is potentially destructive of value (Negri 2003). This mixed utopic and dystopic representation of time in capitalism has always existed, but the contemporary politics of the public sector and of debt reduction emphasize the passage of time as destructive to the realization of value. The dominant model of governance is as a medium for the speedy circulation of capital rather than the slow repetitive maintenance of processes of social discipline, redistribution, and accumulation. The dream of repetition in time is being overcome by a demand for speed of realization of revenue, driven by the short-termism of financial credit speculation itself. Although Sampson and Wu (2003) and Levinson (2006) saw the consequences of this in relation to shipping as a private industry, they did not address its wider significance. In this section, I have begun to broaden out their perspective. This allows us to track a key change in emphasis in the representation of time in recent neoliberal economic and political practices. These focus on its destructive, external force that threatens the realization of value. Now, I wish to turn to the consequences of these policy changes for the timescape of labour and the senses of workmanship of river pilots who work the Hooghly. This will show ultimately that it is not to the temporal fixes of credit that we owe whatever temporary stability there exists in contemporary capitalism. If it exists at all, it is due to emergent, piecemeal solutions for the contradictions produced by the anti- or afunctional practices of contemporary capitalism. These 'fixes' have no teleology or single characteristic, but emerge from diverse ethics and experiences of what it is that makes human labour productive.

The timescape of shipping on the Hooghly, predictive technologies, and a sense of workmanship

Members of the Marine Department in the Kolkata Port live and work according to the unrelated temporal rhythms of the river, international shipping trade, and bureaucratic decisions. To orchestrate their work within this complex timescape in which incommensurable rhythms intersect, they must rely on the calculations of predictive technologies. Central to these calculations are the imaginary track lines that mark safe paths across the fifteen sand bars that lie between Kolkata Port and the sea 125 kilometres away at Sagar Island. Charts of the river divide it into 1,200 metre sections named after the governing bars in those segments. Every 500 metres on the charts are depth readings stretching horizontally across the river. But along the track lines that stretch vertically down the charts there are depth readings every metre. Unstable parts of the river are measured daily by hydrographic launches and larger survey vessels nearer the sea. The charts give the depths at the minimum low tide recorded, but actual depths will vary according to the rise and fall of the tide. The charts are also marked with longitude and latitude positions so that they can be used on the river itself for navigation. The charts are updated every twelve days, but track reports – Excel spreadsheets of the depths on each track down the river – are issued each evening for the next day. The predictive track lines are made from a 110-year history of naming and repeated measuring creating a specific map of the river that is officially secret knowledge. These tracks and daily depth readings form the basis for the calculations that are given the most importance in the bureaucratic planning of work on the river – the draft prediction and the allocation of ships to pilots.

The draft prediction brings the rhythms of international trade in relation to the cycles of the Hooghly. The minimum depths for the tracks each month are predicted a month in advance by the river and port harbour masters, and the head of the hydrography department. On the basis of this, the port issues a maximum draft (underwater depth of a ship, distance from the lowest part of the keel to the waterline at which the vessel is floating – i.e. how large and/or heavily loaded a ship can travel upriver) allowable in the river for each month, on the basis of which shippers in India and abroad in Sri Lanka, Singapore, China, and Vietnam book cargos in and out of the port. This figure entirely determines the size, type, and loading of ships that are sent into the Kolkata and Haldia ports. It is calculated by adding the current depths of the river from the track reports to the height of the tide predicted from the Central Survey of India data published in the port's tide table. These tidal heights are based on harmonic analysis of actual observations at stations along the river during the period from 1975 to 1984. But this probability prediction is in fact merely a partial estimate of the behaviour of the river since actual tidal behaviour and the silting of track marks are highly unpredictable, depending on weather patterns and unforeseen patterns of shoaling. There always has been and always will be an uncertainty produced by this calculative certainty that has to be negotiated by the actual labour of river pilots as they navigate the ships that have been booked on the day of sailing. In addition, the draft prediction in itself brings incommensurable and potentially contradictory rhythms of commerce and the river into relation through the calculation of tides and virtual tracks in the river.

This uncertainty has recently increased. Since 2002, the published predicted drafts have improved, apparently showing that the river has deeper depths for more months of the year, enabling shippers to make greater profits by sending more cargo upriver on fewer larger and more heavily loaded ships. The river seems to have fallen in line with the rhythms of capital and trade, allowing the generation of more profits for shippers and traders through an increase in 'time economy': a shorter time between investment and return. But a probability calculation on the basis of historical data has in fact taken on a new form. It has acquired a greater virtuality or distance from the actual dangers of navigation as a result of attempts to serve the rhythms of capital accumulation with an infrastructure produced from deficit. Frustrated by the lack of central government investment in dredging infrastructure or resources for river training and the falling traffic at the port owing to falling depths, managers now make the draft prediction on a different basis. The required under-keel clearance between the base of a ship and the bed of the river has been secretly reduced. Now on some stretches on the Hooghly river pilots work with a clearance of less than 10 centimetres.

The other core element of planning of work on the river is carried out by the river harbour master and his deputy. They decide five days in advance of the arrival of shipping how traffic will be routed up and down the river. There is always pressure from the shippers to get their specific ship into or out of the port before any of the others because only a certain number of vessels can make it up or down the river in one tide. Shippers always aim for greater speed of journey and loading and unloading to maximize their profits by cutting the cost of payment for crews, berth hire space, and storage space in the port. The riverine tides and depths in the Hooghly determine the

Journal of the Royal Anthropological Institute (N.S.), 71-88
© Royal Anthropological Institute 2014

assignment of traffic through the Kolkata port system and the rhythms of trade to and from Eastern India and Nepal in the ports of Colombo and Singapore. Yet within these constraints there is much negotiation with shipping agents over the timing of the allocation of berths and pilots to their vessels. A day before sailing, the deputy river harbour master assigns pilots to specific ships. More experienced pilots are always given longer vessels: in fact the ranks of a pilot – first, second, or third grade – determine the size of vessels they are permitted to navigate.[3] Similarly, first-grade pilots are given vessels with deeper drafts, with anything above 6.9 metres always piloted by them. It is a matter of prestige if you are given a deep-drafted or large-size vessel, and sometimes more junior pilots are allocated these since there is a limited pool of men who can be called upon for any one scheduled sailing. The orders are issued to specific pilots the afternoon before sailing.

But the allocation of ships is frequently a point of fierce dispute because in the interests of the realization of profit it contains omissions in its calculation of danger and difficulty. The hull shape and the engine power of ships greatly affect how ships can be handled in the river and whether they can be brought safely up- or downriver in different tidal strengths and weather conditions. Yet these measurements are not part of calculations of when and how ships should be timed for sailings. Instead, officers turn to a qualitative measure of 'skill' in the bodies and minds of pilots themselves. Officers claim that they allocate ships according to the skill and 'strength of heart' of pilots – fitting the character of the ship to the characters of men.

River pilots, on the other hand, did not accept this deflection of a quantitative omission into a qualitative measure. They quite bluntly stated that because the allocation of jobs intentionally did not take into account the engine power of ships or the predicted strength of the tide, they often had to refuse ships in order to preserve themselves from dangerous situations. When negotiations over refusals fail, officers themselves take the controversial ships or loads themselves. They are proud of this work, suggesting, as one senior officer put it, that 'only we are capable of taking the risk'. This invocation of skill, individuality, and the excitement of danger is a consistent pattern in the Marine Department. Skill is another name for the ability of a pilot with his body and mind to overcome the omissions and contradictions created by predictive technologies and work practices that tie together the conflicting rhythms of trade and capital generation with those of the recalcitrant river. It is a hierarchical measure that automatically gives authority to Marine Department officers with their 'experience', demonstrated by their willingness to take refused ships up and down the Hooghly.

The sense of workmanship of river pilots is shaped by the way in which their labour strains to bring together these incommensurable temporalities and predictive technologies into a single journey. When they take command of a container ship to guide it safely up- or downriver, they do not simply enter into a domain of time-discipline in which they have to complete a task in relation to the tide and a deadline. They also experience the journey as a product of a deep time-depth of historical knowledge of the river manifested in charts, technologies, and their own skill. In addition, as they move in the waterscape, wrecks, man-made spurs, abandoned vessels, and beached buoys that must be navigated round create a sense of both historical depth and transition. At the same time, their labour involves a skilful manipulation of the non-human rhythms of the river and of the vessel they command. The use of different technologies in combination with each other, such as the chart and echo-sounder, demands a pacing of the body in relation to the various pieces of machinery and the river itself. In addition, the

already complicated timescape of the Hooghly is also permeated with the ritual significance of the River Ganga. River pilots would assert that the river was a place of
technological skill and labour and a man-made river that has taken its current physical
form in the scale of human history as a result of the drainage and spurs of the British.
However, everyone called the river the Ganga and claimed its origins in the Adi-Ganga.
Their complex experience of the timescape of labour can therefore not be encapsulated
by a focus on knowledge practices, technology, time-discipline, or abstract representations alone. It is formed from the intersection of all of these and the ways in which their
labour has to orchestrate and reconcile incommensurable rhythms.

The sense of workmanship emergent from this timescape of labour emphasizes the
navigation of the ship as a moment of freedom and agency in which you open yourself
up to an intuitive fusion between yourself and the forces operating around you. You
seek a fusing with the ship and the river and the forces of wind, waves, current, tide, and
depth. All bureaucratic constraints fall away as your individual power becomes amplified by connection with the ship and the river and the wider forces of the universe.
River pilots young and old repeatedly spoke of how on the river what attracts them, as
36-year-old Sudhir said,

> is the autonomy and freedom of the work. When I am in charge of a ship I don't give a damn about
> anyone else, not the harbour master, not the chairman, not anybody – nobody is over you at all. I am
> totally in charge of a 170 lakh machine. I take the decisions then, and if something happens, then I am
> responsible and I know I have done the right thing. No one else commands you at all.

But this responsibility also contains the thrill of feeling your individual power becoming amplified through its fusion with other agencies. For example, a 35-year-old pilot,
Atin, spoke of piloting in the following terms: 'You pilot with something inside you,
with your strength, and the ship becomes part of your limbs, part of yourself, when you
are in charge of it. You are no longer a malleable, weak creature'. Captain Wadia, a
renowned pilot in his eighties, spoke of why he loved being on the river so much: 'It is
the ship-handling. You are an insignificant pilot on the bridge but you are handling
thousands of tons of machinery, and this thrilled me'. In fact, Wadia's interpretations of
the freedom and constraint of ship-handling have structured most of the current pilots'
interpretations of the work process since he either trained them or coached them for
their exams. When I asked him to give me ship-handling lessons, he made the schema
explicit. The pilot's universe on the river is divided into forces that are under degrees of
individual control. Under direct control are the engines, propeller, rudder, anchors,
moorings, and the ship's inertia. Not under your control are the wind, the waves, the
current/tide, and the depth. The work of ship-handling is to open yourself to these
forces in order to adjust your actions to them. This is why pilots aim to achieve on
board an intuitive fusion within them of the 'feeling of the ship' and the 'feeling of the
river'. This is not simply an attitude of mastery of the distinct vitalities and agencies of
the ship and the river, but an approach that makes you entirely open to them in order
to respond to them. The best pilots were seen to turn their feeling for the river into a
love for the river. Captain Wadia was emblematic of this love, demonstrated by his
refusal to retire and continuing work on ships at anchor in his eighties.

The pilots' ethic of opening themselves to other forces and vitalities ultimately led
some of them to idioms that suggested that there were intrinsic commonalities between
human and non-human forms of life. For example, Captain Wadia used the philosophy
of Vivekananda to express this:

> Vivekananda explains that there is actually an impersonal god and God is in everything. Everything animate and inanimate is part of God, so the way you treat other people, that way you are treating God also. This is what made me love the river – it was part of God. And ships too are part of God, and I always considered them alive.

Although this is a particular framing, this sensibility is entirely characteristic of all the river pilots I met. Ships and the river were attributed a life that the pilot had to fuse with in an amplification of his individual agency.

Given this ethic, what most excited river pilots about processes of navigational technology was the possibility that it would bring them as individuals into a closer relation with the forces that affected their labour on the river. The ideal technologies are ones that make this fusion of men, ships, the river, and the universe more complete. All pilots romanticized the old navigational technologies or rules of thumb that meant you could use your body itself to measure distance and direction.

Within this sense of workmanship, accidents are a terrifying collapse of pilots' agency. As Ajeet put it when describing the effect of his accident on him:

> My hands began to lose power. I could not properly grip the ladder on the ships. Suddenly all my face went black. I began not to be able to even go out of the house into a taxi. My muscle power collapsed. I am losing power – I lost all of my power.

All pilots, young and old, like Ajeet, described accidents as a piling on of unpredicted, incalculable circumstances that left them experiencing a personal crisis expressed in uncontrollable bodily responses. Captain Wadia, for example, described his first accident in 1964:

> I had a collision at Moyapur and an accident there also ... I stayed on the ship for two days. As the tide moved, the ship tilted left then right. I was shaking when I finally got off the boat. I stayed on it to try and do something to rescue it. But the tide scoured the sand away from the ends and she broke her back. When I fell asleep in my bed, I was turning and holding one side of the bed after the other like I was moving on the ship as she tilted in the tide.

Tapan also spoke in these terms, describing how after hitting a jetty at Haldia, his wife would hear him calling out headings in his sleep, replaying the experience that left him disturbed: 'When I was first working, I hit a jetty at Haldia. I would see it again at night in my dreams. My wife said I would call out in my sleep, "Astern, starboard" '.

For all pilots, these failures of agency can only be overcome by making accidents productive. They must be used by pilots either to generate new individual skills that can be passed on to other pilots or to form new technical solutions that make pilots safer and bring them into closer relation with the river. Accidents demand a practical intervention which will help pilots to move even closer to the agency of the river. Consider the following exchange when Tapan was trying to comfort Ajeet over his accident.

> *Tapan*: Accidents are good.
>
> *Ajeet*: Yes, accidents give you the knowledge to pilot. Accidents give you practical knowledge of the river.
>
> *Tapan*: Yes. When you are a branch pilot and testing the young pilots in a few years' time, you will be able to ask them the most difficult questions!

At the most quotidian level, accidents are reworked as transmissible knowledge in the telling of stories to fellow or junior pilots. They are in fact essential to the process of education among pilots. Whenever I asked pilots to explain their work to me, they would always gravitate towards a discussion of accidents that they had experienced. They would also swap these stories with each other. Very often I realized that as people started to describe accidents to me in general terms, I had heard the story told exactly the same way by the person who had the accident. Captain Wadia's ship-handling lessons were built around his recounting of his various accidents as illustrations of general principles. This response, of course, helps to contain any broader questioning of the conditions and contradictions of the complex system of calculation, work process, and prediction that has combined to produce the accidents. The pilots' sense of workmanship that they are heroic amplified agents in communion with the forces of the river and ship unintentionally produces this redirecting of the breaches of accidents into questions of better piloting knowledge.

This practice for making accidents productive is long-standing and quotidian for pilots, but sometimes accidents such as Ajeet's result in them pushing for new techno-logical interventions. How are these innovations a reworking into technology of the ethical duty of care that pilots assert for each other? What do they reveal about the temporal and technological fixes of contemporary capitalism? These questions can be answered by turning next to a discussion of the electronic charts that were introduced during my year of fieldwork.

Affect, ethics, and technological fixes: electronic charts and the pilots' guild

The most conservative response to Ajeet's accident came from marine officers, who simply assimilated it to hierarchies of skill, putting it down to inexperience. They wanted nothing to change at all as a result of the event and actively blocked the attempts of pilots to make electronic charts of the river. The river pilots bitterly resented these attempts to block the development of the charts. They approached the chairman of the port directly and set about collecting data from each other, making and then testing the new electronic charts on the river.

Yet this project was in its own way a limited solution shaped by the pilots' ethic of labour and the lack of union radicalism in the Pilots' Association. The charts were a technological device that would allow pilots to make more dangerous manoeuvres and 'adjust' themselves to the declining work conditions in the port. Although this became clear from discussions with many pilots, here I will draw on conversations with Captain Verma, a high-level office-holder in the River Pilots' professional body. For Verma and the other river pilots, the new electronic charts were inseparable from the ethics and knowledge of the Pilots' Association, which was understood primarily as a guild of secret knowledge. Verma explained the organization in the following terms:

> We are a close-knit family. If any one of us is having a personal problem, we extend help to each other. If any one person has a problem like an accident, I feel that I did something wrong when I was training them. We are not a union. We also pass on secret knowledge to each other so that way we are a guild too. If one member has a problem, then there is a problem among all the members. Recently one member [meaning Ajeet] became very ill and I personally went to the chairman to ask for the money for treatment and we all supported him and his family together.

At its heart the guild was understood by Verma and other pilots as a mechanism for the transfer of knowledge between older and younger generations. As Verma put it:

Journal of the Royal Anthropological Institute (N.S.), 71-88
© Royal Anthropological Institute 2014

> In our training we transfer our values like a father to a son. No one has been able to write a manual in how to navigate this river. I have seen people try to write it down. No book can be right because the channel is always shifting and you learn from your superiors. You can't write our knowledge down.

The transfer of this knowledge was essential to prevent accidents. Verma described the passing on of ship-handling knowledge that would help their juniors in unexpected circumstances as 'our collective responsibility as seniors'. The new electronic charts were simply the extension of this secret guild knowledge and ethic into a new medium. Verma expressed this by first telling me of the inalienable genealogical relationship between the river, pilots, and charts: 'Most of the places in the river were discovered by pilots. The charts and our training are marked by their names'. He then told me that once he had been sailing with an English captain upriver named Harwood, and it turned out that he was the grandson of a Bengal pilot. Verma said: 'I showed him the chart and said, look, here is your grandfather's name here on Harwood Point. His grandfather's name remains on the river'. Then Verma turned to the electronic charts on his laptop and said:

> Look at the electronic chart. Look at all these pilots' names – Preston Tower, Black's Point. They named these places so their grandsons could remember them and they could continue in their minds that way. See Sidney point, Edward's creek. Here are the fathers of the service.

He forged a patrilineal line of inheritance that inevitably linked the organic life of generations of pilots to the technology of charts and the river itself. Electronic charts were simply another manifestation of this knowledge and inheritance. The idiom for this came from a broader repertoire of inheritance. When I asked Captain Verma if the river had any special significance for him, he described how for fifteen days before Mahalaya (the arrival of Durga during the annual festival),

> I go to the ghat [place of worship on the waterfront] and I think of my forefathers and offer to the Ganga. I remember seven generations of ancestors at that time. It is a good time to remember my legacy and inheritance. I ask them to bless me so I will do my duties. I remember each of them by name and think of them all individually.

It was this same idiom of legacy and the river that Verma projected onto the charts, making them a sign of inevitable connection between pilots and the Hooghly.

This emphasis on electronic charts as the natural consequence of the pilots' legacy and as the correct solution for Ajeet's accident limited the implications that could be drawn from it. As Verma and other pilots too explained it, the new technology would mean that:

> You can work with a lesser width of channel because you can have a very high accuracy of location. We can reduce the channel to 1,000 feet width from 1,500 feet for 120 miles of the river, so we will have to dredge a smaller space in the river. This will mean an increase in drafts and less of the channel to dredge so it will save money too. The chairman rang me up last week and said posterity will remember you for what you have done for the port.

This was a technical intervention that would place pilots in tighter navigational situations. It would allow them to 'adjust to' rather than challenge the contradictions of the predictive and planning technologies in the port. It deflected from any discussion of the safety of working conditions and it supported a de-politicized concept of a guild of pilots joined in collective secret knowledge. Created from a sense of workmanship generated by a timescape of labour, this technology provided a temporary fix for the contradictions of a public-deficit-driven extraction of resources from infrastructure towards debt repayment. It is only through the introduction of these electronic charts that Kolkata continues to receive the consumption goods symbolic of 'globalization', international shippers in China and Singapore can secure profits, and the government can repeatedly draw revenue towards its repayment of international debts. It is through small piecemeal, popular moves such as this one driven by affect and ethics that current contradictory forms of neoliberal policy and capitalism can continue. These have been sidelined in our analysis of contemporary capitalism quite simply because we have taken representations, predictive devices, knowledge practices, and time-discipline singly as sites of analyses. Instead, as I have done here, we need to restore their mediation in acts of labour. Then we can uncover the affects and ethics of capitalist time, which are emergent from practices of time-discipline and abstract time-reckoning, but not containable within their logics. It is in relation to these affects and ethics, as well as from infrastructures and abstractions, that rhythms of capital circulation and the contingent realization of capitalist value emerge. Capital can no longer be understood as a teleological process working through history enabled by abstract knowledges and reckonings of time. It is instead an immanent and uncertain effect of acts of labour in the world.

Conclusion: labour, mediation, and heterochronies

There is a shared problem in recent discussions of accidents, predictive technologies, and technological practices. This is that they are analysed as if they could be separated out from the complex timescapes of labour that they are part of. This has meant that predictive technologies have been understood primarily as knowledge practices that reflect and produce abstract representations of time, space, and capital (Aneesh 2006; Miyazaki 2003; Riles 2004). Accidents have been analysed as spectacular phenomena external to the ethical and working life of institutions (Law & Mol 2002; Perrow 1984; Schivelbusch 1987; Žižek 1999). However, such approaches leave out two significant domains of reality. First, they underplay the fact that workplaces are cross-cut by multiple, often contradictory, representations, disciplines, and technologies of time. Secondly, they ignore the complex ethical senses of workmanship that emerge from the work process, the technological interventions that develop from this explicit 'tinkering towards the good' (Law & Mol 2002: 85), and the diversity of representations of the relationships between the human and the non-human. My argument here has been an attempt to build on this pioneering work, but also to correct these omissions. I would suggest that it is impossible to understand the growing instability of capital accumulation and the ethical and political responses of workers to this unless we take such an approach. My perspective here has also been an attempt to contribute to the exploration of what might be called the popular working life of technology. Long ago, Latour (1996) discussed the relationships between technology, ethics, and passion in *Amaris*, but my approach differs from his since it moves beyond the projects of specialist scientists and bureaucrats to an examination of technological ethics that emerge from the work process and timescape of labour. This does not draw on a single experience or concept of the relationship between the human and the non-human. Instead there are a diversity of boundaries and relationships dependent on the experience of labour and skill itself.

The focus here on the mediations in labour of the contradictions generated within contemporary capitalism throws new light on the influential theories of Harvey and Castree. First, their predictions that credit provides a temporal fix for the instability of the over-accumulation of capital only work if we leave out of view current deficit policies and neoliberal state practices. When credit relationships are mobilized in a manner that leads state agencies to extract value from infrastructure and public sector labour rather than investing and redistributing capital, credit does not provide a fix. Instead it produces a mounting contradiction of extraction towards the top of pyramids in governments and in international capital markets that will not prevent over-accumulation and will not enable circulation. In addition, such measures make the act of production and labour of circulation harder to realize, as we have seen on the Hooghly, producing greater short-term instabilities for public and private agencies rather than resolving these. This new role for state institutions in relation to international credit agencies is based on an accentuation of the dystopian representation of time in capitalism, as a destructive external force that must be overcome, rather than as a neutral, abstract, iterative medium for long-term accumulation and social discipline. It is this representation that is dominant in neoliberal deficit reduction policies and short-term capitalism – a fact that has often been glossed as a new emphasis on space/time compression and 'real time'. This is not just a desire for speed; it is a negative chronotope of time as anti-processual, corrosive, and threatening to the realization of profit. Most importantly, the ethnography of river pilots working on the Hooghly suggests that whatever limited and temporary stability there is in the contradictory network of capitalist circulation is generated from contingent ethically and affect-driven practices that are piecemeal and diverse. These emerge within and from mediating acts of labour, not from the large-scale teleological temporal fixes that Harvey (1982; 1989; 2005) and Castree (2009) describe. Unless our theoretical and ethnographic accounts take notice of this central mediating role of labour, they will remain profoundly incomplete. This is equally true for our understanding of markets, governance, production, or finance.

We now have the analytical challenge of tracking more widely the complex terrain of capitalist social time and temporalizing practices, leaving behind our assertion that they are characterized solely by an abstract, homogeneous form of time. As this ethnography of river pilots has shown, time-reckonings and knowledge practices generate multiple contradictions and incommensurabilities. As a result, social time in capitalism is heterochronic and the circulation of capital will repeatedly emerge as an ethical, affective problem of attempting to reconcile diverse, recalcitrant rhythms and representations (Althusser & Balibar 1970; Marx 1992 [1885]; Negri 2003). We have too often glossed this immanent complexity as solely a matter of abstract time-discipline and/or a desire for speed. The circulation of capital will continue as long as we labour to conjoin together abstract reckonings of time, predictive devices, social rhythms, and our ethical relations to each other. If we should stop our labour and contemplate the social heterochronies that we exist within, then what politics and forms of life would become possible? Ajeet was forced to do this in the wake of his accident. Yet he experienced this not as a release, but as an unbearable failure and a loss of agency. How might it be possible to de-individualize our experiences of social hetereochrony and not lose our selves that are formed from the labour of mediating conflicts in time? How could Ajeet recognize that his accident was beyond his control and still be a man of skill with the potential for heroic agency? This is the productive and compelling ethical dilemma that capitalist time offers us.

Journal of the Royal Anthropological Institute (N.S.), 71-88
© Royal Anthropological Institute 2014

NOTES

This work is based on research funded from 2008 to 2010 by the ESRC. This included one year of continuous fieldwork on the Hooghly river and archival work in the Kolkata Port Trust offices. This was followed by return visits in 2010 and 2011. I would like to thank the river workers and their families, who taught me their trades and welcomed me into their homes.

[1] Pseudonyms are used throughout this paper to protect my informants' identities.

[2] I have checked the accounts from 1950 to the present published in the archives of the Board Meetings of the port available in the Port Trust Library, Kolkata.

[3] First-grade pilots have more than twenty years of service; second grade more than four or five years of service; third grade less than four years of service.

REFERENCES

ALTHUSSER, L. & É. BALIBAR 1970. *Reading Capital*. London: New Left Books.

ANEESH, A. 2006. *Virtual migration: the programming of globalization*. Durham, N.C.: Duke University Press.

ARENDT, H. 1958. *The human condition*. Chicago: University Press.

BEAR, L. 2011. Making a river of gold: speculative state planning, informality and neo-liberal governance on the Hooghly. *Focaal* **61**, 46-60.

——— 2012. Sympathy and its material boundaries: necropolitics, labour and waste on the Hooghly. In *Recycling economies* (eds) C. Alexander & J. Reno, 185-203. London: Zed Press.

——— 2013*a*. 'This body is our body': Vishwakarma puja, the social debts of kinship, and theologies of materiality in a neoliberal shipyard. In *Vital relations: modernity and the persistent life of kinship* (eds) F. Cannell & S. McKinnon, 155-78. Santa Fe, N.M.: School for Advanced Research Press.

——— 2013*b*. The antinomies of audit: opacity, instability and charisma in the economic governance of a Hooghly shipyard. *Economy and Society* **42**, 375-97.

BESTOR, T. 2001. Supply-side sushi: commodity, market and the global city. *American Anthropologist* **103**, 76-95.

BIAO, X. 2006. *Global bodyshopping: an Indian labour system in the information technology industry*. Princeton: University Press.

BLOCH, M. 1977. The past in the present and the present. *Man* (N.S.) **12**, 278-92.

CASTREE, N. 2009. The spatio-temporality of capitalism. *Time and Society* **18**, 26-61.

CORBRIDGE, S. & J. HARRIS 2000. *Reinventing India: liberalization, Hindu nationalism and popular democracy*. Cambridge: Polity.

DEV, S.M. & J. MOOIJ 2002. Social sector expenditure in the 1990s: analysis of central and state budgets. *Economic and Political Weekly* **2**, 853-66.

FREEMAN, C. 2000. *High tech and high heels in the global economy: women, work and pink-collar identities in the Caribbean*. Durham, N.C.: Duke University Press.

GRAHAM, S. & N. THRIFT 2007. Out of order: understanding repair and maintenance. *Theory, Culture & Society* **24**, 1-25.

HARVEY, D. 1982. *Limits to capital*. Oxford: Blackwell.

——— 1989. *The condition of post-modernity*. Oxford: Blackwell.

——— 2005. *A brief history of neoliberalism*. Oxford: University Press.

HOPE, W. 2006. Global capitalism and the critique of real time. *Time and Society* **15**, 275-302.

INGOLD, T. 1993. The temporality of the landscape. *World Archaeology* **25**, 152-74.

LANGLEY, P. 2008. Sub-prime mortgage lending: a cultural economy. *Economy and Society* **37**, 469-94.

LATOUR, B. 1996. *Aramis, or, the love of technology*. Cambridge, Mass.: Harvard University Press.

LAW, J. & A. MOL 2002. Local entanglements or utopian moves: an inquiry into train accidents. In *Utopia and organization* (ed.) M. Parker, 82-105. Oxford: Blackwell.

LEVINSON, M. 2006. *The box*. Princeton: University Press.

LI PUMA, E. & B. LEE 2005. Financial derivatives and the rise of circulation. *Economy and Society* **34**, 404-27.

MACKENZIE, A. 2001. The technicity of time: from 1.00 oscillations/sec to 9192631770Hz. *Time and Society* **10**, 235-57.

MACKENZIE, D. 2006. *An engine, not a camera: how financial models shape markets*. Cambridge, Mass.: MIT Press.

MARCHAND, T. 2010. *Making knowledge: explorations of the indissoluble relation between mind, body and environment*. Oxford: Wiley-Blackwell.

MARX, K. 1992 [1885]. *Capital*, vol. 2. London: Penguin.

MASSEY, D., P. QUINTAS & D. WELD 1992. *High-tech fantasies: science parks in society, science and space*. London: Routledge.

MAY, J. & N. THRIFT 2001. Introduction. In *Timespace: geographies of temporality* (eds) J. May & N. Thrift, 1-46. London: Routledge.

MIYAZAKI, H. 2003. The temporalities of the market. *American Anthropologist* **105**, 255-65.

MUNN, N. 1992. The cultural anthropology of time: a critical essay. *Annual Review of Anthropology* **21**, 93-123.

NEGRI, A. 2003. *Time for revolution*. London: Continuum.

PERROW, C. 1984. *Normal accidents: living with high-risk technologies*. New York: Basic Books.

PICKERING, A. 1995. *The mangle of practice: time, agency and science*. Chicago: University Press.

——— 2008. New ontologies. In *The mangle in practice: science, society, and becoming* (eds) A. Pickering & K. Guzik, 1-26. Durham, N.C.: Duke University Press.

POSTONE, M. 1993. *Time, labour and social domination*. Cambridge: University Press.

RICHARD, A. & D. RUDNYCKYJ 2009. Economies of affect. *Journal of the Royal Anthropological Institute* (N.S.) **15**, 57-77.

RILES, A. 2004. Real time: unwinding technocratic and anthropological knowledge. *American Ethnologist* **31**, 392-405.

ROSE, N. 1999. *Governing the soul: shaping of the private self*. London: Free Association Books.

SAMPSON, H. & B. WU 2003. Compressed time and constraining space: the contradictory effects of ICT and containerization on international shipping labour. *International Review of Social History* **48**, 123-52.

SCHIVELBUSCH, W. 1987. *The railway journey: the industrialization of time and space*. Berkeley: University of California Press.

THOMPSON, E.P. 1967. Time, work-discipline and industrial capitalism. *Past and Present* **38**, 56-97.

UPADHYAY, C. 2009. Controlling offshore knowledge workers: power and agency in India's software outsourcing industry. *New Technology, Work and Employment* **24**, 2-18.

ZALOOM, C. 2006. *Out of the pits: traders and technology from Chicago to London*. Chicago: University Press.

——— 2009. How to read the future: the yield curve, affect and financial prediction. *Public Culture* **21**, 245-68.

ŽIŽEK, S. 1999. *The sublime object of ideology*. London: Verso.

Pour le travail physique : l'accident d'Ajeet et l'éthique des accommodements technologiques dans le temps

Résumé

À partir d'une ethnographie des pilotes qui conduisent les porte-conteneurs sur la Hooghly, l'article plaide pour que l'on mette l'accent sur le travail physique comme acte de médiation dans les espaces-temps des lieux de travail mondialisés. Il élabore une nouvelle approche du temps capitaliste, qui tente de combiner la récente attention portée aux pratiques du savoir avec une focalisation marxiste plus ancienne sur le rôle médiateur du travail physique. Les bureaucrates soumis aux cadences du remboursement de la dette publique jouent un rôle extractif sur la Hooghly et entraînent le déclin de l'infrastructure. Les contradictions des politiques gouvernementales rendent de plus en plus difficile la navigation sur le fleuve, avec pour conséquence de fréquents accidents. Les pilotes fluviaux « s'accommodent » de ceux-ci par des interventions technologiques dictées par l'éthique ou le « sens du travail bien fait » qui émergent de leurs actes de travail physique dans des espace-temps spécifiques. Sur la Hooghly, le capital continue de circuler à travers ces petits mouvements « bricolés » dans lesquels le temps est un problème éthique, affectif et technique, plutôt qu'à travers les grands accommodements temporels décrits par Harvey et Castree. Nous devons donc repenser radicalement notre approche du temps dans le capitalisme, en allant au-delà des récits existants qui le présentent comme une mesure abstraite de la valeur ou comme une source de discipline temporelle. Le temps capitaliste est hétérochrone et provoque des tentatives pour concilier des rythmes et représentations divers et récalcitrants par le biais de notre travail éthique et physique.

Political times

4

Historical narrative, mundane political time, and revolutionary moments: coexisting temporalities in the lived experience of social movements

SIAN LAZAR *University of Cambridge*

This paper responds to the challenge to conceptualize political activity through temporal as well as spatial perspectives, and does so by means of a discussion of the different temporalities experienced by union and social movement activists. It is based on fieldwork with activists from two public sector workers' unions in Buenos Aires and residents and street vendors' organizations in the city of El Alto, Bolivia. I discuss two coexisting temporalities, or social experiences of time (Munn): 'historical time', a sense of emplacement within a historical narrative of political action that looks back to the past and to illustrious ancestors and forwards to an imagined set of possibilities for the future; and 'attritional time', one of constant protest or negotiation, the continuance of the day to day of political life when there is no resolution in sight to a particular conflict or problem, coupled occasionally with a dramatization of what can become quite banal over time. Finally, I discuss a kind of event-based mediation between different temporalities, specifically revolution as a clash or meeting of attritional time and historical time, coexisting but separately experienced temporalities. This mediation involves both the revolutionary actions themselves and the practices of hailing, both contemporaneous and retrospective, which include scholarly research as well as other forms of social commentary. I suggest that this hailing might be in part enacted through a promise or assertion of discontinuity and rupture in the flow of time (Harris), even when events may not have been experienced as such at the time itself. Thus, different social experiences of time meet in a politics of time, to co-construct *kairos*, or revolution.

This paper responds to the challenge set by the editor of this special issue to conceptualize political activity through temporal as well as spatial perspectives. It does so by means of a discussion of the different temporalities experienced by union and social movement activists in Latin America, mainly public sector workers' unions in Buenos Aires in 2009. I suggest that Argentine public sector unionists operate within varying coexisting temporalities, which I understand to mean social experiences of time (Munn 1992). I discuss two such temporalities in some detail here, and name them 'historical time' and 'attritional time'. 'Historical time' is a sense of emplacement within a historical narrative of political action that looks back to the past and to illustrious ancestors and forwards to an imagined set of possibilities for the future; 'attritional time' is one of constant protest or negotiation, the continuance of the day to day of political life when there is no resolution in sight to a particular conflict or problem, coupled occasionally with a dramatization of what can become quite banal over time.

Historical time and attritional time are not necessarily competing temporalities, but they have different political effects and ramifications. Occasionally, they come together, either in conflict or perhaps through some kind of mediating event such as 'a revolution'. So the second main aim of my paper is to explore those moments when experiences of time become a *politics* of time, using the particular example of the Bolivian 'revolution' of 2000-5 (Dunkerley 2007; Hylton & Thomson 2007), as experienced by residents' and street vendors' organizations in the city of El Alto, Bolivia. I ask what makes mundane political time ('attritional time') into something astonishing, even revolutionary; what makes an event? 'Revolution' is – among other things, of course – a kind of event-based mediation between different temporalities, which involves both the revolutionary actions themselves and practices of hailing, both contemporaneous and retrospective, which include scholarly research as well as other forms of social commentary. Those practices of hailing thereby evoke and/or constitute the social experience of time of commentators, including anthropologists, historians, journalists, and so on. I suggest that the hailing itself might be in part enacted through a promise or assertion of discontinuity and rupture in the flow of time (Harris 1995; 1996; 2004; 2006), even when events may not have been experienced as such at the time itself. So, I argue that different social experiences of time meet in a politics of time, in some cases to co-construct revolution.

My analysis here goes somewhat against the grain of most writing on social movements, which has tended to produce mostly spatial metaphors as a means of understanding their politics and praxis. Ideas of inclusion/exclusion, networks, meshworks or rhizomatic forms, the commons, the Multitude, the right to the city, 'political society', civil society, framing, capacities, and so on, are all highly spatial.[1] That is not to say that the scholarly work I refer to here is ahistorical or has no theory of change; to the contrary. Rather, I want to suggest simply that it tends to privilege the topographical over the temporal in its analysis of the experience of contemporary social movements. My ethnographic data suggest that for activists, being part of a social movement is as much about inhabiting different lived social experiences of time as it is about participating in networks, fighting for inclusion, and so on. This paper attempts to explore some of the ramifications of that recognition and foreground (some of) the temporal aspects of social movement activism.

In doing so, it speaks to a different literature, namely that on the 'event'. By juxtaposing the experience of ordinary, everyday time with the sense of living in and making history, I aim to investigate what constitutes an event. Alain Badiou (2003; 2005) tends to construct 'the event' by virtue of its particularity, recognized mostly *post facto* as (crudely) the rupture revealing universalizing truth – as with the exemplar of St Paul's conversion. What we might call an anthropology of events (such as Das 1995; Humphrey 2008; Robbins 2007; 2010; Sahlins 1991), also points to the newness – and 'bigness' – of particular happenings that are constituted as events. But the temporality involved in this recognition is one of before and after: before everything changed, after everything was changed. There is also a kind of lurking definitional circularity: an event is an 'event' because it is recognized as an event. My paper aims to complement this literature by exploring how events might be constituted in lived time; what makes ordinary time into astonishing time, and how the revolutionary potential inherent in ongoing political activity is released.

Journal of the Royal Anthropological Institute (N.S.), 91-108
© Royal Anthropological Institute 2014

'Historical time': emplacement within historical narratives

Social experiences of time may be explored through a discussion of both representations and phenomenology of time (Hodges 2008; Munn 1992). The first temporality (or temporal representation) that I propose here is a sense of emplacement within a historical narrative of political action that looks back to the past and to illustrious ancestors and forwards to an imagined set of possibilities for the future. Such a narrative tends to involve a linear sense of time, albeit one that does not flow smoothly but is punctuated by iconic events, epochs, and people.

I conducted my fieldwork in 2009 with activists from ATE and UPCN, two public sector workers' unions. ATE (Asociación de Trabajadores del Estado, Association of State Workers) is a progressive, leftist union, which places great emphasis on its autonomy from party politics, and on internal democracy. UPCN (Unión del Personal Civil de la Nación, Union of National Civil Servants) is much more orthodox and Peronist, and proudly holds what it calls an 'officialist' position with respect to incumbent governments – who are of course its affiliates' employer as well. ATE affiliates range from health workers in municipal hospitals to more middle-class civil servants in central administrative entities, or academic researchers, scientists in state-run laboratories, and so on. UPCN dominates among the middle-class civil servants who work in ministries and other administrative entities, but has affiliates across the range of government offices, albeit mostly at a national rather than municipal level. The majority of my informants were 'delegates', that is, representatives for the affiliates in their workplace – the equivalent of shop stewards in UK terminology. Some were leaders at higher levels of the organization.

In interviews, my informants would often take me through their version of the history of the Argentine labour movement, in response to my general questions about unionism itself. They would stress in particular the relationship between unionism and Peronism, which has been very complicated given the different expressions of Peronism in Argentina – from the mid-century version of Juan Perón himself to that of Carlos Menem in the 1990s. The latter was highly contentious and very much associated with structural adjustment, an issue of particular concern to state workers' unions because of the importance of privatization policies. Historically informed discussions of state-union relationships were very much how people would contextualize themselves *for me* when I was interviewing them or discussing my research with them, and in that sense they constituted a public narrative, albeit one that was remarkably consistent across a range of informants, and also reproduced in other forums, such as training sessions for new activists, or public assemblies.

Considering the interview materials from ATE in particular prompted me into providing historical context in the subsequent writing process, even if informants did not themselves always give an extensive historical background. As the fieldwork progressed, I came to understand, for example, that one crucial aspect of ATE's narrative of self-presentation had a very clear historical trajectory. ATE's self-identification is very much as an alternative to a corrupt Peronist form of unionism; informants spoke of two different *modelos sindicales* (models of unionism), interpretation of which requires an understanding of the historical background to each. ATE is very closely associated with the project of the CTA (Central de los Trabajadores Argentinos), which is an alternative workers' central to the dominant Peronist trade union confederation, the CGT (Confederación General del Trabajo). From the mid-twentieth century on, the CGT has very much enjoyed a 'professional' relationship with the state, and especially the Peronist party. From 1955, the Peronist unions were the backbone of resistance to military regimes, and unionists suffered considerable persecution in the Dirty War of 1976-83. However, there have always been tensions between the bureaucratic unionism of leaders prepared to negotiate with government and employers and more radical tendencies on the shop floor. ATE's contemporary political project with the CTA stakes a claim to be the inheritor of the more radical currents, which were known in the 1960s as *clasismo*, and which in some stories even go back to the anarchist activism of the early twentieth century.

The proposal of an alternative *modelo sindical* was a trope repeated by ATE activists throughout interviews, training sessions, and in published materials. It involved a critique of the CGT unions in the present and the past, and an attempt to construct an alternative political project for both the labour movement and society more widely through the CTA itself. For the former, ATE activists placed considerable emphasis on two main aspects: first, their attempt to preserve autonomy from political parties; and, second, their focus on internal democracy, especially associated with the holding of assemblies. Pablo Sanseverino described this new form of unionism as promoted in ATE as follows:

> Well, the unionism of ATE, within the state, is a unionism that defends autonomy from parties, autonomy from the state, from the boss. In this sense, it's a fundamental difference, one could say, fundamentally different from the other union, which is UPCN, because that's a union which we say is of (dependent on) the state ... Another fundamental characteristic for me is that in ATE, we say, the assembly decides. We're not a union of management, we are a combative union, and it is from this [self-]definition that we take forward the mandate of the workers' assembly.

Claudio Lozano, one of the most important political figures of the ATE/CTA, argued that the CTA was a response to the loss of power for unions in the mid-1970s that resulted from the 'economic, social and political restructuring' that Argentina underwent. He argued in an interview that there were three basic answers to this problem for unions. The first was to become *sindicatos empresarios*, or business unions which seek to make profit not through the support of their affiliates but through becoming important actors in the privatization process, especially the privatization of pension funds. The second response that some unions adopted was to ally themselves with the political system, as happened with Menemist unionism. 'And the third response', Lozano said,

> is that expressed by the CTA, where there is an attempt to seek the recovery of capacity and influence in favour of the workers. [But this is] not through saving the union structure – which is the case of the business model, nor through adhesion and subordination to the dominant political system, but instead by finding a new political and organizational form that permits all the workers to express themselves in a new situation. And there a new organizational form was born ... Now, [what's important is] the theme of proposing a rupture in history, proposing the theme of autonomy of workers or of workers' organizations with respect to the state, the parties and the bosses. Why is this a historical rupture? Because the *modelo sindical* that has been dominant in this country had formed itself in a context of development of the internal market and industry, had opened a space for possible – beneficial – social agreement, between businessmen and workers, and unions, and this goes throughout Argentine history, and it's the history of Peronism.

The CTA contemporary project for society more widely was symbolized for some activists by the initiative of the Constituyente Social.[2] This is a series of meetings held across Argentina, a process that began in 2007-8, culminating then in a national meeting held in Jujuy in October 2008. A subsequent national meeting was held in Neuquen in November 2009, and there have also been multiple regional and local meetings in preparation for the national gatherings. The Constituyente Social is a kind of Argentine Social Forum. Groups affiliated to the CTA – which includes both unions and territorial organizations, as well as some indigenous organizations – meet to discuss common political projects, which a campaign document produced by the communication team summarized as 'wealth *redistribution*, participatory and integral *democracy*, national and community *sovereignty*, plurinational integration in *Latin America*' (emphasis in original).[3]

In some ways, the Constituyente Social is a utopian project, but it is important to note that what the future will be is quite intentionally kept indeterminate. Process is the issue; democratic discussion itself is what is most important. In this, the Constituyente Social has commonalities with the World Social Forums, alterglobalization movements, and contemporary European anarchist currents, for all of whom process is praxis. The future (near and far) is indeterminate, but it is possible to prefigure it by engaging in the kind of democratic discussion and consensus-building internally (to the movement) that is desired for wider society. The anthropologist and activist Marianne Maeckelbergh explains prefiguration as follows:

> In my experience as an activist, practising prefiguration has meant always trying to make the processes we use to achieve our immediate goals an embodiment of our ultimate goals, so that there is no distinction between how we fight and what we fight for, at least not where the ultimate goal of a radically different society is concerned. In this sense, practising prefigurative politics means removing the temporal distinction between the struggle in the *present* towards a goal in the *future*; instead, the struggle and the goal, the real and the ideal, become one in the present (2009: 66-7).

So, the 'near future' is evacuated (Guyer 2007) in these processes, because they do not constitute a state-, party-, or vanguard-led project with a clear programme to be implemented from the top down. The CTA is not an anarchist organization, but the Constituyente Social has taken on some of the anarchist insights of the future as unknown and unknowable, to-be-constructed. Politically, this has meant that the 'concrete' or programmatic results of different instances of the Constituyente Social have been quite limited, and focused on practical questions: specifically, a proposal for a universal child benefit, which was in fact introduced by President Cristina Kirchner in late 2009. However, according to its supporters, the ultimate benefit of the Constituyente Social may be that of networking or the discussion itself and for itself. As much as it is influenced by contemporary alterglobalization activism, this is also part of a Latin American tradition of social movements and NGOs as networks: from feminist *encuentros* in the 1960s through UN conferences and their preparation in the 1990s to contemporary networked activism (Alvarez 1998; Escobar 2009).

UPCN informants were less likely to present a clear linear political project stretching from the past to the present. They tended to focus in interviews and other practical activities on collective bargaining agreements and more immediate issues. But with respect to what it means to be a Peronist, historical time was absolutely crucial, and it flowed through kinship relations. People said that being a Peronist was 'in the blood', or 'from the cradle': taught to them by their parents and/or grandparents through the medium of stories, mostly of Evita (discussed in more detail below). Memory and history were central to such narratives, and evoked – and thus constituted as experience – a particular kind of historical time.

Journal of the Royal Anthropological Institute (N.S.), 91-108
© Royal Anthropological Institute 2014

A tendency to divide the past into quite clearly defined periods was one of the most important aspects of interview data, informal conversations, and official materials produced by both unions, as well as of scholarly accounts in Argentina. These ran from the first Peronist regime in 1946-55, which was often felt to be a kind of golden period by activists from both unions; followed by resistance and 1960s radicalization; the dictatorship of 1976-83; the neoliberal period of 1989-99 (i.e. Carlos Menem's presidencies); to some extent the banking crisis of 2001-2; and the present. A few periods stood out as most important for my interlocutors, especially '76-83 and '89-99, and to a lesser extent '46-55. For many, these periods represent a golden age in both political and economic terms ('46-55), followed by the nadir of political degradation in the time of the dictatorship, when unionists and workers were targeted for political repression, and a number of my informants had to operate from hiding; then the neoliberal period, which was often viewed as one of economic degradation, where privatization policies especially affected state workers. It should be said, however, that in both the latter cases, economic and political degradation respectively were not absent, just subordinate in common representations of the ills of the age.

A further important epoch for unionists' historical narrative of political activism was the recovery of internal union democracy after the intervention and repression of the dictatorship, which is known as *recuperación*, and which formed a fundamental part of older unionists' narratives and images of organization and activism. Both ATE and UPCN underwent a process of *recuperación*: UPCN had been 'intervened' during the dictatorship, which meant that a leader had been imposed upon the union by the military junta, and once democracy returned, a new set of young leaders emerged from within the union, untainted by associations with the military. ATE had not been intervened, because its leadership was already very close to the junta: Secretary General Juan Horvath was especially connected to Admiral Emilio Massera. A group of young activists who had been operating clandestinely during the dictatorship formed the grouping called ANUSATE (Agrupación Nacional Unidad y Solidaridad a ATE) and fought and won the internal union elections of 1984. Néstor Llano, the president of the *agrupación* in 2009, recounted:

> When we won in '84, we took over our union with 56,000 affiliates and a hugely important debt. The union was practically bankrupt ... We found a union with 56,000 affiliates, with debts on all sides, completely disorganized, atomized, each person defended his place. That's to say, a whole collective construction that took many years [to build] had become atomized in that period, each person took care of his own business in the country, looked after his farm (*cuidaba su quinta*). We had to reverse this, during many years debating with the comrades (*compañeros*), winning elections [in different parts of the union structure, including at provincial level], putting forward work projects, modifications for the statutes, financial control, and so on.

Miguel Romero, a long-standing ATE leader, connected the recovery process to the process of developing a new *modelo sindical* of the type discussed above:

> Well, [the recovery] was a very difficult, very traumatic period. First because we received the union completely dismantled and without economic resources. We had to reconstruct it again, and [do that] through the conception of a *modelo sindical* distinct to what was there before ... There we began a whole job to restructure ATE into a *modelo sindical* of participation, of internal structures that were much more agile, much more really expressive of the will of the comrade (*compañero*).

ANUSATE, now known as the 'green list', continues to dominate ATE, and its victory in 1984 is extremely important to them: for example, a video of the history of

ANUSATE was shown right at the beginning of a two-day training session for ATE delegates. This underlined the official position that the story of the recovery of the union should be a key inspirational trope for all ATE delegates, even those from competing electoral lists within the union. Some of the figures who led the recovery of ATE went on to be instrumental in founding the CTA: Víctor de Gennaro in particular, a crucial *referente social* (social reference point) for ATE activists today.

The notion of recovery, *recuperación*, has multiple meanings: in part it is a grasping back of something that had fallen into the wrong hands – like the recovery of stolen goods; the word also evokes recuperation after an operation, the recovery of health after a period of trauma. As such, it should not be understood temporally as a return to a pristine, originary, state, but the trauma is understood as an experience that will inevitably leave scars. Recovery is also an ongoing process: for the majority of ATE activists, autonomy from political parties must be fiercely protected, and any potential return to too close a relationship with the government must be carefully guarded against. Indeed, that precise concern split the CTA in two in late 2010/early 2011: one CTA led by Hugo Yasky, who is a teachers' union leader and was CTA Secretary General since 1997; and a rival one led by Pablo Micheli, former Secretary General of ATE Nacional, who criticized Yasky for being too close to government.

As well as being incomplete in the sense that it needs to continue, complete recovery of what was lost is not always felt to be possible: for example, and with respect to a different trope of recovery, Peronists in both unions do look back nostalgically to the golden period of the mid-twentieth century, and seek inspiration in it, but do not really imagine that they will be able to recover it fully. Nor do they completely idealize it, but ATE activists in particular often feel that contemporary Peronism, including Peronist unions, has betrayed the promise of that early period.

It is probably the case that ATE had a more explicit conceptualization of its place in a particular historical narrative than UPCN did, but the issue I want to highlight at this point is the fact that periodization itself is very common, both in my interviews and in scholarly accounts of political history and the labour movement. Indeed, there is a kind of feedback loop, as scholars speak with activists, and activists read scholarly works and/or media pieces in part shaped by journalists' understandings of key scholarly figures,[4] and so on. The representations of past political time in this way create a temporal flow through the historical narrative which is divided by particular well-defined epochs. Olivia Harris's work (1995; 1996; 2004; 2006) inspires us to be attuned to temporal representations of epochal time, although in this particular case, the sense of epochal time I am evoking does not require a complete rupture in between the periods in the way that revolutions, conquest, or, indeed, some narratives of Christian conversion do (Robbins 2007). But nor is it a Braudelian *longue durée* continuity; rather, the epochs flow into each other, like coloured stripes in woven textiles.

The narrative flow of epochal time is not only divided into identifiable periods, but also punctuated by key events. These tend to be specific events in people's workplaces, such as a particular campaign against the firing of a group of people or individuals, changing an employment contract, making a collective bargaining agreement, and so on. In that sense, they bleed somewhat into the 'attritional time' I discuss below. Key events can also be political events, such as a particular presidential election, or a demonstration in favour of, say, collective bargaining rights.

Such key political events may also be experienced in a repetitive and cyclical way, as they are subsequently commemorated each year on the date they occurred. In particular, on 17 October Peronists celebrate the 1945 demonstrations led by Eva Perón that secured Juan Perón's release from prison; on 24 March each year civic groups and ordinary Argentineans commemorate the beginning of the 1976 coup; on 29-30 May, many Argentineans remember the Cordobazo of 1969,[5] albeit usually without the attendant large-scale demonstrations of the former two dates. Antonius Robben (2007) argues that mass, often violent, street demonstrations have punctuated Argentine political history and changed its course at several significant moments. To the above examples, he adds the demonstrations greeting Juan Perón's return from exile at Ezeiza airport on 20 June 1973 (which became a massacre), the protests against the Falklands war in 1983 (which toppled the dictatorship), and the riots of December 2001 in response to the financial crisis. Here, hindsight is crucial, as certain crowd events come eventually to signify something crucial at different scales, both nationally and in the local workplace, while others do not appear to change the course of history. I discuss this issue in further detail below.

Commemoration of important dates, through memory and reflection as well as actual physical mobilization, creates a strong sense of what Guyer describes as 'a time that is punctuated rather than enduring: of fateful moments and turning points, the date as event rather than as position in a sequence or a cycle' (2007: 416). One might remain sceptical about her contention that we are seeing a 'rising awareness' of such a sense of time – in that there is no evidence that this kind of awareness is an especially recent phenomenon. But in Argentina at least it is a very powerful mediating practice of temporal representation, especially of the past. Further, as some events and dates come to be symbolic in the flow of narrative time, so do particular people. We can of course point to Juan and Eva Perón, for the case of the Peronists. A discussion of the multiple practices of evoking their presence within UPCN and other CGT unions would require much more space than is available here.[6] However, a brief list of such practices would include the commemoration of 17 October, frequent references in everyday talk to Juan Perón's sayings, posting and viewing his and Evita's speeches on YouTube, studying his speeches in the training sessions for new UPCN delegates, and displaying photographs of the couple in the entrance halls and offices of leaders. Other means of evocation include narrative: Peronists told me stories of Evita – how she had given a family member a sewing machine, how she had founded a local hospital – and it is these stories that are transmitted through the generations and that make Peronists, 'from the cradle'. Finally, in large-scale demonstrations of the CGT, enormous photographs of Juan and Eva Perón flank the speakers' stage, in a conscious evocation of past CGT demonstrations (see Figs 1a, 1b, and 2). All these practices bring Juan and Eva Perón into the present.

Such practices of making the past present are not confined to traditional Peronists. For example, for ATE, Germán Abdala is a crucial figure, or *referente social*. He is a powerful symbol of the persistence of the *clasista* movement and the 1970s opposition to bureaucratic unionism and dictatorship. Abdala died from cancer in 1993, and his death continues to be commemorated by ATE militants, in homages on its anniversary, also the naming of new ATE delegations or offices, and so on. His image features in the large banners displayed by ATE at demonstrations (see Fig. 3). He was a leftist militant in the 1970s, and then a protagonist, with Víctor de Gennaro, in the post-dictatorship recovery of ATE. Although a deputy for the Peronist Partido Justicialista, Abdala broke away from Menem in opposition to his neoliberal reforms. He and de Gennaro founded the CTA in 1992. He is spoken of with great warmth and passion by many ATE

Figures 1a, 1b. CGT demonstration, 30 April 2009. (Photograph by the author.)

Figure 2. CGT demonstration, 31 August 1951 (in the same location as Figure 1b). (Wikimedia Commons.)

delegates; and many UPCN delegates also praised him in interviews, not least because he was the sponsor for the law that introduced collective bargaining to the public sector. As with Juan Perón, but to a lesser extent, there are books, films, film clips on YouTube, and blog, newspaper, and magazine articles about Germán Abdala, most of them produced by ATE. They give his biography, discuss his politics, and quote his speeches: for example, one ATE video is called 'Germán by Germán' and is a collection of clips of his political speeches. This kind of political-cultural production reflects and evokes the (much vaster) body of work associated with Juan Perón. It is a very powerful form of iconic afterlife, also enjoyed by figures such as Eva Perón, Che Guevara, and so on.

From the mediating practices described in this section, it should be evident that historical time and memory are of crucial importance for the shaping of political activism in these unions. It is perhaps what Jane Guyer called 'a regime of dated time'

Journal of the Royal Anthropological Institute (N.S.), 91-108
© Royal Anthropological Institute 2014

Figure 3. ATE demonstration, 22 April 2009. (Photograph by the author.)

(2007: 417), albeit with much more content or more meat on the bones of the dates than she implies. It is also a regime of time that shapes the past, especially the immediate past. In contrast, the 'near-future temporal frame' (Guyer 2007: 417) is actually left quite indeterminate: the future is open, not quite stated. Activists do not on the whole seek to construct a knowable utopia, either in the near or distant future; in fact in their daily political life, much of what they do is reactive, to events and to rumours of events.

'Attritional' time

This reactive mode is part of the second social experience of time that I discuss in this article, namely a kind of 'attritional' time, one of constant protest or negotiation. It is the continuance of the day to day of political life when there is no resolution in sight to a particular conflict or problem, coupled at times with a dramatization of what can become quite banal over time.

One example of this from my fieldwork in Argentina is a conflict over the 'modernization' (privatization) of the Teatro Colon, Argentina's pre-eminent opera house. In an example of neoliberal economic policies in miniature, there was a sustained attempt in recent years to change this state-owned opera house from what the workers call a 'factory theatre' – one that puts on its own productions using its own technical and artistic workforce – to a venue for productions mounted by other (subcontracted) theatre and opera companies. This involved both the reduction of the workforce and a highly contentious refurbishment of the building. Some of the workers, led by key figures in the ATE local delegation, have been resisting this process, a resistance which has involved a series of almost constant mobilizations. Indeed, 'a state of permanent mobilization' can even be declared, as in early 2009. Mobilizations include assemblies, demonstrations of different kinds, press conferences, support festivals, and they occur at different frequencies, but up to once or twice a week for months at a time; they are punctuated by particular scandals and events, such as parliamentary hearings, court cases, a building inspection, and so on. Between early February and late August 2009, there were twenty-three separate mobilizations that I knew about.

More generally, ATE itself almost does not stop demonstrating, apart from during holiday months. Delegates attend local and city-wide assemblies, marches, blockades, days of action, protest festivals, Constituyente Social meetings and other CTA demonstrations, and so on, even when not in direct conflict with their employer. They are on constant alert to react to government/employer initiatives both real and potential, such as policy changes like the proposed lowering of the age of criminal liability in the city of Buenos Aires; employer initiatives such as not renewing some people's contracts, firing others, and reorganizing offices; squatter clearance; rises in fuel bills; and they also instigate recurrent demands for wage increases. Finally, each month, ATE and associated groups hold a demonstration outside the national statistics office when inflation figures are released.[7]

Individual demonstrations were an opportunity for the repetition of particular political arguments and the constant rehearsal and refinement of political narratives and understandings, in formal speeches and audience/participant commentary. This repetition is participation in attritional time, the mundane, repetitive, constant struggle that makes up political activism in the everyday. It can be extremely draining, as UPCN delegates often pointed out when discussing ATE's particularly combative approach to their employers. For example:

> Because ATE – ATE is confrontation, ATE is struggle, ATE is conflict, and life just can't be like that. ATE in itself is – well, everything is struggle-conflict, struggle-conflict, struggle-conflict, and that is not a reality that a worker wants. A worker wants to work, s/he wants to work. After that, better conditions, better benefits, all the rest. ATE begins with the struggle, ATE is stoppage, ATE is strike, ATE is conflict. That's what an anarchist wants, a political activist. For this reason, I have never felt represented by ATE (anonymous UPCN delegate).

> – What I mean is, I can do a strike or a mobilization tomorrow, but the day after, every day, no. If I have to live from stoppage to stoppage, it's unsustainable, there isn't a worker in the world who can support it.
> – It creates a lot of anguish, it's impossible (Fernando de sa Sousa, Marcela Manual: UPCN delegates)

None the less, for many the participation in attritional time is also coupled with underlying senses of fun and drama that pull in slightly different directions. Demonstrations are often entertaining, fun, and inspiring. They reaffirm collective faith in the overall struggle for class liberation, against neoliberalism, and so on; they are chances for people to meet and maintain friendships with like-minded fellows and reaffirm their commitment to the cause and to each other; and to feel that they are doing something worthwhile. Further, there is the possibility that each demonstration could be, potentially, a key moment in the struggle.

That said, currently, I am unclear whether this last feeling was one shared by my informants. While in Argentina, I assumed that they continued to demonstrate and mobilize because each demonstration could prove definitive in some way, but the more I reflect on my material, I wonder if that analysis has more to do with my own personal desire for these events to have some significance. Certainly, I kept searching for the event that would or could resolve all the structural contradictions against which the unions were struggling – the revolution – and of course it never happened and (probably) never will. The Teatro Colon workforce was successfully reduced, and the refurbishment was conducted in what the workers maintain is an extremely damaging way. Legal struggles continue, to defend those workers particularly targeted by the management, and I receive regular emails notifying me of press conferences, court cases, and

Journal of the Royal Anthropological Institute (N.S.), 91-108
© Royal Anthropological Institute 2014

other incidents. The monthly demonstrations outside the national statistics office also continue; struggles over intended reorganizations at the local government audit office have neither abated nor been resolved; and so on.

The ultimately unfulfillable desire for certainty, or for demonstrations to have a real effect, is, I suspect, one of the elements that lead people to drop out of activism. However, those middle-aged and older activists I knew seemed on the whole comfortable with the ongoing and attritional nature of their struggle. This was in part because many of them successfully folded it into the first temporality I discussed, seeing themselves as a small part of a much larger narrative, a longer tradition of struggle. Others perhaps simply enjoyed the repetition, the quotidian nature of activism. Nevertheless, for both groups, the future is one of continued struggle, not one of utopia achieved. It is indeterminate.

Events and revolutions

Some events might mediate these different temporalities, often in quite a dramatic way: as coexisting but separately experienced temporalities crash together in specific revolutionary moments, and historical time as a series of periods punctuated by key events is constituted through the lived practices of attritional time. For Argentina, Robben's work, discussed above, gives us some indication of the kinds of events that became important constituents of historical time. Another example from Latin America is the 'revolutionary cycle' of 2000-5 in Bolivia (Hylton & Thomson 2007). In this section, I explore the latter example in some detail, to examine what makes those moments of political time special, what makes them into an event.

Approaching such a question from a consideration of temporality offers a different perspective from the rather more spatial metaphors of most literature on social movement politics. One helpful temporal analytic is the concept of *kairos*, which comes originally from theory of rhetoric.[8] For Antonio Negri (2003), '*kairos*' is a moment of rupture where the 'to-come' is made evident, imaginable as the point in time when the arrow is released from the bow, indeed as the point of the arrow itself. In a later formulation, he describes it with Hardt as 'the opportune moment that ruptures the monotony and repetitiveness of chronological time' (Hardt & Negri 2009: 165). Carolyn Miller (1992) argues that *kairos* is a qualitative term for time, in contrast to the quantitative term *chronos*. The precise relationship between the two is crucial, and she explains it through a description of a debate between the rhetoricians Lloyd Bitzer (1968) and Richard Vatz (1973): 'Bitzer would say that *kairoi* are important exigences punctuating *chronos*, special moments of opportunity that present themselves every now and then ... Vatz would hold that *every* moment along the continuum of *chronos* has its *kairos*, which can be seized and developed in some way with imagination' (Miller 1992: 312, emphasis in original). So, applying these concepts to social movements and revolutionary time, the question becomes how to either recognize or create the *kairos*, the special moment of opportunity for revolution within the *chronos* of everyday political time? Or, put differently, what makes an event an event in Badiou's sense? What turns attritional time into a revolutionary moment, or links attritional time to astonishing time, thus making historical time?

Yet another way of asking the question would be to phrase it in terms of mediation, and explore moments of mediation between material time and social experiences of time, drawing on Gell's distinction between 'A-series' and 'B-series' time (Gell 1992, following McTaggart). For Gell, 'A-series' time names senses of past, present, and future,

Journal of the Royal Anthropological Institute (N.S.), 91-108
© Royal Anthropological Institute 2014

accessible to ethnographic knowledge largely via temporal representations. 'B-series' time is more material and objective, to do with time as a relation between before and after, which situates events as like beads on a necklace. Hodges argues that 'what Gell's B-series amounts to is a metaphysical statement about the objective, autonomous nature of real time', while A-series time is 'the subjective, tensed existence involving past, present and future relations that comprises everyday human time perception' (2008: 404).

Utilizing this distinction brings into view a set of 'A-series' representations or temporalities alongside those of the activists themselves, namely those of scholars and other commentators: historians, journalists, and so on. Hindsight – or co-creation of the past – is crucial here, for my own experience of both revolutionary moments and mundane political time (*kairos* and *chronos*) is that the two are not so different *while they are happening*. What makes them different is their effects, or perhaps more properly their perceived effects and constructed coherence *after the event*. Here, scholars and political commentators from the media play a crucial role in constructing a narrative framework and reworking past events to fit it, in collaboration with participants in those events. This is inevitably a multi-layered process, as everyone participates in a co-construction of a narrative, creating *kairos* retrospectively.

The first workshop paper on which this essay is based was presented on the day after Tunisian president Zine El Abidine Ben Ali was forced out of office. Although the participants commented on these events – inevitably, for this was a workshop on temporality and social movements – it was not evident at the time that they would be the precursor to something even more substantive. Subsequently, it became clear that something was (is) happening; and a series of events congealed into what we now know as the Arab Spring. This naming shows the importance of attentiveness to the processes of hailing that make a revolution in the contemporary world. Those hailings have their own temporality or temporal sequencing: different participants co-create a hegemonic narrative out of a fluid set of events over a period of time after the events that are being hailed actually took place. I will use the example of Bolivia in the first five years of this century to illustrate my point.

The latest 'revolutionary cycle' in Bolivia (Hylton & Thomson 2007) is generally agreed to have begun in April 2000, with what is known as the 'Water War' in Cochabamba, when residents managed to expel the French-owned water utility company by means of massive street protests against water privatization. Concurrently, peasants in the highlands were blockading roads, and they repeated their blockades in September 2000; also in 2001 and 2002; while lowland coca-growers continued their protests against the coca-eradication policies and violations of human rights in the Chapare region. By February 2003, the wave of mass mobilizations reached El Alto, with a week-long riot in the city (and also in La Paz) prompted by an IMF-proposed increase in income tax. A stand-off between the police and the army led to several deaths; also looters and demonstrators attacked the headquarters of political parties, the town hall and customs depot of El Alto, the Coca-Cola factory, and BancoSol (a bank owned by the President, Gonzalo Sanchez de Lozada). In October 2003, another wave of massive street protests and blockades centred on El Alto, but also including La Paz and the surrounding countryside, culminated in a traumatic week that saw around eighty deaths of demonstrators. Sanchez de Lozada then resigned in favour of his Vice-President, Carlos Mesa, and fled the country for exile in Miami. At that point the protests became street parties, which were later described to me by the sociologist Silvia

Rivera Cusicanqui as 'a euphoria of democracy'. Subsequently, the events of October 2003 became known as the 'Gas War', since one of the points of commonality for the different protesters was opposition to the terms of privatization of natural gas resources to foreign enterprises.

In fact, the Gas War became the Gas War over time, not during the events themselves and in the immediate run-up to them, nor, for many, in the period shortly after. In El Alto, just prior to October 2003, civic organizations were leading mobilizations about several issues: proposed house registration procedures in the city; a new tax code; a proposed prohibition of blockades; and the selling-off of the country's gas reserves. When one studies the newspapers of the time, and the reflections of participants gathered soon after, it appears that the spark that finally lit the tinderbox in El Alto and eventually led to the resignation and fleeing of the President on 17 October was the government's decision to start killing protesters. This began a few weeks beforehand, when the army was ordered to shoot at protesters in a highland village called Warisata, on 20 September. In December, my informants were calling the events 'Red October', but gradually one of the issues that had been at stake at the time – i.e. the fate of the country's natural gas reserves – came to define the events. Today, few people call it anything but the 'Gas War'. It is now even perceived by some scholars as a revolution, or at least a revolutionary moment (Dunkerley 2007; Hylton & Thomson 2007). Although I was not in El Alto at the beginning of October, I can attest to the fact that at the end of September there was no inkling of an imminent revolution, even among highly politically active people in the city. Does a revolution need a build-up? The most intense week of protests itself was certainly felt as something special, not to say shocking, as numerous people recounted to me later. But a coherent narrative of the 'Gas War' coalesced considerably later, indeed over the course of months afterwards, not even weeks.

Part of the reason for that is probably the fact that over the course of 2005, as President Carlos Mesa failed to satisfy the social movements that he was adequately dealing with the natural gas question, protests multiplied and eventually he also had to resign. After a transition period, in December 2005, the *cocalero* leader Evo Morales was elected President; widely regarded as the first indigenous President in Latin America. Early in 2006, he nationalized the natural gas and hydrocarbon industries.

The narrative that links all these events has by now coalesced into one about sovereignty, control over natural resources, and indigeneity (Albro 2005; Hylton & Thomson 2007). This is not incorrect by any means, but it excludes a number of different possibilities which were at the time latent in the events themselves. My own reading places more emphasis upon the fact that the citizens of Bolivia objected to the killings of demonstrators; they objected to the state turning upon them. While the questions of national sovereignty and anti-imperialism were absolutely crucial to many Bolivians, the catalyst for the astonishing moments of riot and presidential resignation in October 2003 was the deaths of demonstrators, in my view. People told me of their desire to remove a murderous President, but that call did not incorporate consideration of what would happen afterwards. Why should it? As with the Tahrir Square demonstrations, it is clearer to demand the resignation of a President than to articulate utopian or real alternatives for the future – especially if, as now, political agendas must be articulated within only 140 characters.

Returning to Bolivia, an analysis that privileges time might take a slightly different tack. Evo Morales's victory in the December 2005 elections can be seen as a culmination of the street politics of the previous five years. It can also be seen as the expression of a generalized exhaustion with dramatic mobilization. When revolution becomes routinized, attritional, it can be very draining, and in mid-2005 residents of El Alto were tired of constant demonstrations against the regime. However, they were not willing to give way and accept its neoliberalism, so highland Bolivians resorted to what they called the 'electoral way' ('*via electoral*'), and elected an alternative, one who was more 'like them', to the presidency.

My discussion of October 2003 leads me to raise some questions about how acts become events. As Bruce Kapferer points out, drawing on Marshall Sahlins's Hawaiian work: 'Events are not natural phenomena. They are always constructions and do not exist as events apart from this fact ... [E]vents achieve their import and effects through the meaning or the significance that human beings attach to them, and it is this which yields their generative impact' (Kapferer 2010: 17). Thus, 'happenings [are] made into events' through the construction of significance. Following Olivia Harris (1995; 2004), I want to suggest that a key aspect of the processes of attributing meaning in this way is the constitution of discontinuity. Constant protests seem to become constructed as an event when they lead to some kind of rupture, although the precise moment of rupture is not always easily identifiable. In the Bolivian case, Sanchez de Lozada's escape to Miami and the consequent democratic euphoria on the streets might constitute the key rupture of the Gas War; but equally, Evo Morales's election as President, and the overturning of 500 years of colonization that it represented, might be far more important; or so might the actual nationalization of the hydrocarbon industry in early 2006.

For a revolution to be hailed as such, it appears to be crucial to constitute a given set of moments as event-as-rupture. The search for discontinuity seems constitutive of revolutionary temporalities as experienced from outside the 'revolution' itself. Recall Hardt and Negri's definition of *kairos*, or Badiou's definition of the event as a moment of rupture that reveals a truth (Badiou 2003; 2005). Fernand Braudel famously questioned this prioritization when he made a contrast between the French Revolution and the Industrial Revolution, arguing that the latter was by far more important in its implications for the development of the modern state. He viewed history as to be found in 'enduring and continuous time' (Harris 2004: 165). The emphasis on discontinuity, as Olivia Harris pointed out, is a key part of how most anthropologists, historians, Westerners and Christians experience and depict time (Harris 1995; 1996; 2004; 2006). Joel Robbins (2007) made a similar point for what he called 'Christian time'; although he also argued that anthropologists' disciplinary emphasis on continuity makes it hard to see rupture and change, for example in Christian conversion. His description of the paradox of 'so robust an anthropology of resistance [existing] alongside so slim an anthropology of revolution' (2007: 10) highlights how for him revolution is itself defined through rupture. Marshall Sahlins thought that 'what makes an act or incident an event is precisely its contrast to the going order of things, its disruption of that order ... In the general category of human actions, historical events are a subclass only, consisting of those actions that change the order of things' (1991: 45-6). Similarly, Veena Das defines 'critical events' as events after which 'new modes of action came into being which redefined traditional categories ... Equally, new forms were acquired by a variety of political actors' (1995: 6), again emphasizing the new. Thus, anthropologists also have an identifiable social experience of time, or temporalizing practice, at the moment of hailing historical events and analysing others' temporalities. Harris (1995) particularly demonstrated this when she argued that

Europeans are so inclined to view the Conquest as a dramatic moment of discontinuity that we create a blind spot that affects our interpretations of Amerindian versions of history. This particular temporalizing practice of commentary and analysis *qua* hailing meets the participants' experiences of time as both historical and attritional, and contributes to the co-construction of significance.

Conclusion

In this paper I have reflected upon the interaction between different social experiences of time, principally what I have called historical time and attritional time. Argentine unionists, especially in ATE, experience historical time as participation in a historical narrative, with a relatively coherent version of the past as a flow of time divided into epochs or periods and punctuated by particular events and people. That time flows to the future, but the future is indeterminate; albeit one that is most likely to consist of continued struggle, even if it might be one that is constructed through prefigurative practices in the present. Here, historical time meets the second kind of time I proposed, namely attritional time, which is a kind of continuity. That continuity contains within it the constant possibility of discontinuity or rupture (the *kairos* within *chronos*). The point of rupture is the point at which attritional time meets and constructs historical time. That said, actual desire for rupture may in practice be more that of outside commentators (including myself) than of the activists.

There are specific practices of mediating the different temporalities: for example, in historical time, practices of protest and commemoration make the past present, in daily life and in political protest. Historical time is experienced through the telling of the linear, flowing yet punctuated narrative, for the purposes of training new delegates or enlightening a researcher; but also through more cyclical practices of commemoration. People are made into icons and ways of bringing the past into the present through imagery in offices, at demonstrations, in naming practices, the everyday use of Perón's sayings, the study of his speeches, posting and viewing them on YouTube, showing them to new recruits, repeating the story of recuperation, of the union's path to health, and so on. All these are acts of making historical time present. What I have called attritional time is lived through repetition of political activity, political arguments, rhetorical strategies, visual and mobilizational practices such as demonstrations, assemblies, and so on.

Finally, this paper has also discussed a kind of event-based mediation between different temporalities: specifically, revolution as clashing or meeting of attritional time and historical time. The processes of this kind of mediation involve both the revolutionary actions themselves and the practices of hailing that are both contemporaneous and retrospective. Tentatively, I want to propose that this hailing might be enacted through a promise or assertion of discontinuity and rupture, even when events may not actually have been experienced as such at the time itself. Anthropologists and historians, as well as other social commentators, are complicit or even necessary participants in these hailing processes, which reveal much about 'our' own social experience of time. Thus, different experiences of time meet in a politics of time, to co-construct *kairos*, or revolution.

NOTE

   I want to thank the seminar organizers both for prompting me to think through my material in a way that was very new to me, and for commenting so perceptively on early drafts. I am particularly grateful to Laura Bear in this regard. The research in 2009 on which this paper is based was carried out with financial assistance from the Wenner-Gren Foundation.

[1] See, for example, Alvarez, Dagnino & Escobar (1998); Chatterjee (2006); Escobar (2009); Hardt & Negri (2000; 2005; 2009); Harvey (2012); Juris (2008); Melucci (1989).

[2] The nearest translation for *Constituyente Social* would probably be 'Social Constitution-Building'. Asamblea Constituyente (Constituent Assembly) is the term for the series of assemblies held to rewrite constitutions – and Asambleas Constituyentes have happened across Latin America in this context (e.g. Brazil, Colombia, Bolivia). Constituyente Social refers to this tradition, but is related to society rather than political constitution – the meetings aim to rewrite society itself, albeit with a very strong focus on the role of the state in such a process.

[3] 'DISTRIBUCIÓN de la riqueza, DEMOCRACIA participativa e integral, SOBERANÍA nacional y comunitaria, LATINOAMÉRICA integración plurinacional' (*http://www.constituyentesocial.org.ar/IMG/pdf/ideas_campanas-2.pdf*, accessed 10 January 2014).

[4] For example, Germani (2006 [1956]) and Torre (1998).

[5] A series of street demonstrations and strikes in Cordoba against the military leadership of Onganía, and associated very strongly with *clasista* oppositional unionist currents (see Brennan 1993).

[6] Indeed there is a wide literature – both fictional and academic – on the iconization especially of Evita (e.g. Eloy Martinez 1997; Fraser & Navarro 1996).

[7] Since 2007, ATE and others have argued that the national statistics office has been subject to government interference, aimed at disguising the true rate of inflation.

[8] With thanks to Nick Long for introducing me to this idea.

REFERENCES

ALBRO, R. 2005. 'The water is ours, *carajo!*' Deep citizenship in Bolivia's water war. In *Social movements: an anthropological reader* (ed.) J. Nash, 249-71. Oxford: Blackwell.

ALVAREZ, S.E. 1998. Latin American feminisms 'go global': trends of the 1990s and challenges for the new millennium. In *Cultures of politics, politics of cultures: revisioning Latin American social movements* (eds) S.E. Alvarez, A. Escobar & E. Dagnino, 293-324. Boulder, Colo.: Westview Press.

———, E. DAGNINO & A. ESCOBAR 1998. *Cultures of politics, politics of cultures: revisioning Latin American social movements.* Boulder, Colo.: Westview Press.

BADIOU, A. 2003. *St Paul: The foundation of universalism* (trans. R. Brassier). Stanford: University Press.

——— 2005. *Being and event.* London: Continuum.

BITZER, L. 1968. The rhetorical situation. *Philosophy and Rhetoric* 1, 1-14.

BRENNAN, J. 1993. Working-class protest, popular revolt, and urban insurrection in Argentina: the 1969 'Cordobazo'. *Journal of Social History* 27, 477-98.

CHATTERJEE, P. 2006. *The politics of the governed: reflections on popular politics in most of the world* (Leonard Hastings Schoff Lectures). New York: Columbia University Press.

DAS, V. 1995. *Critical events: an anthropological perspective on contemporary India.* Oxford: University Press.

DUNKERLEY, J. 2007. *Bolivia: revolution and the power of history in the present.* London: Institute for the Study of the Americas.

ELOY MARTINEZ, T. 1997. *Santa Evita.* London: Anchor.

ESCOBAR, A. 2009. *Territories of difference: place, movements, life, 'Redes'.* Durham, N.C.: Duke University Press.

FRASER, N. & M. NAVARRO 1996. *Evita: real lives of Eva Perón* (Revised edition). London: André Deutsch.

GELL, A. 1992. *The anthropology of time.* Oxford: Berg.

GERMANI, G. 2006 [1956]. La integracion de las masas a la vida politica y el totalitarismo. In *Gino Germani: la renovacion intelectual de la sociologia* (ed.) A. Blanco, 201-21. Bernal: Universidad Nacional de Quilmes Editorial.

GUYER, J.I. 2007. Prophecy and the near future: thoughts on macroeconomic, evangelical, and punctuated time. *American Ethnologist* 34, 409-21.

HARDT, M. & A. NEGRI 2000. *Empire.* Cambridge, Mass.: Harvard University Press.

——— & ——— 2005. *Multitude.* London: Hamish Hamilton.

——— & ——— 2009. *Commonwealth.* Cambridge, Mass.: Belknap Press.

HARRIS, O. 1995. The coming of the white people: reflections on the mythologization of history in Latin America. *Bulletin of Latin American Research* 14, 9-24.

——— 1996. The temporalities of tradition: reflections on a changing anthropology. In *Grasping the changing world: anthropological concepts in the postmodern era* (ed.) V. Hubinger, 1-16. London: Routledge.

——— 2004. Braudel: historical time and the horror of discontinuity. *History Workshop Journal* 57, 161-74.

———— 2006. The eternal return of conversion: Christianity as contested domain in Highland Bolivia. In *The anthropology of Christianity* (ed.) F. Cannell, 51-76. Durham, N.C.: Duke University Press.

HARVEY, D. 2012. *Rebel cities: from the right to the city to the urban revolution.* London: Verso.

HODGES, M. 2008. Rethinking time's arrow. *Anthropological Theory* **8**, 399-429.

HUMPHREY, C. 2008. Reassembling individual subjects: events and decisions in troubled times. *Anthropological Theory* **8**, 357-80.

HYLTON, F. & S. THOMSON 2007. *Revolutionary horizons: past and present in Bolivian politics.* London: Verso.

JURIS, J.S. 2008. *Networking futures: the movements against corporate globalization.* Durham, N.C.: Duke University Press.

KAPFERER, B. 2010. Introduction: in the event. Toward an anthropology of generic moments. *Social Analysis* **54**: 3, 1-27.

MAECKELBERGH, M. 2009. *The will of the many: how the alterglobalisation movement is changing the face of democracy.* London: Pluto.

MELUCCI, A. 1989. *Nomads of the present: social movements and individual needs in contemporary society.* Philadelphia: Temple University Press.

MILLER, C. 1992. *Kairos* in the rhetoric of science. In *A rhetoric of doing: essays on written discourse in honor of James L. Kinneavy* (eds) S.P. Witte, N. Nakadate & R.D. Cherry, 310-27. Carbondale: Southern Illinois University Press.

MUNN, N. 1992. The cultural anthropology of time: a critical essay. *Annual Review of Anthropology* **21**, 93-123.

NEGRI, A. 2003. *Time for revolution.* New York: Continuum.

ROBBEN, A. 2007. *Political violence and trauma in Argentina.* Philadelphia: University of Pennsylvania Press.

ROBBINS, J. 2007. Continuity thinking and the problem of Christian culture: belief, time, and the anthropology of Christianity. *Current Anthropology* **48**, 5-38.

———— 2010. Anthropology, Pentecostalism, and the new Paul: conversion, event, and social transformation. *South Atlantic Quarterly* **109**, 633-52.

SAHLINS, M. 1991. The return of the event, again: with reflections on the beginnings of the Great Fijian War of 1843 to 1845 between the kingdoms of Bau and Rewa. In *Clio in Oceania: toward a historical anthropology* (ed.) A. Biersack, 37-100. Washington, D.C.: Smithsonian Institution Press.

TORRE, J.C. 1998. The ambivalent giant: the Peronist labor movement, 1945-1995. In *Peronism and Argentina* (ed) J. Brennan, 125-40. Wilmington, Del.: Scholarly Resources.

VATZ, R.E. 1973. The myth of the rhetorical situation. *Philosophy and Rhetoric* **6**, 154-61.

Narration historique, temps politique séculier et moments révolutionnaires : coexistence des temporalités dans l'expérience vécue des mouvements sociaux

Résumé

Le présent article relève le défi de conceptualiser l'activité politique du point de vue à la fois temporel et spatial, au moyen d'une discussion des différentes temporalités vécues par des activistes de mouvements syndicaux et sociaux. Il se base sur un travail de terrain avec les activistes de deux syndicats de la fonction publique à Buenos Aires et avec des habitants et des associations de marchands de rue d'El Alto, en Bolivie. L'auteure aborde deux temporalités ou expériences sociales du temps (Munn) coexistantes : un « temps historique », sens de la localisation dans un récit historique de l'action politique qui se tourne vers le passé et les ancêtres illustres, d'un côté, et vers des possibilités futures imaginées, de l'autre ; et un « temps de l'attrition », de protestations ou de négociations permanentes, continuation du quotidien de la politique en l'absence de résolution d'un conflit ou d'un problème donné, couplée parfois avec une dramatisation de ce qui peut devenir banal avec le temps. Pour finir, elle discute d'une sorte de médiation opérée par l'événement entre différentes temporalités, et plus précisément de la révolution comme collision ou rencontre du temps de l'attrition et du temps historique, dans des temporalités qui coexistent mais sont vécues séparément. Cette médiation implique aussi bien les actions révolutionnaires elles-mêmes que les pratiques d'acclamation contemporaines et rétrospectives, qui incluent les recherches académiques et les autres formes de commentaire social. L'article suggère que cette acclamation peut être réalisée, en partie, par une promesse ou une affirmation de discontinuité et de rupture dans le flux du temps (Harris), quand bien même les événements n'auraient pas été vécus en tant que tels en leur temps. Différentes expériences sociales du temps se rencontrent ainsi dans la politique du temps pour co-construire le *kairos*, ou la révolution.

5

Rethinking reproductive politics in time, and time in UK reproductive politics: 1978-2008

SARAH FRANKLIN *University of Cambridge*

This paper explores two different but interlinked and contemporaneous debates over reproductive politics in which we can observe at least three distinct combinations of time. In the first part, I describe the shift in the 1980s to a 'biologized' time by British Christian Right-to-Life groups, who began to use a secularized ontogeny to promote and defend a religious definition of 'the way, the truth, and the life' – an altered 'theo-ontology' based on the equivalence of the absolute value of human life, the truth (of biological life), and faith in Christ (as everlasting life). In the second part, I describe a differently 'remixed', and opposing, ontology (secular and semi-secular, using a hybrid bio-legal chronometry but orientated toward the timeless horizon of progress) that characterized the debate over the future of *in vitro* fertilization in the same period, leading up to the adoption of the first Human Fertilization and Embryology (HFE) Act in the UK in 1990. In the third part, I examine the legacy of these debates insofar as they are evident in the more recent political conflicts accompanying passage of an amended HFE Act in 2008 and the debate over so-called 'cybrid embryos'. These episodes reveal how social movements 'are profoundly shaped by mediations and conflicts between diverse representations, technologies, social disciplines and rhythms of time'. I argue that the varied constructions of temporality in reproductive politics evident in these three distinct episodes are crucial to anthropological understandings of the meaning of 'biological control' in the context of stem cell research, cloning, tissue engineering, and reproductive biomedicine.

In her discussion of the role of progressive genealogical time in English models of kinship in *After nature*, Marilyn Strathern underscores the 'formulaic' capacity of biological development to signify 'natural time' as one of the 'facts of life'. For the English, she notes, 'the temporal sequencing of generations is irreversible. Indeed the English are able to point to "biological" experiencing of temporality as vindicating a linear conception of it ... A life has a demonstrable beginning and end in this view, and biological time is irrefutable evidence of linearity' (Strathern 1992a: 62). Linear time was biologized in the context of Darwinian understandings of development and evolution, while thus also reconstituting kinship as 'natural', and as Strathern persuasively shows, this 'formula' was reproduced to become the 'irrefutable' logic of inter-generational time. This recursive structure of time, whereby it is 'one-way' and finite in relation to the past, but also capable of signifying open-ended and multiple possibilities

Journal of the Royal Anthropological Institute (N.S.), 109-125
© Royal Anthropological Institute 2014

in the future, allows the world to continue to have, for example, 'more' time, as Strathern points out, just as it has more people. However, as this paper suggests, the reproduction of biological time has, as Strathern would have predicted, not quite reproduced itself exactly. This can be shown in terms of both how the 'irrefutable facts' of biological time have been used to construct quite opposite models of biopolitics in the past, and, somewhat differently and more recently, how 'biological time' has been reconfigured in relation to the future of 'biological control'.[1]

This paper explores biological time in the context of two British social movements concerned with the 'facts of life' as well as the future of science – both of which used specific moments in time to anchor their arguments in 'irrefutable' natural fact. In the first part, I describe the shift in the 1980s to a 'biologized' time by Christian Right-to-Life groups, who made a deliberate and politically motivated decision to begin to employ the language of biogenetics to defend foetal personhood, and thus foetal rights. In the second part, I describe the equally strategic decision by the pro-embryo research lobby to employ the open-ended temporal and spatial language of scientific progress to defend the value of human embryo research. These two debates, which were in some ways direct reversals of one another, occurred simultaneously during the 1980s and culminated in the successful passage of the first Human Fertilization and Embryology (HFE) Act in the UK in 1990. In the third part, I examine the legacy of these debates in relation to the more recent political conflicts accompanying the amendment of the HFE Act in 2008, and in particular the debate over so-called 'cybrid embryos'.

'Biologized' time in the context of the Alton Bill

The Alton Bill, which was introduced into the UK Parliament in 1987, was aimed at reducing the upper time limit of legal abortion to eighteen weeks, based largely on the claim that technological improvements enabled an earlier age of foetal viability. More broadly, this well-organized parliamentary initiative led by one of the UK's most prominent Catholic MPs (David Alton) represented the culmination of a lengthy period of preparation by the UK Right-to-Life movement to challenge the 1967 Abortion Act. The abortion debate in the UK, like its predecessors in the US, centrally concerned the role of scientific and clinical expertise in the definition of viability, and thus the question of the 'objective' criteria on which abortion law should be based. This framing of the debate in relation to objective scientific facts was itself the subject of extensive critical analysis, and the focus of academic research, such as that I carried out as a graduate student while writing my Ph.D. in the late 1980s. At the time, as part of a working collective at the Birmingham Centre for Contemporary Cultural Studies (CCCS), my colleagues and I critically analysed the extent to which 'the Alton Bill debates were centrally about the role of medical experts, scientific knowledge and technological innovation in contemporary British culture' in ways that had direct consequences for reproductive politics. This was due to our sense that 'although feminists have won short-term gains [in defeating the Bill], we fear we may be losing the larger struggle over commonsense assumptions about abortion'. Thus, we set out to examine 'the legacy of the Alton Bill debate and what it revealed about popular perceptions of abortion, motherhood, scientific medicine and new reproductive technologies' (Science and Technology Subgroup 1991: 147).

A number of important political shifts had preceded the introduction of the Alton Bill, including the conservative political influence of Thatcherism, and the corresponding return of 'Victorian Values' concerning the family, gender, and sexuality (Cannell

1990). The context of the Alton debate was also shaped by the rising influence of new medical technologies, in particular foetal imaging technologies such as ultrasound, but also improved neonatal care facilities which could potentially lower the upper limit of foetal viability (Gallagher 1987). The widespread adoption of ultrasound technology as a routine component in prenatal care from the 1960s onwards played a particularly important role in a shift toward the recognition of 'foetal personhood'. Beginning in the United States as early as the 1970s, a corresponding political shift began to become apparent within the Right-to-Life movement away from a strictly theological definition of human life (as a gift from God) and toward more 'objective' technological and scientific definitions of the biological threshold of foetal viability – measured as the capacity to survive 'independently' (i.e. from the mother, although not from techno-logical support). The American feminist political scientist and reproductive rights activist Rosalind Petchesky was the first to make this shift explicit in her much-cited 1984 publication *Abortion and woman's choice*, in which she argued that: 'Increasingly, in response to accusations of religious bias and violations of church-state separation, the evidence marshalled by the anti-abortionists to affirm the personhood of the fetus is not its alleged possession of a soul, but its possession of a human body and genotype' (1984: 334). As Petchesky noted, the emergence of a powerful new discourse of foetal personhood relied not only on the affirmation of a set of universal human biological facts, but also on the increasingly routine use of technology (ultrasound), through which these facts could be witnessed, documented, and affirmed. As she characterized this shift in her now classic 1987 essay on 'Fetal images: the power of visual culture in the politics of reproduction':'Aware of cultural trends, the current leadership of the anti-abortion movement has made a conscious strategic shift from religious discourses and technologies to medico-technical ones, in its efforts to win over the courts, the legis-latures and the popular "hearts and minds" ' (Petchesky, 1987: 264).

Critical to the 'cultural trends' described by Petchesky was the increasing impor-tance, and ubiquity, of the visual interface between medical-scientific images of the human foetus and popular culture through various forms of media. This trend, epito-mized by the innovative and still influential imagery of the Swedish photographer Lennart Nilsson, whose delicate and evocative full-colour foetal portraits began to be published by *Life* magazine in the mid-1960s, united improved foetal imagery with the rapid proliferation of popular formats for their consumption, including glossy maga-zines, film, television, and, later, advertising. It was thus the power of the combination of new types of scientific imagery of unborn foetal life and wider audiences for their consumption which, in Petchesky's view, motivated a strategic political turn by Right-to-Life activists toward the harnessing of this powerful new tool in the effort 'to win over the courts, the legislatures and the popular "hearts and minds" ' (1987: 264-5).

However, the shift away from traditional religious language toward modern medical imagery was also discursively strategic as a form of political camouflage, harnessing, as it did, the power of 'objective' biological models of human life. Unlike the explicitly religious discourse of ensoulment, the biogenetic model of humanity is both secular and scientific, emphasizing the shared, universal possession of certain natural, heritable and recognizable attributes, including developmental potential. As the political oppor-tunity to challenge the upper time limit of abortion by 'witnessing' the seemingly objective biological facts of foetal development, such as its possession of a unique genetic fingerprint or its recognizably human anatomy, became increasingly obvious during the 1980s, their tactical utility likewise became more attractive to anti-abortion

activists. Right-to-Life campaigners on both sides of the Atlantic, including the organizers of the Alton campaign, drew explicitly on this new strategy. Increasingly, the
unborn foetus became, in the British Right-to-Life discourse of the late 1980s, a separate, individual human entity, whose independence of will, and entitlement to protection under the law, could be attested to by its independence of biological body and
possession of a unique biogenetic identity. As an undated pamphlet published by the
British Catholic Right-to-Life organization, LIFE, succinctly stated the case, in the
words of a medical scientist:

> The genetic pattern of this separate individual is as different to the mother as it is to the father. It can
> in no way be considered as part of the father, nor can it in any way be considered part of the mother.
> This new identity is unique.

Or, as another pro-Alton poster from the late 1980s claimed of the newly animated
foetal individual:

> He has likes or dislikes for sweet or sour fluids, he is developing tastes for music and may jump up and
> down to the beat; he is learning to recognise his mother's voice; he can be alarmed by loud bangs, and
> he is, of course, sensitive to pain.

These appeals to the biological reality of foetal autonomy were designed to elicit
support for foetal rights on a new tactical terrain for the Right-to-Life movement. In
place of the potentially 'biased' and domineering discourse of biblical authority, a new
commonsense 'obviousness' of humanity based on the possession of a unique
biogenetic identity and a recognizably human body functioned as a call to a new kind
of witnessing to the miracle of life. With this call, Right-to-Life activists also proposed
a particular relationship between the inadequate present and the desired future in the
context of debates about abortion. Using the well-established legal principle of viability
to argue for a reduced upper time limit to abortion, Right-to-Life groups sought to
establish a cross-over rhetoric that would harness mainstream biological discourse to
appeal more widely to a secular audience. In other words, they sought both to make
their arguments more popular, and to alter the terms of debate over abortion, by
emphasizing biological development rather than divine authority – albeit through the
quasi-theological concept of witnessing. In terms of the questions this volume poses
concerning the politics of temporality, this call by Right-to-Life activists is thus an
example of how 'representations of the relationship between a desired future and an
inadequate present animate political acts within social movements', yet, interestingly,
not an appeal that 'brackets political time off from other representations and rhythms
of time' (as the organizers' statement put it), but, rather one that achieves the reverse –
by embedding the religious time of theo-ontology within the secular time of biology.

The 'mixed' chronotype of embryo research

The highly publicized and often dramatic contestations surrounding the Alton Bill
during the late 1980s, in which a tactical temporality of developmental biology was
employed to gain political ground in the battle to lower the upper time limit for legal
abortion, were interestingly paralleled and reworked in the closely proximate, and
simultaneous, public and parliamentary debate over assisted conception and embryo
research which extended from 1980 to 1990. Triggered by the birth of Louise Brown in
1978, which was seen to reveal the existence of a 'legal vacuum' concerning assisted

conception, a lengthy process of deliberation and consultation, both within and outside Parliament, was begun with the publication of the Warnock Report in 1984 (and has not really ceased since then in the UK). In the human fertilization and embryology debate, both biological development and biological facts played a somewhat different role from that described above in the context of the Alton Bill. Indeed it is possible to argue that the debate over the precise details of human conception, rather than gestation, revealed a reverse process – a 'Christianization' of biology, in the form of pro-embryo research arguments emphasizing a parliamentary duty of care, an obligation to the reproductive future of the population, and the necessity for scientific progress (Franklin 1997). Just as in the context of the Alton debate, where a desired future is contrasted with an inadequate present, so too was the debate over the future of assisted conception, and in particular that of human embryo research, fundamentally based on a defence of the value of scientific research. However, and as we shall see below, the argument from biology in favour of protecting human embryo research as a source of progress for the benefit of humanity deployed a different set of 'core symbols' and favoured images, as well as an alternative means of harnessing biological time.

To remind us briefly of the unprecedented UK debate concerning 'human fertilization and embryology' that began in 1980 with the commissioning of the Warnock Committee, and culminated in 1990 with the passage of the first HFE Act, it is worth noting that considerable parliamentary time and government resources were dedicated to the promotion of a deliberately lengthy, inclusive, and vigorous public scrutiny of these issues. It is also worth remembering (as I have analysed in much depth elsewhere: Franklin 1993; 1997; 1999a) what an unusual combination of arguments about kinship, technology, and reproductive politics this debate involved. Of course this was a passionate debate, often argued with much feeling, and often invoking distinctive types of personal testimony, imagery, and witnessing. Two of these types of testimony deserve brief mention. One was from Members of Parliament who had themselves had children who suffered from genetic disease – most notably Peter Thurnham and Daffyd Wigley (the latter of whom famously broke the arm off the speaker's chair in one of the more heated debates about the future of embryo research). The other was the frequent 'conversion testimony' from MPs and Lords who had visited assisted conception units where they had personally met women and couples whose own lives had been transformed by the option of pursuing new techniques such as *in vitro* fertilization (IVF).

As Marilyn Strathern (1992b) has memorably argued, these debates were about 'reproducing the future' in more than one respect. It was not only future offspring, but the future of technology that was being fought for by proponents of permissive legislation. Above all, the principle being promoted was of the need to protect scientific and technological progress, from which, it was argued, future human benefits were more likely to emerge, thus relieving the burden of human suffering. Arguments against scientific and technological progress were frequently cast by its supporters as nothing less than arguments against humanity itself. Indeed, noticeably throughout the debate over human embryo research, the future of human technological and scientific progress was often deemed synonymous with life itself, including also the life and health of the population, the future reproductive prospects of infertile couples, and the role of new genetic technologies in the effort to alleviate the severe burden of genetic pathology (Franklin & Roberts 2006; Johnson & Theodosiou 2011).

Thus, for example, in the Upper Chamber, Lord Ennals referred to 'the lives and hopes of thousands of families now and in the future' (HL, 7.12.89, c.1012), whereas, in the House of Commons, Peter Thurnham invoked the hope that couples might 'enjoy marriages in which they can look forward to producing children free of ... dreadful diseases' (HC, 23.4.90, c.62). Lord Jakobovits invoked the effort 'to promote the generation of life for those who would otherwise be infertile' (HL, 7.12.89, c.1492). Through such rhetoric, scientific and technological innovation are woven into the very 'fabric of humanity' and MP Seamus Mallon (HC, 23.4.90, c.68) could state that: 'I am convinced that research and experimentation are a natural part of the development of the human condition. They are almost an essential part of the development of our lives'. As I wrote in my own research on this debate during the 1990s:

> Here, 'embryology', in the sense of the *study* of embryos, is seen in almost organic terms, as an 'essential' component of human development. Hence, embryonic development, the study of this process, 'the human condition' and 'the development of our lives' are linked together by a shared, essential developmental trajectory. It is the striking metonymy of these accounts, whereby each individual trajectory not only 'stands for', but is conflated with, the others which is of note. In sum there is a theme of progress, in its many senses, and particularly in its modernist sense (as a kind of essential truth which is in fact a kind of faith) (Franklin 1999b: 146, original emphasis).

For all of these reasons, which were repeatedly reproduced within the extensive testimony by Members of Parliament concerning the benefits of basic scientific research into early human development, MP Jo Richardson could claim in her summing up of the debates in the House of Commons in April 1990, as a final vote neared, that:

> Research can be beneficial to humankind ... it can be creative rather than destructive. Some of that research will not bear fruit for many years, perhaps not until we in this House have retired or passed on. Therefore, we are legislating for the future and for the future of later generations (HC, 23.4.90, c. 47).

What I want to draw attention to in this extract is not only the quasi-religious imagery of fruitfulness and creation, or the implicit tree of life that will connect these benefits to later generations. In particular I also want to draw attention to the underlying social contract upon which this appeal to legislate in favour of embryo research relies, namely an exchange between life and death. Thus, because IVF requires embryo research in order to be ethically practised (just as it required such research to come into being to begin with), so, as a result, does the 'gift of life' that is IVF require sacrifice, indeed mortal sacrifice – the sacrificial bodies of dead human embryos laid down on the path to new life. Similarly, by less explicit but no less direct an analogy, the lives of parliamentarians and their own offspring are invoked through the mortal language of sacrifice: today, Richardson is saying, we can gift our descendants a creative, beneficial, humane legacy by granting them access to the fruits of knowledge they will otherwise be denied. We may not even live to see this fruit, she reminds her colleagues – indeed we might even be dead, she adds. When she advocates legislation for the future, and for the future of later generations, she is thus linking the tree of knowledge with the tree of life in an ardent arboreal tribute to the benefits of scientific progress – a linkage that implies not only an obligation to the future, but also a duty to uphold and defend these values in the face of opposition.

Here, then, we see the reverse process of that described in the context of the Alton debate, when, during exactly the same time period, the biologization of life by Christian

Right-to-Life activitists was pursued as a tactical political means of *secularizing* the Right-to-Life campaign. In the same way that these activists metonymized biological with divine life – the process of biological development with the gift of life, and faith in biology with faith in the Father – so too were both Christian and secular parliamentarians involved in a similar form of 'cross-fertilization': sowing the seeds of religious devotion in their impassioned defences of science. In the context of the debate over human embryo research, a defence of experimental biology, and of basic science, was couched in the idiom of salvation and of a quasi-religious duty to humanity. Infused with the idioms of life, generation, and sacrifice, the defence of science was not so much timeless as embedded in the forward temporality of scientific and technological progress. Witnessing, used in both contexts, serves as a crucial resource in the rhetoric of persuasion – directed both at the general public, and at the parliamentarians involved in a free, or 'conscience', vote on the limits of the law.

Ultimately, the Alton Bill was defeated, and a compromise measure was introduced into the HFE Bill to lower the upper time limit of abortion. But this too was defeated, resulting in the situation which has prevailed since 1967, namely that abortion is permitted until the twenty-fourth week of pregnancy, but that in cases of substantial risk to the pregnant woman, there is no time limit. Two doctors must agree that the abortion is in the woman's best interest, and that continuing to carry the pregnancy would put the pregnant woman at greater risk than a termination. The abortion must take place in approved premises that are subject to inspection by the Secretary of State.

The primitive streak

The lengthy debate over human fertilization and embryology during the 1980s not only involved interesting new mixtures of Christian and scientific imagery (which in other respects are not really new, since they animate much of Western science, as well as British colonial expansion), but also new mixtures of legal and biological language. One of the most elaborate of these, which introduces another example of the politicization of biological temporality, was the debate over the so-called 'primitive streak'. This curious tale has often been told, but is one that continues to reveal new dimensions (Franklin 1999*a*; Spallone 1996).

In the context of the HFE debate, both the ruling Conservative government (which, under Margaret Thatcher, was very pro-science) and the leading members of the Warnock Committee (namely the philosopher Mary Warnock and the biologist Anne McLaren) were aware of the significant danger of either parliamentary deadlock or defeat on the key issue of embryo research – not least because of its proximity to the intense and unpredictable abortion controversy. Through recent historical research on this period, including interviews with both McLaren (sadly now deceased) and Warnock (who remains deeply involved in this area),[2] it has become possible to explore in depth one of the most important decisions responsible for the eventual success of the HFE Act – the only piece of legislation of its kind ever to come into existence, under criminal law, covering the entire gamut of technologically assisted conception methods (as well as non-technological ones, such as surrogacy and artificial insemination), and thus a piece of legislation whose successful passage into law defied considerable odds.

The strategy initiated by McLaren, and implemented by Warnock (most likely with the help of Thatcher), of avoiding a deadlocked debate on the thorny and intransigent issue of 'the moral status of the human embryo' was simple but effective. McLaren in particular sought to avoid this particular phrase altogether by proposing an alternative formulation.

Journal of the Royal Anthropological Institute (N.S.), 109-125
© Royal Anthropological Institute 2014

In lieu of the philosophically intractable and awkward moral status question, the aim was to provide instead a quasi-biological basis for limiting embryo research – a 'natural line' of sorts (which of course does not exist 'biologically') as a basis for proposed legislation. The need for a 'line to be drawn' itself symbolized the core principle of the proposed Act, namely that some form of limitation to research was essential. The 'natural line' proposed by McLaren had the added advantage of establishing a kind of compromise: in exchange for allowing a strictly limited amount of embryo research, such research would be subject to the very strictest regulatory standards, including a dedicated 'watchdog' body, which would have at its disposal the use of criminal sanctions. The new HFE Authority would be ultimately responsible to Parliament, but it would draw up and enforce a 'Code of Practice' – by which all fertility treatment and all embryo research in the UK would be tightly controlled and licensed. Here, as in the exchange of embryo sacrifice for future human lives, was a second 'deal': in exchange for allowing a limited amount of research, the limits would be enforced by Parliament itself.

Strict enforcement of the limits to permissible research had, as a consequence, to have a credible basis in law, and ultimately this was found in the form of a natural fact of biological temporality manifest as a stage in early embryonic development known as the formation of the 'primitive streak'. The basis of this argument was initially made to Warnock by McLaren, and later by both of them to the entire committee. The logic was impeccable – if biologically a bit of a stretch. In effect, McLaren drew on her prodigious knowledge as one of the world's leading mammalian developmental biologists (and the first woman to hold office in the Royal Society) and her equally renowned abilities as a communicator (Warnock has described her as the best teacher she has ever met) to provide the committee with a thorough grounding in human embryonic development. Included in this instruction was a description of the process by which, after approximately fourteen days, the primitive nervous system of the developing embryo begins to become differentiated from the parts of the embryo that will go on to become the placenta, the supporting tissues and nutritive elements necessary to support pregnancy – but not the actual foetal body itself. In other words, at approximately fourteen days, with the formation of the emergent spinal column, visible as a tiny 'streak' on the body of the developing conceptus, a 'natural' dividing line separates the formation of a distinct human individual from its supporting environment, and thus also provides a morally sound (and anatomically convenient) point in the otherwise continuous process of early development at which to determine a 'natural' legal limit.

The so-called 'fourteen-day rule' proved a success with the committee, and later became one of the core elements of the Warnock Report (published in 1984). It was in turn imported into the proposed HFE Bill, and has since proven to be the signature element of one of the UK's most famous pieces of twentieth-century legislation. This principle, through which the time of the law (two weeks) and the time of biology are united, has been widely emulated all over the world. Moreover, this widespread adoption of the fourteen-day rule has prevailed in the face of significant doubts concerning its legitimacy from philosophers, biologists, legal scholars, and theologians. Critics, for example, have pointed out that the terminology of the so-called 'pre-embryo', brought in to distinguish the pre-fourteen-day entity from its biological sequel (and to attribute a lesser humanity to the former), is not a proper scientific term at all, but a convenient piece of made-up quasi-scientific jargon (Harris 1985). Others have noted that the fourteen-day rule, although supposedly based on the formation of the primitive streak, is in fact entirely arbitrary, since the streak sometimes emerges at fourteen days, but may emerge at twelve, or fifteen, or sixteen (Spallone 1996). The convenient two-week limit has also been criticized by feminists for the same reasons foetal personhood arguments have been – because they reinforce a patriarchal and masculinist equivalence between the 'individual' foetal body and foetal personhood, when in fact the foetus is never an 'individual' at all as long as it is inside a woman's body (Franklin 1991). From the point of view of anyone who believes life begins at conception, the primitive streak argument – however scientific or unscientific it may be – purports an indefensible divide between protected and unprotected human life.

Here, then, as above, is not so much a bracketing off of a separate kind of political time as an example of what Mikhail Bakhtin (1981) might call the formation of a distinct chronotope: the generic time of a specific event-space that allows certain kinds of things to happen.[3] However, the breach in developmental time signified by the emergence of the primitive streak is not intended *only* to be a distinct time-space event; indeed it is imagined to belong to the biological time of life itself, and to all of humanity, in perpetuity. Biological development is a useful idiom precisely because of the extent to which it can be seen as a non-specific discourse of temporality, existing in a realm that is both supra-legal and scientifically verifiable. Paradoxically, though, it can *only* be a distinct time-space event (such as the formation of the primitive streak) that enables the law to 'make a new kind of time' (a fourteen-day rule) if this time-space event (a precise phase in biological development) is *not* specific unto itself, but rather belongs to an objective world of natural facts that are universally valid, neutral, 'timeless', and true.

Leaving aside the somewhat paradoxical features of the fourteen-day rule, what we can observe here is an excellent example of what the organizers of the seminar series on which this volume is based described as 'the complex temporal reality of political events such as campaigns, protests and revolutions'. It can be added that the fourteen-day rule is is also an example of the highly contested nature of time-events and chronologies in politics. A further point, which as we shall shortly see has acquired increasing political importance, is that both the teleological and ontological constitution of the primitive streak-as-legal-limit argument are *mixed*, or *hybrid* – drawing together *a surfeit of seemingly overlapping logics* (moral, legal, biological) to constitute a single, decisive moment in time – thus achieving by a kind of condensation, or 'layering', parliamentary consent to a 'line' that is (by other reckonings) neither logically nor morally legitimate (or momentary, single, scientific, or decisive).[4]

Above all, what can be observed by comparing the uses of biological time and temporality in the context of two simultaneous British debates over reproductive politics in the 1980s is the extent to which time and temporality operate as spaces of conversion. As Judith Butler notes in her analysis of time as a component of cultural and sexual politics, these are 'already imbued with the problem of time, of progress in particular, and in certain notions of what it means to unfold a future of freedom in time' (2008: 1). How temporality is organized, argues Butler, 'already divides us' because its organization both reveals and conceals 'which histories have turned out to be formative' and 'how they intersect – or fail to intersect with other histories' (2008: 1). In the case of the borrowing of secular time by Right-to-Life abortion activists, in order to further their political goal (to ban all abortions) by disguising it as modern, rational, and scientific, biological temporality performs a function of conversion: by camouflaging Christian fundamentalist tenets in the cloak of biogenetic reason, it becomes possible to ground a religious argument in allegedly secular biological facts. Similarly, the primitive streak argument posits a universal developmental event – a biological fact of life – in order to convert a pragmatic legal objective into a simple matter of deductive biological reasoning. Again, time and temporality provide a space for reworking one idiom as another, repositioning the form of one temporality as the content of another's time.

Thus the primitive steak argument relies both on a 'moment' in time (as do many accounts of conception) and on the form of temporality, or chronotope, which determines what kind of time this is, and what it can contain or signify. What is noticeable about the impassioned invocation of the reproductive time of future generations from the pro-embryo research lobby in the HFE Act debate is its ironic relationship to the identical form of time depicted by the Right-to-Life lobby in their effort to protect the future lives of the unborn. Here, then, we have what the seminar organizers (see above) call the conflict in 'what it means to unfold a future of freedom in time', but evinced through similar genres of time. It is thus the composition of time and the mobilization of different temporal configurations that offer what Strathern (1992a) has identified as the 'plural universe' of temporality.

The case of the primitive streak similarly demonstrates how the mobilization of plural temporalities can be strategically orientated toward specific political goals – through what we might denominate as 'chronopolitical' conversions.[5] Through the figure of primitive streak are combined the 'natural' temporality of the biological and the statutory time of the law in the form of an apparently self-evident empirical reality, appearing as a visible line. The aim of this strategic alignment of biological development with legal requirement is politically pragmatic: the intersection they create is both a deliberately diversionary tactic (to avoid the 'moral status of the human embryo question') and strategic (by providing a legitimate basis for future governance of human fertilization and embryology). Both past time (in the form of the 'pre-embryo') and future time (in the form of legalized human embryo research) are conflated through a layered temporal construct that functions as a conversion device (to convert an early human embryo from a continuous path of development into a partitioned process of transformation). That this logic contradicts itself (since a human embryo used for research or clinical purposes must be continuously developing in order to be useful for either medicine or science) is not only why, but also how, its 'chronopolitics' are manifest. In the British debates over abortion law and the HFE Bill in the 1980s, time and temporality were crucial political resources in a battle over 'which histories have turned out to be formative' and 'how they intersect – or fail to intersect with other histories' (Butler 2008: 1).

Of course, we should not expect the law to be other than a fiction to itself that is upheld by other means – including symbolic and performative devices, such as protocols, procedures, and elaborate recording apparatus (hence the elaborate rituals of Parliament). For the law to reproduce itself credibly and effectively, there must be disagreement and debate. As Warnock herself stated, the basis of the law need not be 'right' in order to be 'alright' to enough people that it is workable. Thus it is not surprising that the various kinds of 'leakage' from the first incarnation of the HFE Act, passed in 1990, have required periodic visits from the parliamentary plumbers. The next, and last, example moves us forward in time to the Act's amendment by Parliament, a process referred to as the HFE Act II, and introduces a new chrono-typic event that poses the question of hybrid temporalities in the context of new biological mixtures. This debate concerned the formation of admixed human embryos for research, using the eggs of cows combined with human nuclei to create new biological tools. These were also known as the cybrid chimera debates of the early twenty-first century, which dominated the politics of HFE Act II much as the embryo debates had dominated the politics of HFE Act I two decades earlier (a politics that is very much with us in 2014 due to what we might call HFE Act III – the current effort to dissolve the HFE Authority).

Human admixed embryos

During 2008, an eventful year for reproductive politics in the UK, the thirtieth anniversary of the birth of Louise Brown almost exactly coincided with the unamended passage of a new HFE Bill ('HFE Act II'). In conspicuous contrast to the US, the UK strengthened its position as the most highly regulated but scientifically permissive climate for human embryo research anywhere in the world. Uniquely in Europe, human embryo research in the UK, including human embryonic stem cell derivation, has had consistently strong support from all of the major political parties, the major religious groups, and the general public, as does the production of cloned human embryos for research and human-animal, or 'cybrid', embryos. Indeed this area of research is something of a jewel in the crown as far as UK bioscience and biomedicine are concerned and is one of the very few areas not to have received extensive budget cuts under the current Coalition government's draconian plans to reduce the nation's budget deficit (although, as noted above, the HFE Authority itself may, ironically, not survive in its present form much longer under the new emphasis on 'austerity').

As part of my ongoing ethnographic research on human stem cell research in the UK, I attended one of the major demonstrations outside Parliament in support of, and against, the new HFE Bill at a key point during its passage through Parliament in 2008. It was a beautiful sunny day and it was a short bike ride from my office at the London School of Economics down the Embankment to Old Palace Yard in Westminster, where I arrived just after 1 p.m. In the announcement of the 12 May pro-embryo research demonstration, 'Show Your Support', organized by the office of MP Evan Harris (the *de facto* leader of the pro-embryo research lobby), it was suggested that:

> In recent months there has been intensive lobbying of MPs, particularly from groups who are opposed to embryo research to continue in the UK, including embryonic stem cell science and the animal-human hybrid work. MPs may not have heard quite so clearly from those who strongly support the proposals in the Bill, and know that it is vitally important that the legislation is not watered down.

It went on:

> A YouGov poll in August 2005 showed that 77% of people accept embryo research for life-threatening diseases. But for far too long, the most prominent shows of feeling on this issue have come from those who wish to impede carefully regulated embryo research and important and ethical clinical interventions like preimplantation genetic diagnosis.

The announcement concluded that on 12 May, just before the start of the Bill's Second Reading in the House of Commons,

> hundreds of patient groups would join with scientists, doctors and other supporters to represent the breadth and depth of support for the Bill, and in particular to confirm support for the government proposal that embryo research should continue in the UK, and should include animal-human hybrid work as well as embryonic stem cell science.

In fact, on the day, there were fewer than a dozen patients and representatives of patient groups available to comment to the media – most of whom had left by the time I arrived. The only scientists present were those who had taken time off from their work at the Guy's Hospital research centre near Borough market, where the first UK human embryonic stem cell lines were derived in 2003 (Franklin 2007). The fear that the pro-embryo research lobby would be swamped by the Right-to-Life rally also scheduled the same afternoon just before the start of the Second Reading, at 2 p.m., proved groundless, as it too was poorly attended and lack-lustre, the weather perhaps too glorious to support a mood of indignation.

Riding back to my office to watch the Second Reading live on Parliament TV, I reflected on what a different situation it had been in the late spring of 1990 when the first HFE Bill was passed. Then, not so long after a Private Members Bill introduced by MP Enoch Powell had attempted to ban embryo research entirely, the question of how Parliament would vote on the amendment to allow embryo research was far from certain. The Right-to-Life lobby were much larger and more well organized, and on something of a crusade. In a dramatic show of opposition to abortion, they had showered the chambers of Parliament with postcards emblazoned with images of aborted foetuses.

However, the reduced size and fervour of the demonstrations for and against embryo research were not the only measure of the difference between 1990 and 2008. Looking back, we can see that although some forms of reproductive technology – such as cloning, human-animal hybrids, and stem cells – still engender controversy, the logic of progress associated with assisted conception has been sedimented into a naturalized trajectory of intervention in the name of human betterment in which technological manipulation of human embryos is not only a viable alternative to 'natural' reproduction, but also *a necessary path* to the continued improvement of human health. If severe, debilitating, and destructive conditions can be potentially alleviated through embryo experimentation, this is a path that must be followed out of an ethical responsibility not to deny future generations the fruits of promising scientific research. In a sense, the connection between IVF and generation which we saw in the earlier episodes of reproductive politics discussed above has become more visible, and more unquestionable, as the dominant discourse, characterized by a general isomorphism between improvements to human health and well-being and the ability to culture human (or partially human) embryonic life 'in glass'.

The early twenty-first-century debate over cybrid embryos (e.g. mixed animal-human embryos) in the UK suggests that the cultural shift in reproductive politics over the past thirty years is not only a process through which the axiomatic status of natural facts has been displaced, but also one through which a newly naturalized, and quasi-theological, discourse of progress has become a form of moral commonsense. Here again is the recombinant mixture of past and future temporality as a form of chronopolitical mechanics. In the presumed utility and moral legitimacy of cybrid embryo research, we see not only the chronic failure of the anti-abortion rhetoric I wrote about as a graduate student in the 1980s, but also its complete, and almost burlesque, conversion into a form of quasi-religious faith in human salvation, expressed, celebrated, and defended as a duty to protect experimental science. Whereas the Right-to-Life movement turned to biological science as a strategic means of secularizing the abortion debate in the 1980s, but lost its way politically on this ground, the scientific lobby's turn to the quasi-theological language of witnessing, salvation, and the relief of human suffering has prevailed, ironically establishing a new temporality of 'marching forward into the unknown' as a moral obligation that has gained widespread public acceptance. It has even become a source of British national pride.

Journal of the Royal Anthropological Institute (N.S.), 109-125
© Royal Anthropological Institute 2014

This conversion, whereby religious content was given secular biological form in one context, and biological science was embedded in a chronotope of salvation in another, has yielded an interesting chronopolitical comparison, whereby not only has the former effort lost ground to the latter, but it has also become a debased political currency in the process. Hence, for example, very much in contrast to the debate that took place in Parliament throughout the 1980s concerning embryo research, in which the Right-to-Life movement appeared to be gaining ground, the high-profile UK debate in 2008 concerning human-animal hybrids, or cybrids, relegated the Catholic Church Right-to-Life position to the 'extreme' fringe of public debate. Cardinal Keith O'Brien's strident 2008 Easter sermon condemning the revised HFE Bill was widely perceived to damage the reputation of Catholicism in the UK. 'It is difficult to imagine', O'Brien (2008) claimed, 'a single piece of legislation which, more comprehensively, attacks the sanctity and dignity of human life than this particular Bill':

> What I am speaking of is the process whereby scientists create an embryo containing a mixture of animal and human genetic material. If I were preaching this homily in France, Germany, Italy, Canada, or Australia I would be commending the government for rightly banning such grotesque procedures. However here in Great Britain I am forced to condemn our government for not only permitting but encouraging such hideous practices ... This Bill represents a monstrous attack on human rights, human dignity and human life ... One might say that in our country we are about to have a public government endorsement of experiments of Frankenstein proportion. May God indeed help us to be Missionary at this present time and to hand on the saving message of Jesus Christ in a world which does not seem prepared to receive it.

Among those challenging this view was the prominent geneticist Mary Seller, also a Christian, whose commentary on cybrids published in *The Tablet* (Seller 2008) cited the teachings of Jesus Christ as a motivation not only to heal the sick but also to marvel at the splendour of God's creation.

> God certainly intends healing of the sick. Jesus always healed when he encountered a person in need: he never passed one by. Indeed he often flouted authority to do so: he healed on the Sabbath, he touched untouchables, and vociferous criticism did not stop him. Furthermore, he gave power and authority to his disciples to go out on the highways and byways to do likewise. If today we are able to heal anyone through our new scientific endeavours, it is an expression of our discipleship, and can also be construed as another way in which we legitimately 'Play God'.

Seller's pragmatic interpretation of Christ's teaching neatly encapsulates the mainstream UK position of support for science based on a sense of moral duty to explore new avenues for the relief of human suffering. In her view, God's intentions are consistent with instrumental intervention, including biological experimentation. She invokes a tradition of active, mobile evangelism – flouting the state's authority to take to the road, 'the highways and byways', with tools to heal the sick. Scientific research, in this view, is no less than a form of discipleship.

In their press release, 'Human admixed embryos', prepared to accompany the debate in Parliament on human-animal hybrid embryos, the Genetic Interest Group (2008), representing patient groups in favour of the new legislation, took a similar view – describing the human *in vitro* embryo as 'a vital tool to advance the progress of research into the potential of embryonic stem cells' and thus as 'a potentially vital avenue for research which could greatly increase our understanding of serious medical conditions such as Parkinson's, motor neurone disease, Alzheimer's disease and cystic fibrosis'. Such a statement strongly reinforces the initial UK government position set in place by the debate over Warnock – that some embryo research should be permitted in the effort to provide relief from human suffering – whilst also confirming, as does passage of the new legislation unamended, that this position has stood the test of time. As the (lack of) cybrid debate reveals, support for this view has, if anything, been strengthened to the extent that the value of the *in vitro* human embryo culture system as both *a tool and a way* has come to occupy the moral high ground. The strategically recombinant chronopolitics introduced by McLaren, endorsed by Warnock, and implemented by Thatcher's government over an unusual prolonged period of parliamentary debate has become, in Butler's words, the history that 'turned out to be formative' (2008: 1).

Conclusion

During the 1980s, many feminists were deeply concerned about the strategic adoption of a secularized biological time of foetal development by the Right-to-Life movement. This seemed a worryingly effective chronopolitical strategy, and one that was gaining ground by employing an already established, powerful idiom of development – namely biological science. I have referred to this as the 'time of biology' or 'biological time'. However, what emerged out of the clash of reproductive aspirations that occurred when the pro-embryo research lobby squared up against the Right-to-Life movement in the UK in the 1980s was that, somewhat ironically, an almost reverse scenario emerged – in which scientific progress emerged as the triumphant form of temporality, framed within a quasi-theological idiom of duty to humanity, and ethical obligation to future generations, by 'marching hopefully' into uncharted biological territory. This duty was then codified in law, inaugurating a social contract, or exchange, legitimating the sacrifice of existing human embryos in the name of future human health, prosperity, and progress. A specific 'time event' – namely the 'natural fact' of the 'primitive streak' – proved to be a crucial basis for this shift. The 'legal fiction' of the 'fourteen-day rule' entrenched the power of the progress argument – so much so that it now seems all but unassailable in the UK, whereas the Right-to-Life advocates appear to be at a loss to capture the public imagination, or the common ground of commonsense consensus, as they once did. Their chronopolitics, their version of history, and their attempt to reduce the upper time limit of abortion have failed: their history is not the formative one. Among other things, this reversal suggests that time is an important, but undertheorized, resource in the mobilization of social movements – and that it can operate as both form and content in political struggles.

Returning to the linearity of biological time described by Strathern at the outset of this paper, we can thus conclude that its 'literalism' serves more than one function, and is recursive in more than one sense for 'the English'. Taking 'literalism' in its Bakhtinian sense to mean what is generic to representation, as evidenced by how the chronotope formally structures not only written texts, but also the worldviews within which they operate, we can interpret the contrast between two social movements in the 1980s over reproductive, or biological, time as one not only of tactics but also of ethical culture, or, as Foucault (1990) described it, of biopower. While both pointing to specific moments in biological time, and insisting on their literalism, the two movements were also pointing in different directions, ethically, politically, and legally. While both employing the language of witnessing and conversion, the linear passage of time being pulled into focus by the two sides of the debate, and the 'natural facts' the passage of time 'revealed', were also clothed in the empirical robes of 'objective fact'. At once represented as 'obvious', two different versions of early human development *in vivo* were situated within the 'literal' narration of biological facts, but utilized as symbolic political resources. This contrast thus also confirms that what 'the English are able to point to' when they invoke 'the "biological" experiencing of temporality as vindicating a linear interpretation of it' (Strathern 1992a: 62) is not obvious at all. Symbolically, ethically, 'literally', 'objectively', legally, politically, and culturally, such 'pointing' is, in fact, highly ambivalent. 'Biological time' may provide 'irrefutable evidence of linearity' (Strathern 1992a: 62), but this linearity is never sufficient evidence in itself to reveal what 'biological time' means. 'Biological time' turns out to be an inherited cultural resource, a chronotopic one perhaps, which is as malleable as any other.

A coda to this observation would be that we might expect biological time 'itself' also to change, and thus also its meanings to 'the English'. Significantly, this is exactly what happened in the period separating HFE Act I from its successor incarnation in HFE Act II, for it was in 1996 that the successful cloning of Dolly the sheep confirmed not only that biological development can be reversed, but also that it is possible to induce the 'backwards' de-development of mammalian cells. The importance of this new and unexpected discovery for understandings of developmental time is why cybrid embryos were needed to further the exploration of the possible health benefits of human embryonic stem cell therapy – now a major focus of scientific research in the UK and elsewhere. Of the many recursions the 'literal' meanings of 'biological time' can offer, we now, it appears, have not only 'more' time, but also more kinds of time, and thus more opportunities to be both literal and objective, as well as ethical and political, about going backwards as well as forwards within them. As Alice once had to learn, from her new location on the other side of the looking glass, times and temporalities do not all run alike: even when they are moving in the same direction, as the Red Queen points out, the fastest runners might be standing still:

> '[I]n our country,' said Alice, still panting a little, 'you'd generally get to somewhere else – if you run very fast for a long time, as we've been doing.'
> 'A slow sort of country!' said the Queen. 'Now, here, you see, it takes all the running you can do, to keep in the same place. If you want to get somewhere else, you must run at least twice as fast as that!' (Carroll 1998 [1871]: 345).

NOTES

[1] The term 'biological control' is used in the context of contemporary bioscience to refer to the increasing ability to manipulate biological components and pathways, including biological 'time', technologically and experimentally.

[2] With funding from the Wellcome Trust Medical Humanities programme, Martin Johnson and I have interviewed two dozen of the 'key players' in the emergence of IVF and human embryo research during the post-war period in the UK. These interviews are now archived at the British Library as part of a project on the emergence of mammalian developmental biology in the UK.

[3] Bakhtin borrows from Einstein's relativity theory to define the concept of the 'chronotope' as a form of literary representation. He argues in *The dialogic imagination* (1981) that it is a form of 'time-space' that allows time in literature to become visible by being 'thickened'.

[4] Significantly, by Strathern's account (1992a; 1992b), this plural, or 'merographic', time of the primitive streak 'chronotope' is *exactly what makes it modern*. Modernity, as Appadurai (1996: 1) notes, 'belongs to that small family of theories that both declares and desires universal applicability for itself' (thus non-reflexively instantiating the paradoxical terms of its own foundational narrative). Indeed the primitive streak example serves as a useful parable for modernity in many other ways too – not least its simultaneous invocation and erasure of the primordial.

Journal of the Royal Anthropological Institute (N.S.), 109-125
© Royal Anthropological Institute 2014

[5] The term 'chronopolitical' has been variously used in the past: for example, by George Wallis (1970) to describe a time of political transition, and by Paul Virilio (2007) to describe the effect of speed on politics and the relationship of space to time. For a review that is relevant to the contributions to this volume, see Klinke (2013), in particular the discussion of 'heterotemporality' to refer to a crucial element in modern geopolitics.

REFERENCES

APPADURAI, A. 1996. *Modernity at large: cultural dimensions of globalization.* Minneapolis: University of Minnesota Press.

BAKHTIN, M. 1981. *The dialogic imagination* (trans. C. Emerson & M. Holquist). Austin: University of Texas Press.

BUTLER, J. 2008. Sexual politics, torture and secular time. *British Journal of Sociology* **59**, 1-23.

CANNELL, F. 1990. Concepts of parenthood: the Warnock Report, the Gillick Debate, and modern myths. *American Ethnologist* **17**, 667-86.

CARROLL, L. 1998 [1871]. *Through the looking-glass and what Alice found there (The annotated Alice: Alice's adventures in Wonderland and through the looking-glass).* New York: The New American Library.

FOUCAULT, M. 1990. *The history of sexuality*, vol. 1: *An introduction* (trans. R. Hurley). London: Penguin.

FRANKLIN, S. 1991. Fetal fascinations: new dimensions to the medical-scientific construction of fetal personhood. In *Off-centre: feminism and cultural studies* (eds) S. Franklin, C. Lury & J. Stacey, 190-205. London: HarperCollins.

——— 1993. Making representations: the parliamentary debate on the Human Fertilisation and Embryology Act. In *Technologies of procreation: kinship in the age of assisted conception* (eds) J. Edwards, S. Franklin, E. Hirsch, F. Price & M. Strathern, 96-131. Manchester: University Press.

——— 1997. *Embodied progress: a cultural account of assisted conception.* London: Routledge.

——— 1999*a*. Dead embryos: feminism in suspension. In *Fetal subjects, feminist positions* (eds) L.M. Morgan & M.W. Michaels, 61-82. Philadelphia: University of Pennsylvania Press.

——— 1999*b*. Making representations: the parliamentary debate on the Human Fertilisation and Embryology Act. In *Technologies of procreation: kinship in the age of assisted conception* (eds) J. Edwards, S. Franklin, E. Hirsch, F. Price & M. Strathern, 127-65 (Second edition). London: Routledge.

——— 2007. *Dolly mixtures: the remaking of genealogy.* Durham, N.C.: Duke University Press.

——— & C. ROBERTS 2006. *Born and made: an ethnography of preimplantation genetic diagnosis.* Princeton: University Press.

GALLAGHER, J. 1987. Eggs, embryos and foetuses: anxiety and the law. In *Reproductive technologies: gender, motherhood and medicine* (ed.) M. Stanworth, 139-50. Cambridge: Polity.

GENETIC INTEREST GROUP 2008. Human admixed embryos. Press release (available on-line: *http://www.geneticalliance.org.uk/docs/BriefingStemCellResearch.pdf*, accessed 28 January 2014).

HARRIS, J. 1985. *The value of life: an introduction to medical ethics.* London: Routledge.

JOHNSON, M.H. & A.A., THEODOSIOU 2011. The politics of human embryo research and the motivation to achieve PGD. *Reproductive Biomedicine Online* **22**, 457-71.

KLINKE, I. 2013. Chronopolitics: a conceptual matrix. *Progress in Human Geography* **37**, 673-90.

O'BRIEN, K. 2008. Cardinal O'Brien's sermon. 23 March (available on-line: *http://news.bbc.co.uk/1/hi/scotland/7308883.stm*, accessed 28 January 2014).

PETCHESKY, R.P. 1984. *Abortion and woman's choice: the state, sexuality, and reproductive freedom.* Boston: Northeastern University Press.

——— 1987. Fetal images: the power of visual culture in the politics of reproduction. *Feminist Studies* **13**, 263-92.

SCIENCE AND TECHNOLOGY SUBGROUP 1991. In the wake of the Alton Bill: science, technology and reproductive politics. In *Off-centre: feminism and cultural studies* (eds) S. Franklin, C. Lury & J. Stacey, 147-8. London: HarperCollins.

SELLER, M. 2008. Slipping on the slope of progress. *The Tablet*, 5 April.

SPALLONE, P. 1996. The salutary tale of the pre-embryo. In *Between monsters, goddesses and cyborgs: feminist confrontations with science and medicine in cyberspace* (ed.) N. Lykke & R. Braidotti, 207-26. London: Zed Books.

STRATHERN, M. 1992*a*. *After nature: English kinship in the late twentieth century.* Cambridge: University Press.

——— 1992*b*. *Reproducing the future: anthropology, kinship and the new reproductive technologies.* Manchester: University Press.

VIRILIO, P. 2007. *Speed and politics* (trans. M. Polizzotti). New York: Semiotext(e).

WALLIS, G.W. 1970. Chronopolitics: the impact of time perspectives on the dynamics of change. *Social Forces* **49**, 102-29.

Journal of the Royal Anthropological Institute (N.S.), 109-125
© Royal Anthropological Institute 2014

Repenser la politique de la reproduction dans le temps et le temps dans la politique de la reproduction au Royaume-Uni : 1978-2008

Résumé

Le présent article explore deux débats différents, mais liés et contemporains, sur la politique de la reproduction, dans lesquels se manifestent au moins trois combinaisons distinctes de temps. Dans la première partie, l'auteure décrit l'orientation vers un temps « biologisé » dans les années 1980, sous l'impulsion des groupes britanniques chrétiens se réclamant d'un « droit à la vie » qui ont commencé à utiliser une ontogenèse sécularisée pour promouvoir et défendre une définition religieuse « du chemin, de la vérité, de la vie » et ont modifié une « théo-ontologie » basée sur l'équivalence de la valeur absolue de la vie humaine, de la vérité (de la vie biologique) et de la foi dans le Christ (source de vie éternelle). Dans la deuxième partie, elle décrit une ontologie opposée, « panachée » différemment (séculière ou semi-séculière, utilisant une chronométrie hybride à la fois biologique et juridique, mais orientée vers l'horizon intemporel du progrès), caractérisant pendant la même période le débat sur l'avenir de la fécondation *in vitro* et qui devait aboutir en 1990 à la première loi sur la fécondation humaine et l'embryologie (HFE Act) au Royaume-Uni. Dans la troisième partie, elle se penche sur l'héritage de ces débats dans l'éclairage qu'ils jettent sur les controverses politiques qui ont, plus récemment, accompagné l'adoption d'un HFE Act amendé en 2008 et sur le débat autour des embryons dits « cybrides ». Ces épisodes révèlent à quel point les mouvements sociaux « sont profondément modelés par des médiations et des conflits entre des représentations, technologies, disciplines sociales et rythmes temporels différents ». L'auteure avance que les diverses constructions de la temporalité dans la politique de la reproduction que font apparaître ces trois épisodes distincts sont cruciaux pour comprendre, en anthropologie, la signification du « contrôle biologique » dans le contexte de la recherche sur les cellules souches, du clonage, du génie tissulaire et de la biomédecine de la reproduction.

Bureaucratic times

6

The time it takes: temporalities of planning

SIMONE ABRAM *Durham University*

State planning has been a defining means for modern subjects to regulate the passage of time. In practice, it is the focus of multiple conflicts and doubts, which planners attempt to mediate. In this paper, I address the regimes of time that planning both promotes and encounters, and tease out what these imply for anthropology. Using ethnography of Norwegian and Swedish planning offices and their encounters with participatory planning, I question recent claims that there has been an evacuation of the near future or a retreat of administrative intervention. I also suggest that recent anthropological concerns with time have been confined by their attempts to characterize the changing timescapes of specific modal shifts, such as from the modern to the neoliberal. Instead, in my ethnography, I focus not on tracking epochal breaks in time, but on demonstrating how time is manipulated, and how multiple temporalities are performed in ongoing projects of democratic planning.

In defining the modern, it would be uncontroversial to suggest that state planning is an archetypally modern expression of both time and space. The idea of improved futures to be achieved by the rational application of policy and the hygienic distribution of development is emblematic of a modern worldview (see Rabinow 1989), even if practice may fall short of the high ideals that rational planning promises. Wittrock (2000) even locates the key identifier of modernity in the rise of promissory notes, of which governmental plans could be considered an example (see Abram & Weszkalnys 2013). With its concern for improvements and with the future as its object, planning is, by definition, a temporal field, one that is concerned with transformation through time, or what Gisa Weszkalnys and I have described as 'the possibilities that time offers space' (Abram & Weszkalnys 2011: 3). Notions of progress that are implicit in plans suggest that planning time is inherently modern, yet close attention to planning practices indicates that such temporalities are doubted, contested, and mediated. Planning is in fact a particular form of governmental technology through which social discipline, ritual, and rhythm are made present in social life, and in which time is materialized, mediated, or brought into conflict. Planning technologies continue to colonize state practice, despite neoliberal principles of minimizing the role of the state; indeed, it

Journal of the Royal Anthropological Institute (N.S.), 129-147
© Royal Anthropological Institute 2014

appears that as the management of actual services is put out to contract, the role of the state is increasingly bound up in proliferating forms and domains of planning. Concrete modernist architectural city plans of the post-war era have given way to 'aspirational' regional socio-economic future-visions of the twenty-first century. Planning is not going away.

Anthropological approaches to neoliberalized time suggest a break with modernity's temporalities, yet as land-use and development planning move into neoliberalized forms, their temporal frames appear to become more abundant rather than denuded. Movement into the future changes direction, with forecasting challenged by 'backcasting', and planning regulations being implemented retrospectively as well as through ordered progression in linear time. Planning for the future contains more forms of temporality than merely anticipation (cf. Adams, Murphy & Clarke 2009). In contrast to the focus on predicting the future (e.g. Zaloom 2009) or anticipating potential events (Lakoff 2008), a closer look at both ordinary and particular planning practices demonstrates the variation and fecundity of temporal imagination and management that are found in both modern and neoliberal regimes. These have much more to tell us than of the relationship between technology and affect (cf. Zaloom 2009). Contemporary forms of planning continue to envisage long-term futures, and deal with immediate issues, but I argue that they do not evacuate the near future of intention or activity, or of potential (cf. Guyer 2007a). Instead, that near future is becoming a different domain, whose authority is more dependent on appeals to the demonstrable participation of a putative public, while games of control and expertise continue to be played. If anything, it is the near and medium past that are evacuated from the practices of planning professionals and bureaucrats, their relentless focus on worlds yet to be and work yet to be done quickly leaving behind this meaningful past. It is in the encounter with 'ordinary people' – residents, protesters, participants – who bring an unruly past back into the planning process, that planning's selective technologies of moving through time are unsettled.

In this paper, I consider the temporalities of democratic spatial planning, including holistic community planning and land-use planning in Norway and Sweden. While the term 'spatial' indicates a concern with land-use, urban design, spatial distribution of facilities and services, and concrete development, planning practice is full of temporal conundrums. Referring to various instances of planning practice, I will argue that conflicting temporal frames characterize contemporary urban and infrastructural planning, and that widespread forms and norms of social mediation adopted by planners falter through a lack of theoretical and practical attention to temporal contradictions. But first, I will briefly address some of the recent discussions of temporality that help to bring fresh insights into an analysis of planning, which in turn is a site of analysis that offers new dimensions to the understanding of time in anthropology.

Near, present, future, and horizons of time

Current discussions of time in contemporary anthropology have been spurred on by Guyer's thoughts on changing regimes of time in relation to economics and evangelism. Guyer (2007a) argues that economic theories and practices have shifted towards a monetarism that implements immediate controls over money supply with the aim of achieving stability over the very long term, thus evacuating the medium term or the near future of significance or potential for action. This shift away from medium-term regulation (the five-year plan, episodic looking forward and backward, the rational welfare state) is mirrored, in Guyer's analysis, by an evangelical Christian prophetic temporality, in which the lived present is an indeterminate time between the first and second comings, or between a historical past and a timeless future horizon. In this, too, the near future of the human lifetime is postponed in favour of the distant rapture, leaving a focus only on the imminent and stripping it of causalities.

Guyer is hardly alone in her concern for the changing political potential for the future. Pusey (1998), for example, argued much earlier that a shift from public time towards market time is experienced as a shrinking horizon of meaningfully anticipated futures. This temporal perspective is increasingly shared by other anthropologists. Baxstrom, for example, has argued that urban development plans in Kuala Lumpur operate in an everlasting present rather than 'towards an authoritarian, teleological sense of "the future" ' (2012: 135). Referring to this as a 'baroque disposition' (2012: 137), Baxstrom suggests that the primary role of these plans is to demonstrate mastery over a present that is enfolded and multiple, where buildings seem to be demolished and rebuilt at whim in what he calls the 'dizzying eventedness of the present' (2012: 143). This eventedness does not quite correspond to Guyer's notion of punctuated calendar time, but the emphasis on events disconnected in time is shared. Stuff happens, they seem to say, even if we cannot make sense of its sequence.

Guyer's article also intimates a sense of loss in referring to the decline of the near future, of her sense of foreignness in the current present, and the evacuation of a temporal frame that allowed for 'planning and hoping, of tracing out mutual influences, of engaging in struggles for specific goals' (2007a: 409). The mention of planning is instructive, since it is precisely in this middle-distance future that one would expect the ambitions and hopes of spatial planning to be found. Yet even in Baxstrom's instrumental plans, the spectre of the future does not disappear from plans themselves. Plans always gesture towards some version or 'vision' of a future, even if this acts only as a vehicle for present action. It could be argued that the kind of future thus depicted might be changing, however. Vike (2013) notes a shifting of temporal horizons in relation to Norwegian plans. Inspired by Pusey's observations, he has suggested that the future experienced in the Norwegian welfare state is being redefined from an Enlightenment ideal of participatory planning as a means to achieve political mobilization and democratization towards a neoliberalization of planning as a managerial strategy. In Vike's analysis, the conceptualization of politics has been transformed from Utopian Time to Contemporary Time. Utopian Time, as the horizon of the possible, suggests collective movement along a path towards goals which motivate, offer hope, and may instil a degree of patience, even a willingness to make sacrifices towards the greater goal. Contemporary Time, by contrast, as the temporal mode of market transactions, implies a logic of immediate return, equivalent to Utopia Now, or in Norwegian terms, the immediate delivery of universal welfare as an individual right guaranteed by the state. As Vike notes, it becomes increasingly difficult to satisfy demands for Utopia Now with plans that propose an orderly transition towards better services in the future. These gaps between ideology and practice lead inexorably towards pragmatic attempts to tackle overloads in demand, and a corresponding disillusion with the making of visionary plans. If we can have Utopia Now, why wait? Without the rational link between future vision and action, long-term planning is easily seen as 'just words' (Vike 2013).

And yet, observing the world of European state planners today, there is little evidence of any decline in planning activity. On the contrary, over nearly two decades in which I have been observing planning, the numbers and kinds of plans demanded by the state have flourished. For instance, a recent law on planning in Norway proposes that each municipality should adopt a planning strategy within a year of local elections, identifying strategic choices over social development (including long-term land-use, environmental challenges, and the need for further plans – see Miljøverndepartementet 2011). This meta-plan appears to be a tool to promote co-ordination among neigh-bouring districts and among the layers of governmental hierarchy, and as an immediate political evaluation scale – progress towards strategic aims identified at the start of one electoral period will provide benchmarks for the following election (see KS n.d.). It does not replace the ambitious requirement for all Norwegian municipalities to produce comprehensive medium- and long-term development plans, however. On the contrary, the new planning strategy must take account of existing municipal plans, but while planning strategies require broad public debate, they do not entail the same strict procedural inclusion, information, and consultation procedures as municipal plans. How the four-year term of the planning strategy affects the twenty-year horizon of municipal planning remains to be seen, but it would appear that the planning strategy is a means to fill the near and medium-term future with ever more alternative forms of organization rather than to empty it out (see Wilk 2007; Zaloom 2007).

Similarly, even though a new national planning framework for England proposes a blanket approval for 'sustainable development', potentially weakening planning control to the point of inutility, it still insists on a plan-led approach (DCLG 2012). Given the potentially radical changes currently proposed for planning in England (where the end of planning has been mooted among planning practitioners), my intention is not to try to prophesy how these changes might emerge, but instead to consider some of the temporal schemes adopted in plan-led systems in the decades before and after the turn of the twenty-first century, many of which remain in place at the time of writing. Plan-led systems, common at least to Northern European countries, presume a set of planning tools and practices revolving around visions of variably distant futures. In both the UK and Scandinavia, for example, governmental planning systems have been seen by the centre-left political parties as a key route to securing a more participatory democracy, enthusiastically supported by planning theorists inspired by the participa-tory planning movements of the 1960s (see Damer & Hague 1971) and by the New Labour government's 'modernizing agenda', in which inclusive planning would con-tribute to democratic renewal (RTPI 2007).

The question that arises for this paper is whether the temporalities of planning have been evacuated from local government action in the way that Guyer argues that they have from state economics. While the normative academic literature of planning theory acknowledges that planning is a process that implies progress through time, the concept of conflicting temporalities is generally underemphasized in favour of questions of spatial justice. Yet games of temporality are constantly being played. New varieties of future horizon have emerged as well as disappeared, and models of the progression from one to another have been postulated, discarded, and adopted. Political beliefs in participative planning have survived various attempts to create discursive forums, and future-visioning and scenario techniques have come and gone. A brief survey of plan-ning horizons also suggests a range of temporalities in play that are fleetingly concretized into planning documents, documents which give the appearance of solidity and endurance, yet are constantly in the process of revision and reinvention.

There are, despite Guyer's concerns, near- and medium-term plans. Norwegian Municipal Plans, with their horizon of fifteen to twenty years, or the English Local

Development Frameworks with their twenty- to twenty-five-year Core Strategies, are both revised more frequently, suggesting that the near future is still at least rhetorically present in local state planning in neoliberalizing (or, following Guyer, monetarized[1]) economies. Norwegian local planning is marked by the four-year electoral cycle and the annual financial plan. Annual planning takes the form of reporting of service levels, revision of spending plans, and adjusting of service criteria. In other words, the long-term plan is implemented through shorter-term plans. Until the new planning strategy comes into force (see above), planning beyond annual plans has been considered 'strategic'. Municipal plans, for example, are usually considered strategic, and take a standard (or, one might argue, hegemonic) form. An example from a wealthy district near Oslo begins with an outline of the municipality's vision of the future, clothed in the moralized rhetorics of well-being: 'Everyone will have the opportunity for success in their own ambitions, wishes and desires'.[2] At the same time, challenges for the future are outlined, and some acknowledgement may be offered that the future may not always live up to the vision: 'Visions can never be realized, but serve as a guiding star and articulate an ambition'. After a general exposition of this strategic ambition, the plan lays out a series of policies with different temporal horizons. A general development plan includes broad development areas identified in maps covering a thirty-year horizon, while more concrete policies propose to concentrate development in particular areas over the next ten years. Specific developments are sometimes identified, but detailed architectural plans are not considered in the strategic plan. The plan projects forward up to twenty to thirty years, but is revised or rewritten over one or two electoral cycles, so a strategic plan never holds over the whole period of its strategy. While some policies might roll forward into a new plan, others may not, suggesting that there are parallel temporal flows. On the one hand, there is an imaginative future vision in the long term, which itself is revised on a shorter cycle. In the shorter term still, concrete projects are dealt with under a different temporal and spatial framework which is more immediate. And, in practice, imminent political decisions are taken that do not align with the ambitions outlined in the plans. Despite their sometimes grandiose pretentions, plans are not always sovereign.

It is worth noting an issue that we generally take for granted: that spatial and temporal plans are often scaled in proportion. Strategic planning should be large in both scales – a district-wide plan for a twenty-year period might include a note on the development of a plot, but a detailed plan (blueprint) or architectural design for a specific plot to be built in the next year or two would rarely be considered strategic in its own right. The Norwegian plan mentioned above is explicit: the plan's society section translates and concretizes the vision, and the strategic direction and vision are operationalized through the implementation plan and annual reviews. Spatial and temporal scales thus shrink from the abstract vision to the concrete development. Another way to frame this would be to suggest that something one expects to happen in the foreseeable future cannot be seen as visionary. Setting out a plan to build a new office block in a town centre is unlikely to be seen to fulfil a vision of enabling people to achieve their ambitions and desires, or even to make the town the best in the country (another typical strategic planning goal), even if providing more office space for entrepreneurs is a medium-term aim.

These scaling effects were apparent in the preparation of a municipal plan that I followed in 2000 in the same Norwegian municipality,[3] a rural but urbanizing district with approximately 50,000 inhabitants that had expanded rapidly in the preceding

Journal of the Royal Anthropological Institute (N.S.), 129-147
© Royal Anthropological Institute 2014

decades from a comfortable agricultural district to a well-connected set of commuter settlements, where average incomes were above the national mean and an increasing proportion of the population was over the age of 70. The municipality was politically conservative, and in the period I was there was governed by a coalition of Conservative and populist Future parties. From the late 1990s, the Chief Executive, supported by the Mayor, introduced new organizational forms and policies that corresponded to the New Public Management, a process that could be understood as a form of neoliberalization (see Abram 2002). In 2000, the process of preparing a new municipal plan had changed. Until then, municipal plans had generally been prepared by the Chief Planner, circulated for comments among directors of municipal departments (senior administrators), and presented to politicians for discussion and approval. 'Ours is a very written culture', the Chief Planner explained. Inspired by professional debates about inclusive planning, the Chief Planner had proposed a more comprehensive process, where participants would contribute to a more integrated vision of the municipality's future. At the same time, the Chief Executive, a great enthusiast for neoliberal public management, had been approached by a private consultant who argued that municipal planning would benefit from professional management. The consultant was contracted to deliver a new participative plan. His process demanded that a mixed group including both politicians and senior advisers should agree long-term goals, strategic objectives, and concrete policies to achieve them. The consultant was an experienced businessman nearing retirement age, who dressed in suit and tie, and made extensive use of detailed diagrams on PowerPoint slides to demonstrate his ideas. Key words framed in differently coloured circles, with arrows from one to another, popped up on the screen in front of an ambivalent group of local politicians and administrators in rather more relaxed attire. My observations of these meetings recall a sense of circularity and frustration, of people extremely politely resisting the pressure to conform to the consultant's desires, diverting the meetings through detailed discussion of particular municipal issues, and raising queries about the process wherever possible.

The consultant constantly pushed to achieve a set of hierarchical aims, with an overall image of how the municipality should be in the future – 'a good municipality to live in', followed by closer definition of aspects of this future vision with the various municipal activities indicated in a new set of circles. Each activity was to have its own vision, and each was to be identified by a series of elements that could be measured, such as the number of people qualified to do a particular job. And with this mapped out, a series of strategic challenges would emerge that were of more permanent concern in the municipality, each of which could have development goals, sub-goals, and policies. Within this model, the overall aim was to organize all municipal activities into long-term general aims and specific objectives. The consultant seemed to believe that the politicians could identify future visions, goals, and objectives as 'resource persons' independent of their political views. One of the politicians from a small party (the Socialist Left) was concerned that issues under discussion should be shared with her party, and was afraid that when the plan came up for debate later, she would be told 'but you went along with the process'. Another minority party (Labour) politician agreed that if the small parties' views were ignored, they would relinquish any responsibility for the resulting documents. After a fairly lengthy discussion of roles, the consultant broke in to suggest that 'we have to move on, we need to run this process at a certain tempo'. Politicians who felt that their concerns were not represented in the aims identified need not worry, he suggested, since all their proposals had been noted and

Journal of the Royal Anthropological Institute (N.S.), 129-147
© Royal Anthropological Institute 2014

would be considered when the Chief Executive's team continued the planning work later. In addition, he remarked that these were issues that had been discussed several meetings earlier.

Even in this short exchange, we can see time and process being folded and layered, and the near future being filled with concern and action. Municipal time is first layered and hierarchized, with near, middle, and distant future scaled from concrete to abstract concerns. The practitioners attempt to draw routes through the hierarchy to join each concern in order of scale. But the neatness that the consultant sought was constantly challenged as politicians raised problems of integration between channels, seeking to reintroduce conflicting political positions, to cast doubt on decisions made, and to remind the consultant of the requirements of the democratic process. At the same time, the whole process was about time itself. What kind of future should they want for the municipality? How should that be prioritized and articulated? How much time should they give to the process of finding out? When should others have a chance to influence the process? How should time be managed?

One could interpret the situation as left-wing politicians attempting to recapture the near future as political control begins to disappear into contracts and competition. Locally, though, the concerns of those involved in the municipal planning process were not articulated in those terms. The Socialist Left politician referred to above expressed her concerns in a didactic way to the consultant, trying to be positive while explaining her reservations:

> I'm not really sure what I'm doing here, apart from that I think it's really interesting to be part of a discussion about the municipality's future, and I think it's great to look forward more than four years at a time, that's very valuable for me. But the political aspects – I have a party and a group who elected me, and whom I represent, so it's a bit difficult to carry on.

Such a process should include time for her to consult her party colleagues and prepare a position. A correct schedule of action supports the democratic process, and most of those present had reservations about taking short-cuts. The Mayor himself outlined the problem clearly enough:

> It's the overall aim that we politicians signal to the administration that we want, and the administration comes back with the policies that they think are right. They are best qualified to know which policies work best to reach our goals. So we can have a political discussion about what we think, and we have something to hang our debates on, but if we politicians should try to identify the right policies, I have a problem with that.

Not only should there be a correct division of labour, but also a correct order of events. Working towards a joint visionary plan that bypassed other systems would be a temporal problem: one would end up with a set of policies that did not co-ordinate with those coming from the administration, creating disruption and conflict. The political debating chamber was the arena designed to enable conflicts to be aired and resolved, and the political debate was the correct time to air such conflicts and disagreements. This alternative process appeared to be a kind of semi-private arena where the politicians were present not as elected representatives but as 'resource people', whose different concerns were reflected in the choice of majority views as agreed aims, and their differences were hidden under broad thematic phrases. In effect, it cast doubt on their role, the legitimacy of the process, the meaning of the plan, what a private business consultant was doing steering the planning process, and how it would integrate with other formal democratic processes.

Journal of the Royal Anthropological Institute (N.S.), 129-147
© Royal Anthropological Institute 2014

Parallel processes that fail to co-ordinate threaten the temporal coherence of bureaucratic life. Municipal organization is a constant balancing of temporal cycles and of managing the progression through interlocking activities, and of meeting successive deadlines. Deciding the annual budget unlocks the financing for services to be offered, and for the budget to be approved; detailed reports and policies must be prepared by different departments, each feeding into the budget proposal. Each service also works to a committee cycle, through which any new proposal must pass, and at which each report must be approved. Progression through time is thus ordered into cyclical calendars, each of which must feed into the cyclical calendar of the primary committee, the general municipal council. Municipal council meetings are often seen as ritual formal events where prior work is passed through, but they are not necessarily empty rituals.

The Director of Technical Services explained this one evening during a council meeting. Taking a break from the slightly intense discipline of the council chamber, I slipped out into the town hall atrium, where coffee and pastries were laid out, as always, ready for the break. Council meetings were always open to the public, who sat towards the back of the modernist, elegant concrete hall, which was austerely decorated with framed oil-portraits of former mayors. In the atrium, I found the Director sitting back on one of the leather easy chairs listening to a discussion on the annual budget relayed from the chamber over loudspeakers. Asking him what he thought about the evening's meeting, he told me that you cannot understand this meeting in isolation, only as part of a broader series in time as a case passes from committee to committee and changes a little each time it is debated. But he also pointed to another temporal dimension, of experiential learning time, a time of cumulative knowledge gained through presence. Having sat through four yearly cycles of meetings, one learns to interpret the significance of what is being said, he explained. In that evening's meeting, for example, politicians who normally never talk about shifting significant sums of money between sectors were talking about moving millions of kroner. They were discussing taking money from reserves that the Chief Executive did not want them to use, and the Director interpreted it as a sign of their irritation that the Chief Executive had not offered them alternative budgets, as they would expect. Interpreting the Chief Executive's action as an attempt to hide money from them, they were discussing using large quantities of the very reserves he wanted them to save, to do what they wanted to do despite his obfuscation. The interpretation of this meeting as extraordinary was available only to someone with the knowledge of routine practice, and a deep understanding of routine was only available through experience of repetition.

Municipal time and planning time in this Norwegian local authority are both cyclical and hierarchical. Each consists of nested cyclical processes, both in the present and into the future, and each contributes to the creation of moral frames that are also nested and scaled. The aim of strategic planning is to try to maintain the hierarchy between immediate decisions and longer-term goals, to furnish immediate decisions and the near future with coherence by linking them with broader temporal horizons. Each step must be subject to the demands of democratic accountability, and each actor understands that they play a role as a representative of others. Politicians must refer to their parties; directors must seek professional advice from their staff. Requiring each detailed policy to acknowledge the abstract plan can be an effective governmental technology for keeping order in the diverse activities that fall within the remit of the municipality. But the form and content of strategic plans are constantly changing,

Journal of the Royal Anthropological Institute (N.S.), 129-147
© Royal Anthropological Institute 2014

under revised guidance from governmental agencies, or through the constant reinvention of local government management. The interlocking cogs of the municipal cycle are not static, like the cogs of a clock, but progressive, like the drive-wheels of a ship that propel it through the unpredictable waters of time, constantly under maintenance and subject to upgrading of the engine. It is no coincidence that changing the strategic direction of a municipality is likened to turning a tanker – a process that takes some time, and requires many small adjustments of contributory motors if the turn is to be held in control. This is how it is broadly understood by municipal actors, and why it was misunderstood by the business consultant, who tried to short-cut the municipal planning process as though it were a free-standing business 'vision'. As one of the participants noted, democracy takes time; each participant has a hinterland of constituents to consult and confer with.

Time as process, time as learning

One of the great challenges for municipal planning time is to relate different temporal scales of procedural and lived time: how does one relate the horizon of a plan with the lived horizon of a citizen? One planner related his experience of consulting different local groups on the strategic plan of his small rural municipality. He was amused that the residents of the municipal elderly care home agreed that the plan's aims were laudable, but found the twelve-year horizon rather too long. The primary school children, by contrast, found it barely imaginable, and produced drawings of steel and glass skyscrapers in the village as their imagined future. Planning trends favouring increased public participation in the production of strategic plans have only highlighted the difficulties of reconciling different temporal horizons, although the difficulties of participative planning are usually framed in terms of competing interests, or the need that planners feel to educate the public in planning practice.[4]

The anthropological ideal that people should have some kind of sovereignty over their own development does not stand alone; calls for wider public participation in development and its planning were particularly vociferous in the 1960s (Anton 1969; Arnstein 1969; Mogulof 1969; Skeffington 1969). They found a new lease of life in the centre-left European governments from the mid-1990s and have since become a truism in planning studies. Participative planning is not one set of practices, but an umbrella term for the many forms of concern about how the 'public good' is explored, determined, and negotiated in both general and specific terms. Whereas in development contexts, it has often been assumed that the community affected by development is self-evidently the local residents in the development site, in the Western planning context it is impossible to ignore the challenges that public participation poses for the very definition or model of democracy. While the discourse of participative planning conjectures an impersonal, disembodied public as the audience for planning processes, in practice, of course, this public is difficult to recognize in the face of the actual, embodied, and particular persons who turn up to consultation events, for example, or who form campaign groups to challenge policies or decisions. A municipality may struggle to produce a suitable taxonomy through which to understand its public, leaving it struggling to produce the legitimacy it seeks for its actions (see Abram 2002; 2007). In the case of overarching infrastructure development, however, identifying a public and finding a way of building actual social relations with it presupposes a learning relationship on both sides. Theories and guides on public planning strongly advocate early and consistent participative practices, such that public concerns can be considered before the key early decisions are made, and public interest can be drawn into the planning, ensuring that early objections can be co-opted and transformed into supportive criticism.

The kind of strategic plans being discussed in the municipality described above tend to be seen as controlling progression into a slowly emerging future, during which ordered communication between politicians, parties, and constituents can be supplemented by direct surveys of 'user groups' for particular services, for example. In the case of infrastructure plans, however, the future can appear to offer radical change, and the temporal horizon suddenly seems to expand. Rather than projecting forward over the years for a decade or two, the construction of major infrastructure can appear to be decisive for the envisageable future: effectively for all time. Infrastructure planning can thus open out the temporal horizon by proposing action in the near future that will have consequences beyond the lifetime of those involved in the planning. Infrastructure planning helps to highlight the potential for the future to flip from orderly to threatening. A closer look at the attempts of infrastructure planners to be 'transparent' (see Garsten & de Montoya 2008) further highlights the internal contradiction between planning and participation.

Boholm and her colleagues (2000) have written extensively about their research on the planning and implementation of a major railway improvement on the West Coast of Sweden. Boholm herself (2013) describes the design of railway infrastructure as 'hypercomplex'. During the 1990s and 2000s (and ongoing), the Swedish National Rail Administration, Banverket, undertook a project for the Swedish government, to upgrade the single-track railway line between Gothenburg and Lund along the southwestern coast of Sweden. The project was administered through a series of parallel development projects. Banverket approached each municipality with a proposal for the stretch of rail through that municipality, including the main station. The municipalities then considered the proposals, discussed them, and consulted on them. In each case, one or several protest groups appeared with some objection to the proposals, and in each case this led to a broader debate, in some cases protests, and in some cases legal action, public inquiries, and even EU environmental court cases (see Abram & Strandberg 2005). The key issues for debate in each municipality were the safety of running high-speed trains through narrow urban corridors or popular recreation areas, or whether lines should be moved out of town and stations re-sited. Different constellations emerged around each proposal, with one municipality supporting out-of-town station relocation, with opposition from residents' groups, while another municipality supported keeping the station in town, with opposition from residents' groups there. These proposals raised questions about the legitimacy of decision-making processes, how the authorities should respond to protest groups, and how protest groups could make themselves heard. These, in turn, raised questions about how different kinds of knowledge were made instrumental during the debates about the plans.

Formally, Swedish municipalities have a monopoly over municipal planning. As one municipal planner explained: 'The whole legal apparatus is built on the principle that, quite simply, the local society decides over conflicts', but this definition does little to illuminate how 'local society' is constituted. Local politicians claim a privileged ability to understand local society holistically and thus to represent collective interests. One council chair, for instance, summarized this position in contrast to the fleeting interests of other citizens:

Journal of the Royal Anthropological Institute (N.S.), 129-147
© Royal Anthropological Institute 2014

Lots of people ... young families, they look to child-care and schools, that's important, and only that's important. Later it's other things; it'll be care for the elderly that is the only thing one looks to. So it is up to us politicians to try to take account of the whole, for society, and for the consequences.

The politicians described their own role as leaders, or as builders of society: 'to look forward, plan for the future, what's best from a social development perspective'. This role also demanded of their own time, and they contrasted this with what they saw as short-term horizons of private citizens. As one council chair expressed it:

In complex issues, which will affect the future colossally, if you send the question out to people who haven't got stuck into them, who just think about it over a coffee break and then spontaneously choose something, well that's to build infrastructure in a way which I don't think is particularly good, and not one for an insightful politician.

Thus, as well as claiming authority over spatial oversight, and the ability to assess competing interests, the politicians claimed temporal authority.

Their concern with consequences was shared by members of protest groups, who rejected the image of themselves as ignorant and self-interested. On the contrary, they were at pains to point out that they were campaigning for the public good: 'to try to ensure that the national interest is preserved, and that the West Coast line is developed in an optimal way'. Members of the protest groups talked much more widely than others of the temporal context of current dilemmas. They referred to plans from the 1950s and before, and they saw the implications of the current plans potentially lasting into the foreseeable future. But they also described ruptures in this long span, when, for example, after generations of plans identifying transport development located near the motorway, 'suddenly, we were so surprised that the municipality took a decision to develop the West Coast line on the current track, through our recreation area, coastal zone, through the small boat harbour, the town and through the hospital grounds'. Indignant surprise related to what appeared as the sudden unpredictable decisions of the municipality, which until then had followed known policies and procedures.

One way they attempted to secure the quality of the development was by bringing technical issues to the attention of Banverket. What distinguished these protesters from the authorities in our discussions was their marked concern with the past, in contrast to the officials' over-riding concern with the future. There were several examples of historical knowledge being brought into the planning process by organizations set up to make objections to the plans. One group contacted a professor of geology from Stockholm whose Ph.D. supervisor had had his summer house in the area. The geologist had done his dissertation research there, within a kilometre of the proposed tunnel works, and he was commissioned by the group to conduct a safety assessment of the site. He identified a number of critical crack zones and the group tried to bring these to the attention of Banverket. Many of them complained that Banverket had lost the detailed technical expertise it had once had, and they were shocked that the engineers and politicians did not seek to share their detailed historical knowledge of the geology and ecology of the different development routes. While they had sympathy for the heavy responsibilities taken by local politicians, they were critical of what they saw as their failure to live up to the ideal of a rational juridical political decision-making process. What they saw was the less respectable 'realpolitik', provoking righteous protest:

Journal of the Royal Anthropological Institute (N.S.), 129-147
© Royal Anthropological Institute 2014

[I]f they [local politicians] don't decide in your favour, well you just have to put up with it, in a democracy. But when you feel that they won't listen, that they avoid the question, that they change the agenda or act on prior parameters to get the result they first wanted, I react against that.

Municipal planners shared some of this scepticism about Banverket's knowledge. As ome senior planner put it: 'There's been nothing like it since the end of the 1800s in Skåne. So their knowledge about this kind of project had to be built up as they went along, quite simply. Not least the questions of risk and so forth'. The planners' concern was with knowledge to be produced in a forwards trajectory, as historical knowledge had disappeared, a viewpoint shared between the formal actors. Local politicians' remarks on this longer perspective had an entirely forward-looking direction: 'We are evaluating an infrastructure project, and obviously we need a hundred years' perspective ... We have to take the responsibility to look forwards, to plan for the future, as best we can'. The protesters also looked forward, but when they did so, they were also immediately concerned about losing the goods from past development: 'This is our municipality's most important decision for this century at least, and it affects future generations, [our town's] development and North-West Skåne's [the region's] development ... which has a superb communications infrastructure, which they're now frittering away'. A sense of scale is suggested that conjures a long history of slow development, where a sudden rupture imperils the qualities of the future. In this regard, the proposed plan operates as a temporal hinge from a secure past to loss in the present, and from a known future to an unknown future. One might argue that the position of the planners and managers evacuated the *near past* rather than the near future. Historical conditions leading up to the plan were consistently overlooked in planning, while forming the core of the rationalities presented by objectors. Objectors were concerned about changing the temporal direction, so that instead of the steady progress from the known past into an unevented future that they had anticipated, they would be heading into a future that was unknown and highly unstable, while planners could be said to be concerned with the progression from the present towards a planned future-vision.

The greatest concern for the Banverket managers, by contrast, was the time taken to produce the plans for the railway works. A municipal committee chair spelt this out: 'These are projects that take an *incredibly long time* and demand an *incredible* amount of engagement from the municipality' (original emphasis). The project managers most clearly created a proportional relation between time for democracy and time for engineering progress, seeing time taken to make decisions as a delay for building. For managers working in an environment where problem-solving is highly valued, negotiations between state agencies and political debates at the local level appeared to be unnecessary bureaucratic formalism. As a municipal committee chair put it:

We could get the same result considerably more promptly by bringing together the different departments, if we arranged one meeting and went through the matter, adjourned one or two weeks and arranged a new meeting so we could get to a common understanding on the matter.

With some irony, one district rail administration manager questioned whether the drawn-out process is a necessary evil in a democratic society:

So it takes eight years to investigate everything, and two years to build, today that's approximately the relative times. So you have to wonder, which part could be reduced? Or is it an end in itself, to take such a long time so people have time to get used to the change that is on the way?

Journal of the Royal Anthropological Institute (N.S.), 129-147
© Royal Anthropological Institute 2014

The managers were very much aware of the problems caused by a drawn-out state of doubt, including what is known as planning blight: 'People don't know whether to sell their house or move'. In other words, a democratic decision-making process requires an excess of time, and this has costs for those most directly involved. On the one hand, managers criticized self-interested objectors, but sympathized with those affected by planning blight. Their sympathy is not for those who complain when they see that development will affect them personally for the worse, but for those who suffer from a lack of decision which prevents them from pre-empting or counteracting the effects of development. This brings us back to the municipal planners, who were critical of the apparently sudden complaints late in the process, by newcomers to the debate. In their commentaries, they began to explain, and de-legitimize, the participation of protest groups at late stages in the process, insisting, for example, that 'there's been complete political unanimity in getting the West Coast Line; everyone has agreed on it right through the process'. Municipal chairs also struggled with this, perceiving a silent antipathy that could not be addressed, in contrast with the explicit objections that emerged later as a 'normal' part of the procedure. Planners explained late-emerging protest as a sign of process failure:

> Probably the most important experience is that early discussions need plenty of time. It's essential, to raise different viewpoints and alternatives. And in some of those earlier projects there was such a rush to get going, and I think that's really affected those projects. And there's a more general point, in terms of the role and significance of social planning: Democracy takes time.

The municipal planners thus articulated a tension between time, political expediency, and technical solutions. They were able to reason that problems lay in poor public understanding of complex issues, rather than public discovery of errors: 'My general experience of this kind of big project is that people only start to concern themselves when it starts to affect their own back yard, quite simply'. This references the usual 'nimby' ('not in my back yard') accusation, with the inference that self-interest emerges at late stages of a process. A widespread complaint amongst planners more generally, that the 'general public doesn't care', stems from a particular interpretation of the patterns of public engagement in planning processes (Muller & Kohutek 2002; Neveu 2002) and continues despite counter-evidence (Abram 2001) and arguments that interest broadly grows as a project becomes more imminent (Wolsink 2005). The problem with the public was further projected away from the (temporal aspects of) management of the decision-making process onto the lack of rationality amongst the public, as seen by the railway project managers. For the municipal planners, the problem lay not with the overall project, but with the detail, and with the self-interest versus the national or general interest. Difficulties in the process and the emergence of protest at awkward times was not, for them, a question of errors or shortcomings in the detailed planning of the infrastructure, but a general question of interest resolution: '[T]his problem of the balance between general interest and the special interest. It's the basic issue in planning that we are always confronting. It's not unique to this situation'.

This chimes with the suggestions made by protest groups that their arguments were not listened to, but categorized as irrelevant or out of context. Even though the protest groups framed their objections in terms of general environmental questions, regional economic solutions, and so on, in other words, despite using the discourse of government and general interest, it appears that the detail of their arguments was never scrutinized. They were perceived, instead, as posing problems for time-efficiency of planning processes. There was no discussion of local protesters potentially alerting the authorities to technical or environmental problems which might cause significant delays or costs for the overall project further down the line.

This is a generalized problem with participative planning processes that are designed by planners to follow a progression through time which involves initiation into both governmental technologies (how to be a participant) and project aims (learning to share the plan's ambitions). This is at odds with an open process in which meetings are held in public and technical information is shared relatively openly. The contradiction here can be explained relatively simply as an instance of the distinction between knowledge and information. According to Corsín-Jiménez (2011), for information to circulate freely, it must be outside particular social relations. Knowledge, by contrast, is learned implicitly in the context of morally framed relations. When new participants appear at planning meetings sometimes years into the planning process, they may be in possession of information, but they have not been inducted into the shared knowledge of the participants to previous planning procedures. Planners and managers are then faced with the potential necessity to either revisit or rehearse the earlier stages of the planning process. An open public participative process thus presents a contradiction to the idea of progress through participation, since participative processes imply that participants learn from each other and from the experience of participation. The missing element is the learning that is gained from the participation over time. The contradiction is highlighted by the notion of a general public to whom participation must always be open, as noted above. Repeated calls by planners and managers for early participation indicates their reliance on a temporal progression through which participants can learn to share the planners' aims, and different views can be evaluated at the initial stages of any planning. Faced with new objections to early decisions, they found fault with the organization of participation or with the quality of motivation of the participants rather than with the limits to their expectations of their own potential learning from informal participants, or the limits to the compatibility between democratic participative politics and technical design.

Rescaling futures, layering temporalities

A series of relevant temporal frames emerge from this brief foray into an ethnographic field of planning.[5] These could be articulated as follows:

- different futures envisioned in the process of planning, scaled at different degrees of abstraction in both time and space, some of which are textualized in planning documents;
- changes that are happening outside the planning process, which the plans must pay attention to, either through mapping trends, or through noting events or changes at different scales (from demographic changes to international markets to local ecological effects);
- temporal cycles of preparing, making, and agreeing planning documents and their policies;
- the time taken to pursue the process of creating each plan and review it at various points, depending on the scale of the future imagined within it; and
- progress towards planning aims, assessed and evaluated at various points;

Each of these is also subject to temporal cycles on other scales, such as the reformulation of national policies, the electoral cycle, turnover of personnel in the municipal bureaucracy, and so forth. But it would be wrong to assume that each of these temporal frames was static in its own right. They also change, sometimes abruptly, sometimes more slowly. Planning frameworks are subject to national and international fads (see Abrahamson 1991), and policy cycles often vary. But the methods for envisioning the future have also varied, with new techniques appearing at various times. In my own ethnographic research on the creation of future plans (ten- to twenty-year district or regional plans) in England and Norway, I have been concerned with the governmental techniques that organize knowledge about the world into usable information, and the consequences of these both for the people involved in planning and for the people and places planned for (see Abram 2003; 2011). In these cases, future scenarios were imagined based on recent trends. The future was thus extrapolated from experience, and policies were invented to adapt to this (Murdoch & Abram 2002). Such processes could be understood as self-fulfilling prophecies, and objectors to plans often found themselves excluded from the planning process by the kind of 'muting' effects that Edwin Ardener (1975) identified, including those described above. Since then, however, trend-based planning has been challenged by new techniques to create future plans and visions. British planners are increasingly adopting a technique called 'backcasting'. Whereas forecasting takes current trends, extrapolates them to a distant future, and invents policies to adapt to that future, backcasting starts with a desired future and invents policies to achieve it (see Holmberg & Robèrt 2000). The difference may sound subtle, but the concept of time is altered. Whereas forecasting sees the future as the inevitable outcome of the present, backcasting casts the future as a malleable result of present and future decisions. Backcasting thus gathers potential and agency into the near future, such that desired outcomes might be achieved by releasing the near future from merely extending trends set in the past.

Another very brief example will make this more explicit. Planning for housing in England has been subject to a regime of numbers that collects statistical information about household formation, dwelling construction, and a range of demographic and commercial factors, such as the demand for office and domestic space measured through 'vacancy rates' (which record the proportion of such facilities available). Based on trends identified by these numbers, predictions are made about the need for future development. There is a subtle slip in the process between the measurement of past demand and the prediction of future need, but challenging the numbers on this basis is futile as the numbers become immutable in the process of moving up and down planning hierarchies (Murdoch & Abram 2002). The effect is that areas that experience high rates of growth are allocated future development growth, and areas that are well protected continue to be protected. These predictions are then aligned with policies that reinforce the divisive effects. Trends thus procure a forward drive that is unrelated to situated experience. Whereas residents may feel that they need time to adjust to a period of rapid growth, or that they have had their 'fair share' of growth in areas of pressure, the trends ensure that rapid growth continues. Backcasting the future, by contrast, might start with a vision of the kind of development that would be desirable, and adopt strategies to direct growth to areas where it is seen as appropriate. To some extent, the planning in the Norwegian example could be considered a version of backcasting. A deputy director in the municipality described a planning process she had observed in another district, where a public survey had invited residents to say what they wanted from a future district. Suggestions which merely suggested spending money were filtered out, while others were mapped and discussed in political debate, becoming the basis for specific policies, thus working back from a desired future rather than extrapolating from the present.

Both methods of future planning are fallible and subject to political manipulation, of course, and it could well be argued that as models they are rarely applied in any pure form, but the explicit adoption of new techniques indicates that it is possible to recast what the future is, and to reimagine the temporal frame of the passage from present to future envisaged in planning. These methods also imply that time can be imagined forward and backwards, as well as cyclically. Backcasting, as its name implies, works back through time, but planning processes can also be retrospective. Lund (2011) describes how land invasions in peri-urban Peru start with the construction of dwellings and then work backwards towards the retrospective adoption of local planning regulations, perhaps over a lifetime. In my experience of English and Norwegian plans, it is otherwise very rare that the past is considered to any great degree in forward plans. A longer perspective on the historical development of a place, for example, is conspicuously absent from all the plans that I have read, and rather than evacuating the near future, such strategic or forward plans tend, instead, to evacuate the near past (or the distant past, for that matter). This wilful ignorance of time past leads often to both distress and distrust among people who come into contact with plans.

What is perhaps remarkable is how robust governmental planning remains despite the continued hollowing out of the welfare state. As an increasing range of services is organized through contracts with third-party organizations, and criteria for services are organized centrally by state governments, political actors are left with budget responsibility rather than management accountability, and hence with radically reduced political possibilities. It is possible that governments attempt to compensate for the evacuated near future by filling it with land-use plans, but it is equally possible that public servants are using plans to try to counteract the erosion of their roles. However we choose to speculate on the politics of planning, it is clear that governing the future is an ambition that recruits many and multilayered temporalities.

There appears, therefore, to be a lot going on in the neoliberalization of the state that precludes a singular judgement about the effects on temporality of the kind that are often favoured by anthropological publications. In anthropology, discussion of temporalities has been dominated by studies of anthropology's relationships to time and other kinds of reckoning. Postill's (2002) stinging critique of the anthropologists of time is itself concerned with the spread of clock and calendar time, rather than an exploration of the variation and manipulation within this apparently global time schedule. Zonabend (1984) offers recognition that different temporalities flow in parallel, where cycles of different length (diurnal, life-cycle) happen alongside historical and event time, which itself is seen not as unilinear, but as uneven, flowing in fits and starts around the breakwaters of significant eras. Briggs (1992), also, outlines how different temporal schemata may operate in parallel. In contrast, recent discussions of neoliberal time have been much more centred on expert technologies of prediction (e.g. Lakoff 2008; Zaloom 2009), but are similarly singularly focused on one kind of temporality at a time, although Zaloom does offer an ethnography of how the technology is done, as well as how it projects over time. Somewhere between these core approaches, addressing changing regimes of everyday time, asking how anthropology deals with history, or how scientific technologies are used to cope with uncertainty, we need to make room to see the layering and folding of presents and futures that persist from modern into neoliberalizing states. Expert technologies need to be seen in a broader frame, in the light of attempts to derail them, encounters with non-believers, and contradictory temporalities. Planning technologies may seem to presume a particular temporal flow, yet in the practice of planning, the encounter with the non-initiated repeatedly throws up the same problems, preventing planning techniques from rolling smoothly on, and ensuring that the promises of planning remain elusive. Planning itself takes time, and during which circumstances change, ambitions alter, and different participants arrive on the scene, while all the participants (the ethnographer included) continue to learn about the planning process and what it entails.

NOTES

[1] Guyer chooses to focus on monetarism as a theory and professional practice, and not on neoliberalism as an ideology. One reason for this is to recognize that monetarism

> is precisely not just an ideology but also a massive created edifice of specific research and implementation measures in the financial world that has already shaped people's sensibilities and perceptions, if not to the point of a naturalistic acceptance of them as somehow generically human, then at least to the kind of lulled and muted self-referentiality that anthropology has always worked to challenge (2007b: 448).

[2] From *Kommuneplan for Asker 2007-2020.*
[3] Ethnographic fieldwork was supported by the ESRC and the Department of Social Anthropology at the University of Oslo.
[4] For a discussion of the production of a public by public sector agencies, and of the notion of educating the public, see Abram (2011).
[5] For the sake of clarity and brevity, I have mentioned relatively little in this discussion about the effects of investment cycles and developer shareholder demands on the actual physical building process that plans envisage, or about the immediate bureaucratic regulatory practices of development control, planning permission applications, building regulations, or planning-decision enforcement. Each provides a further layer of dispute, uncertainty, and multi-party mediation.

REFERENCES

ABRAHAMSON, E. 1991. Managerial fads and fashions: the diffusion and rejection of innovations. *Academy of Management Review* **16**, 586-612.
ABRAM, S. 2001. Amongst professionals: working with pressure groups and local authorities. In *Inside organisations: anthropologists at work* (eds) D. Gellner & E. Hirsch, 183-203. Oxford: Berg.
——— 2002. Planning and public-making in municipal government. *Focaal – Journal of Global and Historical Anthropology* **40**, 21-34.
——— 2003. *Anthropologies in policies, anthropologies in places.* In *Globalisation: studies in anthropology* (ed.) T.H. Eriksen, 138-57. London: Pluto.
——— 2007. Participatory depoliticisation: the bleeding heart of neo-liberalism. In *Cultures et pratiques participatives: perspectives comparatives* (ed.) C. Neveu, 113-33. Paris: L'Harmattan.
——— 2011. *Culture and planning.* Aldershot: Ashgate.
——— & U. STRANDBERG 2005. Six controversies in search of an epistemology. Gothenburg: CEFOS Working Paper 4.
——— & G. WESZKALNYS 2011. Introduction: anthropologies of planning – temporality, imagination, and ethnography. *Focaal – Journal of Global and Historical Anthropology* **61**, 3-18.
——— & ——— (eds) 2013. *Elusive promises: planning in the contemporary world.* Oxford: Berghahn.
ADAMS, V., M. MURPHY & A.E. CLARKE 2009. Anticipation: technoscience, life, affect, temporality. *Subjectivity* **28**, 246-65.
ANTON, T.J. 1969. Politics and planning in a Swedish suburb. *Journal of the American Institute of Planners* **35**, 253-63.
ARDENER, E. 1975. Belief and the problem of women. In *Perceiving women* (ed.) S. Ardener, 1-17. London: Malaby Press.
ARNSTEIN, S.R. 1969. A ladder of citizen participation. *Journal of the American Institute of Planners* **35**, 216-24.

BAXSTROM, R. 2012. Living on the horizon of the everlasting present: power, planning and the emergence of baroque forms of life in urban Malaysia. In *Southeast Asia perspectives on power* (eds) L. Chua, J. Cook, N. Long & L. Wilson, 135-50. Abingdon: Routledge.

BOHOLM, Å. (ed.) 2000. *National objectives – local objections: railroad modernization in Sweden.* Gothenburg: Center for Public Sector Research (CEFOS).

——— 2013. From within a community of planners: hypercomplexity in railway design work. In *Elusive promises: planning in the contemporary world* (eds) S. Abram & G. Weszkalnys, 51-75. Oxford: Berghahn.

BRIGGS, J.L. 1992. Lines, cycles and transformations: temporal perspectives on Inuit action. In *Contemporary futures: perspectives from social anthropology* (ed.) S. Wallman, 83-108 (ASA Monographs **30**). London: Routledge.

CORSÍN JIMÉNEZ, A. 2011. Trust in anthropology. *Anthropological Theory* **11**, 177-96.

DAMER, S. & C. HAGUE 1971. Public participation in planning: a review. *The Town Planning Review* **42**, 217-32.

DCLG (DEPARTMENT FOR COMMUNITIES AND LOCAL GOVERNMENT) 2012. *National planning policy framework.* London: Crown Copyright.

GARSTEN, C. & M.L. DE MONTOYA 2008. *Transparency in a new global order: unveiling organizational visions.* Cheltenham: Edward Elgar.

GUYER, J.I. 2007a. Prophecy and the near future: thoughts on macroeconomic, evangelical and punctuated time. *American Ethnologist* **34**, 409-21.

——— 2007b. Further: a rejoinder. *American Ethnologist* **34**, 447-50.

HOLMBERG, J. & K.-H. ROBÈRT 2000. Backcasting from non-overlapping sustainability principles – a framework for strategic planning. *International Journal of Sustainable Development and World Ecology* **7**, 291-308.

KS (KOMMUNENES INTERESSE- OG ARBEIDSGIVERORGANISASJON [LOCAL GOVERNMENT ASSOCIATION]) n.d. *Inspirasjonshefte om kommunale planstrategier – et verktøy for ønsket samfunnsutvikling* [Advice on municipal planning strategies – a tool for desired social development]. Oslo: KS.

LAKOFF, A. 2008. The generic biothreat, or, how we became unprepared. *Cultural Anthropology* **23**, 399-428.

LUND, S. 2011. Invaded city: structuring urban landscapes on the margins of the possible in Peru. *Focaal – Journal of Global and Historical Anthropology* **61**, 33-45.

MILJØVERNDEPARTEMENTET [NORWEGIAN MINISTRY OF ENVIRONMENT] 2011. Veileder: Kommunal planstrategi [Guidance on municipal planning strategies]. T-1494 Miljøverndepartementet (available on-line: *http://www.regjeringen.no/pages/17299458/T-1494.pdf*, accessed 15 January 2014).

MOGULOF, M. 1969. Coalition to adversary: citizen participation in three federal programs. *Journal of the American Institute of Planners* **35**, 225-32.

MULLER, B. & P. KOHUTEK 2002. Engaging the new democracy: the power of participation in the post-communist Czech Republic. *Focaal – Journal of Global and Historical Anthropology* **40**, 67-82.

MURDOCH, J. & S. ABRAM 2002. *Rationalities of planning: development versus environment in planning for housing.* Aldershot: Ashgate.

NEVEU, C. 2002. Nimbys as citizens: (re)defining the 'general interest'. *Focaal – Journal of Global and Historical Anthropology* **40**, 51-66.

POSTILL, J. 2002. Clock and calendar time: a missing anthropological problem. *Time & Society* **11**, 251-70.

PUSEY, M. 1998. Between economic dissolution and the return of the social: the contest for civil society in Australia. In *Real civil societies: dilemmas of institutionalization* (ed.) J. Alexander, 40-66. London: Sage.

RABINOW, P. 1989. *French modern: norms and forms of the social environment.* Chicago: University Press.

RTPI (ROYAL TOWN PLANNING INSTITUTE) 2007. *Planning with communities.* London: RTPI.

SKEFFINGTON/MINISTRY OF HOUSING AND LOCAL GOVERNMENT 1969. *People and planning: report of the Skeffington Committee on Public Participation in Planning.* London: HMSO.

VIKE, H. 2013. Utopian time and contemporary time: temporal dimensions of planning and reform in the Norwegian welfare state. In *Elusive promises: planning in the contemporary world* (eds) S. Abram & G. Weszkalnys, 35-55. Oxford: Berghahn.

WILK, R. 2007. It's about time: a commentary on Guyer. *American Ethnologist* **34**, 440-3.

WITTROCK, B. 2000. Modernity: one, none, or many? European origins and modernity as a global condition. *Daedalus* **129**, 31-60.

WOLSINK, M. 2005. Wind power implementation: the nature of public attitudes: Equity and fairness instead of 'backyard motives'. *Renewable and Sustainable Energy Reviews* **11**, 1188-207.

ZALOOM, C. 2007. Future knowledge. *American Ethnologist* **34**, 444-6.

——— 2009. How to read the future: the yield curve, affect, and financial prediction. *Public Culture* **21**, 245-68.

ZONABEND, F. 1984. *The enduring memory: time and history in a French village.* Manchester: University Press.

Journal of the Royal Anthropological Institute (N.S.), 129-147
© Royal Anthropological Institute 2014

Le temps qu'il faut : temporalités de la planification

Résumé

La planification par les pouvoir publics a été un moyen déterminant pour la régulation du passage du temps par les sujets modernes. En pratique, elle suscite de nombreux conflits et doutes que les planificateurs s'efforcent d'aplanir. Le présent article aborde les régimes de temps que la planification favorise tout en les contrariant et met en évidence leurs implications pour l'anthropologie. Grâce à une ethnographie d'agences de planification norvégiennes et suédoises et leur découverte de la planification participative, l'auteure remet en question des affirmations récentes selon lesquelles le futur proche serait évacué ou l'intervention administrative en repli. Elle suggère également que l'intérêt récent de l'anthropologie pour le temps est restreint par les tentatives de caractériser les paysages temporels changeants de changements modaux spécifiques, par exemple entre moderne et néolibéral. En lieu et place, la présente ethnographie s'attache non pas à repérer les ruptures d'époque dans le temps, mais à démontrer comment le temps est manipulé et comment de multiples modalités sont mises en œuvre dans les projets de planification démographique en cours.

Journal of the Royal Anthropological Institute (N.S.), 129-147

7

The reign of terror of the big cat: bureaucracy and the mediation of social times in the Indian Himalaya

NAYANIKA MATHUR *University of Cambridge*

This paper describes the arrival of a man-eating leopard in a small Himalayan town in India and the local state's subsequent struggle to control the big cat. By focusing on what went on within the apparatus of the state during this period, this paper attempts to contribute to the study of modern time in bureaucracy. It argues that the startling inefficiencies in the effective governance and regulation of the big cat stemmed from a clash of various social times that were unfolding simultaneously. It outlines five distinct forms of social time that were in play during this period, which led to long periods of waiting and allowed for the articulation of a searing critique of the Indian state by town residents. Ultimately this paper contributes a rethinking of current theories of bureaucratic time that focus on the production of disempowered waiting, risk analysis, and anticipation. Instead it argues that a study of low-level bureaucrats and citizens shows that a central task of bureaucracy is to attempt to mediate conflicting forms of social time. Moving away from accounts of bureaucratic indifference, this paper depicts failure as an impasse arising out of attempts to bring incommensurable forms and representations of time into congruence. These failures importantly imperil the legitimacy of bureaucrats and can lead to a radical critique of the state.

It was a regular late November morning in the small government office in the Himalayan town of Gopeshwar, northern India, where I was conducting my doctoral fieldwork.[1] I was struggling to decipher the contents of a file while the other four members of the office were busily working on documents of all sorts. The cold had frozen our conversation. All of a sudden, a man burst into the room to announce dramatically: 'The *bagh* [leopard] has returned!' My office-mates gasped aloud in horror. He proceeded to rapidly recite the story: a woman had been climbing to the top of the mountain on which Gopeshwar is located to collect some grass for her goat. Out of the blue a *bagh* leaped up, gouging her face out. Screaming in agony and pain, she fell down the steep slope. The screams attracted the attention of other people nearby, who started making a noise, which scared the *bagh* and, in a trice, he vanished into the bushes. Mercifully, this attack had not proven to be fatal, but the bad news, I was told solemnly, was that the *bagh* had returned to haunt the little town of Gopeshwar again. People in the district office came out of their rooms to talk about the 'return of the *bagh*' in

Journal of the Royal Anthropological Institute (N.S.), 148-165
© Royal Anthropological Institute 2014

hushed and horrified tones. I was still relatively new to Gopeshwar and remained perplexed by all this *bagh* talk. As I had an interview scheduled with a senior official in the district, I could not stay for long but instead hurried over to his office. When I arrived in his room, there were two other top officials of the district already there deep in conversation on the 'return of the *bagh*'. The three of them informed me of the regular appearance of man-eating leopards in Gopeshwar and its outlying regions.[2] Given the unprovoked nature of the attack, the bureaucrats were certain that, yet again, we had a man-eater in our midst. 'So what will you do to tackle the man-eater?' I asked. One of the officials replied matter-of-factly, 'There is nothing we can do about the *bagh* at the moment – hunt him down or even capture him. We will have to wait before he has killed a few people'. As it turned out, the *bagh* did 'kill a few people' before any action was taken against him by the state. For over two months, he haunted the town of Gopeshwar and its surrounding villages, attacking and killing humans and livestock and unleashing what was popularly described as 'a reign of terror'.[3] Perplexingly, and much to the fury of its citizens, the local state appeared incapable of thwarting this terror. I argue here that the state's seeming incapacity to overthrow the reign of the big cat and protect human lives emerged from a clash of conflicting temporal processes and associated material practices that were taking place within its bureaucratic apparatus.

Bureaucratic times

There is a conspicuous absence in anthropology of detailed ethnographic work on time in bureaucracy. Complex timescapes are but rarely evident other than in novels such as Kafka's *The trial* (2000 [1925]), which are able to move away from the homogeneity of linear time. Ever since Weber's influential account of bureaucracy as a product of an increasingly disenchanted modernity, bureaucracies have been *de facto* understood to have institutionalized linear time, be it through law (Greenhouse 1989) or via planning, which is concerned with 'the transition over time from current states to desired ones' (Abram & Weszkalnys 2011: 4). When time is discussed with reference to modern bureaucracy and the state, it is often under the theme of waiting. As Jeffrey points out, 'During the 20th century the increasing regimentation and bureaucratization of time in the West, combined with the growing reach of the state into people's everyday lives, created multiple settings – such as traffic jams, offices, and clinics – in which people were compelled to wait' (2008: 954). The capacity to make its subjects wait is seen as a technique of the exhibition of power by the modern state. 'Waiting', as Bourdieu writes, 'implies submission' (2000: 228). Drawing out the link between time and power, he makes the point that 'waiting is one of the privileged ways of experiencing the effects of power' (2000: 228).[4] The social value of a person can be gauged from how much time he or she has to 'give', with important people always being busy and the time of 'subproletarians' not being worth anything. As Corbridge observes from his work in India: 'Waiting is something that poorer people do' (2004: 184). Auyero similarly notes that in Argentina 'shanty residents are always waiting for something to happen' (2012: 4). His study of the poor's 'grueling pilgrimages through state bureaucracies' leads him to argue that these are 'temporal processes in and through which political subordination is reproduced' (2012: 2). 'Poor people learn that they have to remain temporarily neglected, unattended to, or postponed', thus becoming, in his words, 'patients of the state'. 'In recurrently being forced to accommodate and yield to the state's dictates, the urban poor thereby receive a subtle, and usually not explicit, daily lesson in political subordination' (2012: 9). *Contra* Auyero, however, I argue that waiting for the big cat's reign of terror to end in Gopeshwar did not make the residents of the town patients of the state. Rather, as I show below, they became the state's strongest and most articulate critics. Another influential work on waiting describes it as 'a de-realisation of the present' (Crapanzano 1985): 'Waiting means to be oriented in time in a special way. It is directed towards the future – not an expansive future, however, but a constructed one that closes in on the present ... Its only meaning lies in the future – in the arrival or non-arrival of the object of waiting' (1985: 44). An anxious waiting for a future when the big cat would go away/be killed was very much present in Gopeshwar, but, again, this was not the only affect generated by waiting. There were also expressions of anger, fear, dark humour, along with politicized commentaries on the 'value of life' and the struc-tural inequities embedded in the space of the Himalaya, and even acknowledgements of a grudging respect for the big cat. Not only were the affective experience and political subjectification induced by waiting multiple and contradictory, but also, I argue, the reason the state, in this particular case, made its subjects wait before it allowed for the big cat to be killed was not in order to demonstrate its power or somehow to mould submissive citizens, or because (as was the common refrain in Gopeshwar) it was 'uncaring'. Citizens were made to wait because of contradictions within and between the timing of procedures and long-term temporal aims of state institutions.

The second mode, broadly, through which the question of time is commonly addressed in analyses of modern bureaucracy is by reference to the future. The future is frequently invoked by recourse to the concept of 'risk', which, as Reith notes, has assumed 'a central explanatory role in the indeterminate world of late modernity' (2004: 384). Risk, she writes, 'is defined by and through temporality: the notion of "risk" expresses not something that *has* happened or *is* happening, but something that *might* happen' (2004: 386, emphaisis in original). Reith points out that risk is not 'an objective feature of post-industrial society', but rather 'it is a measure of calculation' (2004: 385); it can 'be defined largely through its attempt to calculate and so manage the uncertain-ties of the future' (2004: 386). The work of Lakoff (2006; 2008) has examined the specific manifestations of this temporal orientation by focusing on 'preparedness' and the method of 'imaginative enactment' through which bureaucracies are tutored in the present in how to react to a potentially catastrophic event in the future. Adams, Murphy, and Clarke (2009) have suggested we now live in regimes of anticipation of risk. My analysis here draws on this work to think through how conservationist regimes that seek to manage the specific risk of the extinction of big cats in the future affect the responses of the bureaucracy to the threat of a man-eating leopard. On the basis of the historical decline in the population of big cats, future projections are constantly made. A long-term risk-aversion strategy aimed at 'saving the big cat' is clearly reflected in the wildlife protection laws, programmes, and agencies that abound in present-day India. But I show how this was not the only risk analysis at work in the bureaucracy; there was also the more immediate and localized risk of losing further human lives if the big cat was not killed. This more immediate risk and how best to avert it consumed senior bureaucrats in Gopeshwar. Both these orientations to risk – the future of big cats as species and the present of the human residents of a marginal Himalayan town located on the Indian borderland – were operating simultaneously, leading to severe contradictions within the district bureaucracy. The risk and anticipation literature importantly notes a contemporary orientation to time that looks to the future, the affects, techniques, and politics such a way of being in time produces, and the forms of expertise and modes of calculation it calls upon. While I draw upon these themes, I argue that there was not just a singular temporal orientation, and also that the bureaucracy was not only orientated towards the future. Rather, there were various bureaucratic temporalities at play that looked to the past, the present, the immediate near future, and a long-term future.

Working through the case of the man-eating leopard of Gopeshwar, I identify five forms of time, which clashed, and allowed for the formulation of stinging pronouncements on the nature of the Indian state (cf. Ssorin-Chaikov 2006). The first four of these were evidenced within the state bureaucracy itself, and hence my focus on thinking through the complexity of 'bureaucratic times'. First and foremost, there is the social discipline of everyday time within the setting of a government office in India (May & Thrift 2001). The everyday life of the state is constituted through the enactment of routine bureaucratic practices centred upon the production, consumption, and circulation of documents and the convening of meetings (Mathur 2010). Secondly, and in contrast to the regularized rhythm of quotidian bureaucratic life, there was a sense of urgency – a palpable immediacy caused by the risk to human lives – that enveloped senior officials as they attempted to 'govern' the big cat. Thirdly, there was a concern with what Guyer (2007) calls the 'near future',[5] which, instead of being 'relatively evacuated', as she puts it, was being constantly contemplated by asking 'what if?'. What if in the near future the town residents were to revolt against the state? What if in the near future the big cat was to become even bolder and enter the district office? What if more than one man-eating big cat was to be on the prowl in this small town? What if we cannot eventually hunt down the big cats? In contemplating what might happen if the big cat was not dealt with, there were also nostalgic representations of the past when state officials were allowed to deal with wild animals immediately and independently. Finally, there was the representations of a long-term temporality which sought to avert the risk of the extinction of big cats, which made its presence felt in the district bureaucracy via the entry of national law that covers (and protects) wildlife in contemporary India. Constituting an absolute other to bureaucratic time were the unpredictable timings of the movement and activities of the *bagh* itself. These remained radically unpredictable and unknowable. It was precisely the unpredictability of what the *bagh* would do next, where and when he would appear, how long he would stay for, when he might return or when he would be hunted down, that led to widespread terror.

'Saving the big cat': the risk of extinction, conservationist impulses, and legal assemblages

The global move towards conservationism combined with the particular history and symbolism of big cats on the sub-continent has led to the construction of a strong big cat preservationist legal regime in contemporary India.[6] Conservationism is premised on the identification of a present that contains a specified population of big cats. It builds upon this worrying present to project a long-term platform of action for the future. The future for conservationist time is one in which the risk of the endangerment of big cats is omnipresent and, hence, all policies are geared towards 'saving the big cat'.[7]

In addition to conservationist impulses, nationalistic pride figures in the protection of India's official national animal and representative in the international animal kingdom, the 'royal Bengal' tiger. In 1969 a Wildlife Board was set up by the

Table 1. Number of tigers and leopards killed in India, 2000-7.

Year	Tigers	Leopards
2000	52	1,278
2001	72	166
2002	46	89
2003	38	148
2004	38	123
2005	46	199
2006	37	160
2007	27	122

Source: Damania *et al.* 2008: 13.

Government of India to ban the export of tiger and leopard skins completely. In 1970 a total ban on tiger shooting was legislated upon, and in 1972 the Wildlife (Protection) Act was introduced into India. In April 1973 a scheme to 'protect the tiger' – Project Tiger – was launched with a budget of 40 million rupees, making it the world's largest conservation project of its time (Rangarajan 1996). Ever since then, efforts to preserve big cats have only increased, spurred also by the global project of 'saving the big cat' (see Jhala, Qureshi, Gopal & Sinha 2011; The Tiger Task Force 2005). The World Bank is just one such powerful international organization that has joined this noble cause. It plans to keep a close watch on the population of tigers and leopards in the world, as Table 1, taken from their recent report, makes clear. The report, entitled, tellingly enough, *A future for wild tigers*, congratulates India on its response to what is described as a big cat 'crisis'. The report notes that in India 'planned allocation for tiger protection will soon be increased to about $150 million over five years. This is equivalent to approximately $20,000 annually per living tiger or about $8 per hectare and amounts to a three- to fourfold increase in the available budget' (Damania *et al.* 2008: 15).

Criticisms of specific aspects of India's wildlife conservationist regime have surfaced, with Saberwal, Rangarajan, and Kothari (2001), for instance, exhibiting the connections between the colonial practice of *shikar* (hunt) and the nationalist project of conservation and their very similar location in elite aesthetics and practices. In a study of man-eating tigers in the Sundarbans in West Bengal, Jalais (2008) brings out the stark distinction between what she terms the 'cosmopolitan tiger' and the 'Sundarbans tiger'. The cosmopolitan tiger for her is one that personifies 'the very universalism of a Western particular – that of "wildlife" and its need to be protected' (2008: 25). Guha cautions against the form of national park management that is at work in much of the global South, which emerges from a 'distinctively North Atlantic brand of environmentalism' (2005: 151). Such an approach argues for vast regions of 'wilderness' to be carved out and emptied of all human habitation and activity. To adopt this approach uncritically, argues Guha, amounts to something akin to a form of 'green imperialism'. The adoption of precisely this logic of demarcated spaces is what led to the description of the Gopeshwar *bagh* as an animal that is 'escaping' from its own territory. The tiny town of Gopeshwar is surrounded on all sides by protected areas (PAs). Close to the town limits on the west is the Kedarnath musk deer sanctuary, which was established in 1972, covering an area of 967 km^2 to protect the now extinct musk deer. To the north of Gopeshwar, covering almost half of the entire district, is the Nanda Devi Biosphere Reserve. What happens when a *bagh* with man-eating predilections

Journal of the Royal Anthropological Institute (N.S.), 148-165
© Royal Anthropological Institute 2014

'escapes' from its own PA-land into human habitations? Quite simply, he unleashes a reign of sheer terror.

The reign of terror, or the radical unpredictability of the big cat

Gopeshwar, never the liveliest of places, became a veritable ghost town over the two and a half months that the *bagh* haunted it. Movement out of one's home was kept to a bare minimum. When travel was absolutely unavoidable, one would hastily scurry between destinations in large groups, never alone. Shops shut well before sunset. Doors were bolted firmly all day and people were wary of as much as stepping out onto the porch. Children, in particular, were strongly guarded by their families. No physical activity involving movement outside of the classroom was allowed in any school or college. Evening promenades were firmly discontinued by one and all. Women, who were in any case rarely seen alone on the streets, now virtually disappeared from the public sphere. Pet dogs were not allowed outdoors either. Orders were given for lights to be installed everywhere. A special request was sent to Dehradun (the state capital) to allow for uninterrupted power supply in the town (unhappily, this demand was not complied with, leaving us plunged in darkness many a night). There was frequent monitoring of the roads by policemen and forest guards, again in large groups. These monitoring groups held large flaming torches or beamed flashlights around. The Government Girls Inter College (GGIC) was shut down for over a month once it became clear that the *bagh*, too, was living in the same colony – Kund – in which the school is located. All large foliage growing in Kund was lopped off in order to lessen the hiding spaces for the new resident of the colony. This did not prevent a woman from falling down a hill and sustaining multiple fractures when she thought she caught sight of the *bagh*. In the neighbouring village of Roli-Gwad, a woman actually lost her life when she mistook a dog for the *bagh* and fell off a tree. Terror over these cold winter months was so palpable that even the movement of a falling leaf was enough for your blood to run cold with fright.

When the *bagh* first arrived and it became increasingly obvious he was a man-eater, his presence was made official by the state through the means of public announcements. A man was hired to walk around town with a huge *dhol* (drum-like musical instrument) slung from a white cloth around his neck. For the first fortnight or so he would go to public spaces such as the office square or around a cluster of houses and, beating the *dhol* to draw attention to himself, would, in a loud yet clear voice, recite details of the *bagh*'s recent activities and list the places and times at which he had been sighted or made a strike on humans. Once the sun had set, there was not a soul to be seen anywhere. Along with the dark, empty roads and spaces came an eerie silence, which was broken only by a piercing siren, a banshee's wail, at dawn. The siren, which would rudely jolt us all out of sleep at 4 a.m., was designed to frighten the *bagh* away from the town precincts. In addition, it daily awakened us anew to his presence – that was only reinforced through the constant *bagh* talk in hushed tones, the accounts in the newspapers, gossip, jokes, and the increasing anger against the state for not doing anything to counter the terror of the *bagh*.

The *bagh* became a larger-than-life presence in our lives in the town over these months. He was not just feared, but also anthropomorphized, to the point that he became a co-resident, one whom we could joke about and get angry at. From our daily conversations about the *bagh*, it would have appeared as if there was just one *bagh*, and that it was a male, being always referred to as 'him', even after it became clear, on the basis of an analysis of pug marks, that the animal in question was a female – that is, it was a *baghin* (leopardess).[8] Over the course of just 2006 there had been three separate man-eating leopards that had 'visited' the region and killed humans. All the *bagh* stories that were related to me, however, referred to him monotheistically, as if there was just one single *Bagh* that was ruling over us at all times, which explains the reference to the 'return of the *bagh*'.

The Gopeshwar *bagh* was most generally considered to be 'cunning' (*chatur*) and entirely 'unreliable' (*bharosa nahin kar sakte hai*). His cunning in locating, stalking, and obtaining human prey despite the precautions taken was incredulously discussed. Furthermore, his ability to just turn up anywhere at anytime (*kahin bhi kabhi bhi*) made him entirely unreliable.[9] So, for instance, one day he turned up outside the district development office that I was working in at precisely 5 p.m. There were loud giggles mixed with fear in the office about the cunning *bagh* who knows very well that the office shuts at that time. In general, the unreliable *bagh* could be seen in the full light of day (*din-dahade*) insouciantly walking around government offices, sunning himself on ledges in full sight of the busy bazaar, taking naps in the town's only public park, and leaving his pug marks in the most unlikely of places such as the village temple entrance. One night the *bagh* decided to spend some time in the District Magistrate's bungalow. This 'visit' was reported on the front pages of all the local newspapers the next day and became the subject of much hilarity for the longest time. On the basis of pug marks, it was clear that the *bagh* walked around the District Magistrate's garden, took a nap near a rose bush, and then made off in the morning before being spotted by anyone, including the various security guards stationed permanently in the compound. The local newspaper headlines the next day ran, '*Bagh* visits District Magistrate (DM), but catches him sleeping'. This incident proved to everyone in Gopeshwar that the *bagh*, too, was fully aware of how incapable agents of the state were and, thus, there was no need to fear them. The *bagh* could (mis)behave as he wished for, as usual, *sarkar* (the state), comprising the DM, who is the highest-ranked state official in the district, and his guards, was sleeping.

The sleeping state: everyday social discipline of government offices

Was the state really just sleeping through the reign of the Gopeshwar *wallah bagh*, as he came to be commonly referred to in the region? I follow the state's activities through an analysis of files and via participation in official meetings that were hurriedly convened during the reign of the big cat as well as my general presence in the main district office. A set of two thick files named 'Attacks by Wild Animals in the District' are maintained in room no. 14 in the District Magistrate's office in Gopeshwar. They are classified by the district bureaucracy as constituting 'sensitive' state matter and, hence, are kept under lock and key in a large steel *almirah*. Following the process whereby documents related to the *bagh* were produced, circulated, and filed, as well as the impact of these very documents on future events – the 'trajectory of work', as Riles (2006: 80) puts it – brings out the local state's tussle with the *bagh* that commonly terrorize this region. The two files contain a variety of documents within them: lists; faxes; telegrams; memos of phone conversations; hunting licences; medical certificates; government orders issued by the Government of India (i.e. from New Delhi); department orders coming from the provincial state's various departments in Dehradun; a copy of the Wildlife Act; Excel sheets of budgets; newspaper cuttings; copies of state-issued appeals; photographs; and, most abundantly, letters, letters, and more letters. From this rich hoard of documents of various sorts, I trace out the process of the government of the big cat, starting with his official declaration as a man-eater.

The Indian Wildlife Preservation Act's (1972) chapter 3, which deals with the hunting of wild animals, begins with the statement: 'No person shall hunt any wild animal specified in Schedule, I, II, III and IV except as provided below'. The leopard or panther (*panthera pardus*), along with the tiger (*panthera tigris*), is listed as a mammal under Schedule I of the Act.[10] Their hunting is absolutely prohibited, barring certain cases, with the one concerning us here falling under the purview of Clause 11 (1) (a), whereby:

> The Chief Wildlife Warden may, if he is satisfied that any wild animal specified in Sch. 1 has become dangerous to human life or is so disabled or diseased as to be beyond recovery, by order in writing and stating the reasons therefor, permit any person to hunt such animal or cause animal to be hunted (Government of India 1972).

The declaration of the *bagh* as a man-eater (*narbhakshee/adam-khor*) was made through the invocation of Clause 11 (1) (a). The Chief Wildlife Warden (CWW) of Uttarakhand is stationed in Dehradun. To get him to order *in writing* that the *bagh* must be hunted down turned out to be no mean feat, one that required gallons of suasive government ink to be spilled, with a flurry of letters and telegrams being sent back and forth before the written declaration was won. Basically, the process of obtaining a hunting licence for a *bagh* consists of convincing the CWW that the *bagh* in question has actually become 'dangerous to human life'. This was achieved by the making of a case by the local state against the *bagh* and in favour of humans. The case was argued, as everything else in the Indian state is, on paper through official documents.

Even after the *bagh* had attacked at least three other humans after the first incident with the woman in Kund, the local state had to struggle to secure the declaration of a man-eater. So the *bagh* kept appearing, even during daytime, in and around Gopeshwar. He carried off a cow and a dog, mauled three humans, and killed two before they could make a serious case against the *bagh*. The first of the victims was a 7-year-old girl on 7 December and then a 12-year-old boy. This boy – Vishal – was killed in dramatic fashion. He was walking home from school on the afternoon of 18 December when suddenly the *bagh* pounced on him from the bushes and carried him off. As this attack occurred in the daytime, it was witnessed by people in the vicinity, who began to create a huge din in order to get the *bagh* to drop his victim. The *bagh* did do so and ran off to a nearby cave to seek shelter. Unfortunately, by this point, Vishal was already dead. The horrified crowd surrounded the cave in an attempt to trap the *bagh*, and senior officials of the district – the Superintendent of Police who heads the police force, and the Divisional Forest Officer (DFO), who heads the forest department – were summoned to the site with their departmental forces to capture it. Despite their presence, however, the *bagh* managed to wriggle out of the cave and escape unharmed.

The events of 18 December led to a great upsurge of anger mixed with fear in Gopeshwar. The DM shot off an emergency telegram to the CWW describing the event and beseeching him to declare the *bagh* a man-eater. He had been sending regular updates to the CWW on the doings of the *bagh* ever since the leopard's 'return' to Gopeshwar and his very first attack on the woman in Kund colony. The DM and the

DFO followed up their written requests to Dehradun with phone calls explaining the enormity of the situation and consistently underlining how *akroshit* (furious) the *janta* (people) were. On 19 December 2006, the CWW sent a letter to the DFO with a copy to the DM recounting the above incident, quoting back the DFO's and the DM's letters to them. He ended by writing:

> Keeping in mind the information provided by you and the DM as well as the anger of the villagers and with the objective of protecting their lives, under Government Order number 111(6)/14-3-107-72 dated 01-02-1973 and the Wildlife Protection Act 1972 and 1991, on the basis of clause 11 (1) (a), I give you the power to catch this particular leopard using a cage, failing which you may destroy him.

The caution with which the letter proceeds is noteworthy. The CWW is squarely telling the DFO and the DM that he is transferring this power to destroy (*nashta*) the *bagh* on the basis of their claims that he is dangerous (*khatarnak*) and given that the villagers are furious (*akroshit*) and the *bagh* may cause further damage to them. Further, it is only if they fail to catch the *bagh* through the means of a cage that they are allowed to kill him. The DM was relieved to 'win' this hunting licence, a document for which he had to, as he said, 'always fight a lot'.

The government of big cats: documents, conflict, and nostalgia

District officials held up the hunting permit as a prize that they had won after a long wait and fight with the CWW. The wait was evident in the fact that it took two deaths, at least half a dozen attacks, numerous official documents, and five weeks to 'win' the hunting licence that would allow the local state to kill the *bagh* legally. The fight was more than evident in the files, which contained a variety of documents prepared by the district furnishing proof that the *bagh* in question was, undeniably, a confirmed man-eater and therefore pleading with the CWW to allow it to be caught or killed. These included daily updates; newspaper cuttings; copies of angry letters written by villagers/ victims/'prominent persons'; some rather gruesome photographs of victims; lists of deaths and injuries; medical certificates testifying that the human deaths had certainly been caused by big cats; and reports sent in to the district headquarter from villages and lower-level administrative staff.

The varieties of what I term 'suasive documents' that the district administration produced to convince its superiors of the facticity of its claims and the enormity of the problem are quite staggering. The rhetoric of these various documents invokes imageries of simultaneously terrified, angry, and helpless masses whilst continuing to follow the rather dry, accepted form and stylistics of the letter-based exchanges that constitute a central mode of communication between state functionaries. To give an instance, the DFO wrote a letter to the CWW in July 2006 requesting that a *bagh* that had been attacking humans in Gopeshwar be declared a man-eater. He began the letter with a detailed and vivid recreation of a bizarre attack by the *bagh* on a group of four women walking at sunset in the middle of the town. This text narrates, step-by-step, the perambulations of the women as they weaved their way through Gopeshwar up till the point they were, all of a sudden, attacked by the *bagh*. The letter goes on to dwell on the injuries sustained, the tears shed, and the anger caused by this alarmingly impertinent *bagh*. The forester adjudges this *bagh* to be 'very dangerous' (*atyanta khatarnak*) as he is exhibiting 'Aberrant Behaviour' (English term used in an otherwise entirely Hindi-language letter). The letter ends with a formal request:

Journal of the Royal Anthropological Institute (N.S.), 148-165
© Royal Anthropological Institute 2014

This sort of behaviour is increasing the possibility of destruction of life in the near future due to which it is imperative to immediately discipline the concerned *bagh*. In order to regulate the concerned *bagh* and seeing the failure of the present efforts to do so, I request you to utilize Clause 11 of the Wildlife Protection Act of 1972 on a priority basis and give me the permission to do the required work at my level to get him killed.

Letters consistently deployed verbs such as 'regulate', 'govern', 'discipline', 'control', or 'curb' with reference to what the state should be doing to the *bagh*. Furthermore, these letters consistently aimed to characterize the *bagh* as extremely dangerous to human lives and thus to the upkeep of 'law and order'. It was easier to issue a death warrant for an aberrant, cunning *bagh* that was behaving like, as one letter put it, 'a real desperado'. Speedier responses to attacks on humans were received in relation to 'high-profile' leopards such as the ones that made the mistake of entering the district headquarters, which was the largest town of the district and was also the place where all the agents of the state resided. Stoler has distinguished various types of 'the unwritten' (2009: 3). An unwritten in the documents on the man-eating big cats files was what the senior district officials had spoken openly to me about on the very first day of the *bagh*'s appearance. Everyone in the district office knew that it would take a lot of convincing by means of a barrage of suasive documents combined with a few human lives to get a written death warrant for the big cat. Tracing the career of the documents in the wild animals file, it emerges as the unwritten code, for only after the death of/attacks on 'a few' people was the declaration ever won.

In my interview with the then CWW, he listed the reasons for his cautious approach to the declaration of a man-eater. He was of the opinion that often a 'stray encounter' between a *bagh* and humans was, in panic, described as the case of a man-eater. He believed it wise to 'wait for a history' of the same *bagh*'s activities to come to light before making an irrevocable 'rash decision'. Therefore he often recommended the capture of the *bagh* in a cage by laying out a trap or by stunning him/her with a tranquillizer gun before 'jumping to the conclusion' that this 'poor *bagh*' (*bichara bagh*) was, indeed, a man-eater. Fresh from the novel and hair-raising experience of living under the terrifying shadow of the Gopeshwar *wallah bagh* for over two months, I could not help but comment that his sympathies seemed to be lying more with what he had just called a 'poor' *bagh* and less with the humans it was maiming, who would definitely not utilize the same descriptor for the said beast. His response was, naturally, to deny such a charge by gently telling me 'in government one must follow the law', proceeded by the reading out of certain clauses from the Wildlife Protection Acts, and the listing of how many 'innocent' *bagh* presumed to be man-eaters had been mistakenly killed in the past.[11] The killing of the 'innocent' *bagh* was a big worry for the Forest Department, but specifically for him, as he was responsible for 'each and every *bagh* in the state' and was answerable to his bosses in New Delhi for every permit that was issued from his office. It 'just does not look good' (*achha nahin lagega*) if we kill too many *bagh*, the CWW told me worriedly. In Gopeshwar, too, bureaucrats referred to how 'bad it looks' (*kharab lagata hai*) to kill too many *bagh*. And, indeed, there was immense pressure on these forest and wildlife officials from within the state bureaucracy to protect big cats stemming from the laws and conservationist pressures I mentioned above. Each and every hunting permit that was issued would go on to be listed as a leopard killed in India in tables such as the one in the World Bank report (Table 1 above). Thus, it was only after incontrovertible evidence had accumulated in documentary form that these officials felt they could safely sign off a hunting permit.

Journal of the Royal Anthropological Institute (N.S.), 148-165
© Royal Anthropological Institute 2014

To return to Gopeshwar, the 'winning' of the prized permit allowed for the local district officials to send out an appeal to professional hunters. Given the 'remote' location of Gopeshwar in a borderland district in Himalayan India, it proved to be very hard to find trained hunters. Local forest officials did not possess the basic equipment such as cages, tranquillizer guns, rifles, and other sorts of ammunition with which they could themselves hunt down the *bagh*. The hunting permit had been won on 19 December, but the *shikaris* (hunters) did not arrive in town until 4 January 2007. By this time, the *bagh* had killed another young woman, taking the total tally thus far to three humans.[12] The *shikaris* made a grand entry into Gopeshwar in an open white jeep, clutching big guns, dressed in camouflage with sunglasses and safari hats. On the very day of their arrival, they publicly declared, much to our collective delight, that the *bagh* now had only three days, at the most, to live. For the next three days, the entire town waited with bated breath. The local newspapers would daily carry photographs of the *shikaris* 'at work' scouring the mountainside dressed in their hunting gear and wielding impressively large guns. Senior officials grumbled that this lot 'looked too Bollywood-ish' actually to be the real thing, but locals seemed to be somewhat comforted by their presence.Ultimately, however, the faith of the locals in the hunters' ability turned out to be misplaced. For over two weeks, the *shikaris* attempted to shoot the *bagh*, but they were unsuccessful in their venture and had to leave the district with their tails between their legs, or, as it was described in Hindi, like wet cats (*bheegi billi*).

Ineffectual as the *shikaris* were, the spectacle of their hunt eased the pressure on the local state to exhibit action. For the very first time since the return of the *bagh* on that fateful November morning, senior officials were not being berated for doing nothing or not caring. Before the arrival of the *shikaris*, there were constant comparisons being made between present-day officials, who were incapable of handling the *bagh*, and men of state of the past, who would have immediately gone out and hunted the beast down. Hussain (2012) has made the point that the hunting of man-eating big cats in India was central to the colonial British welfare-orientated programme of governance. The colonial state saw the 'hunting of man-eating tigers in the foothills and plains as an effort to prevent fierce and unpredictable nature intervening in their day-to-day governance practices in Indian society' (Hussain 2012: 1213). Hussain notes that so important did the British consider it to be able to impose order, 'civilize' the wild nature of India, and exhibit their capacity to protect the natives that in the hunting down of man-eating big cats there was a suspension of fair hunting codes that were otherwise essential to their identity as sportsmen. The hunt has, more generally, been studied as central to the culture of imperialism (MacKenzie 1988; Rangarajan 2005). *Shikar* (i.e. the hunt) in British India 'constituted propaganda: it showed emperor, king, or lord exhibiting power' (MacKenzie 1988: 10). In Gopeshwar, for a brief tantalizing moment, an exhibition of state power was presented in the form of the hired professional *shikaris*. Pandian reads stories on the 'terror of man-eating big cats in India' as colonial accounts that recuperate the figure of the Oriental despot to characterize both the big cat and the preceding rulers in India. The terror is dispelled only through 'the masculine intervention of the white hunter' (Pandian 2001: 87). Yet it was precisely such a masculinist intervention or a forceful display of authority from the state that the residents of Gopeshwar were seeking. The confused and frightened persona of the officials in the face of the terror unleashed by the *bagh* was met with disdain and anger. Orwell's essay 'Shooting an elephant' (2009 [1950]) beautifully captures this pressure on state officials to behave and act as a *sahib* ought to when it comes to an incident such as an animal that has 'gone wild'. In Gopeshwar, oral histories of man-eating tigers and leopards nostalgically recount the time of the British Raj and the early years of Independent India when officials or the local royalty would immediately and personally take it upon themselves to protect their subjects by killing the beast. Today, in contrast, they encounter officials who struggle for ages to 'win' a flimsy piece of paper that would even allow them to commence looking for a hunter.

'Anything might happen': waiting and anticipating the near future

Whilst bureaucrats in Chamoli were preoccupied with enacting the routine procedures of the state, what a disgruntled colonial officer in Orwell's *Burmese days* describes as consisting merely of 'paper-chewing and chit-passing' (1948: 21), the residents of Gopeshwar were boiling over in anger at *sarkar*. On 21 December, at the peak of the *bagh's* reign of terror, a procession of over 100 people under the banner of the district's resident forum took out a procession (*jaloos*) and amidst the beating of drums and cries of 'Uttarakhand *Shasan Hai Hai*' (Shame on Uttarakhand Administration) and 'District Magistrate *Murdabad*' (Death to the DM) met the DM to give him a petition addressed to the Chief Minister. The subject line read, in bold, 'The terror of the man-eating leopard in Gopeshwar, district Chamoli'. It described the spread of terror in different districts of this Himalayan region, one that is regularly reported in local newspapers. 'Yet, the central government, Uttarakhand state government and district administration do not regard it gravely. The state has today put the worth of a leopard greater than the worth of humans. Is there no value left to humans in Indian democracy today?' (cf. Jalais 2005). The letter goes on to list a series of recent attacks by the *bagh*, with a stress on the manner in which in broad daylight (*din dahade*) the increasingly fearless *bagh* was barging into houses and grabbing children/attacking women. 'After the experiencing of these incredible incidents, too, our *sarkar* remains mute'.

In its tone, this petition wished to highlight the urgency of the situation and it made demands related to increasing the speed with which decisions took place. Thus, it sought an immediate amendment to the Wildlife Protection Act with the view of empowering local officials to kill instantly what they knew to be a man-eating big cat. It demanded that compensation for injury or death should paid in due time, especially for the killing of livestock, which was a very common problem. Finally, it demanded that anyone who killed a man-eater should be considered not a criminal but a 'brave' (*bahadur*) person.[13]

Around the time the procession had come to petition the DM, the Gopeshwar *wallah bagh* was being sighted almost every single day and indulging in all sort of 'activities', creating an atmosphere of such intense terror that you could almost see it hanging over us like a cloud in the cold, silent, empty mountain town.[14] During this period, the DM, as the head of the district administration, was under tremendous amounts of pressure and expressed to me in private more than once that he was worried 'anything might happen' (*kuch bhi ho sakta hai*) in the town. The procession that had come to petition him had clearly articulated their fury with *sarkar* for 'doing nothing' and for valuing the *bagh* more than humans. Immediately after the procession, the DM hurriedly called an emergency meeting with all the concerned officers and the Forest Department. In a letter written to various senior bureaucrats in Dehradun after the emergency meeting, he put forth detailed recommendations for the bettering of the situation. These included: provisioning the Forest Department with adequate equipment, such as tranquillizer guns and light cages; the transfer of the power to declare a man-eater from the

CWW to the concerned forest official in order to speed up the process/take care of urgent situations; and the provisioning of a budget with which to award *shikaris* and to pay victims their compensation. Enclosed with this letter was a copy of the *gyapan* he had just received. The high level of fear and helplessness that was being experienced within the state apparatus comes across clearly in this particular letter, where the DM writes of the increase in the attacks on humans by *bagh* in Chamoli and describes the procession that came to meet him:

> On speaking to them I felt that inside the people there is a tremendous amount of anger bubbling due to these incidents and in the near future we cannot overrule the possibility of a violent movement, which could lead to the development of grave dangers for the Forest Department and the district administration.

In this exhaustive letter, the DM put forth a show of unity whereby all the departments of the district were seen to be working in concert to eradicate the *bagh ka atank* (terror of the leopard). The reality of the situation back in the multiple offices in Gopeshwar could not have been more different, however. The schisms within the three primary wings of the local state – the District Administrator's Office, the Forest Department, and the police – came out in plain sight during this period. The myth of the state as a singular unit was sharply dispelled as there was a back and forth on the jurisdiction over, and regulation of, the *bagh*. As a television reporter grumbled to me, the *bagh* had 'become a volleyball ... you go to one office and they say this *bagh* is not mine, go to that office. When you go to that office, they say this *bagh* is not mine, go to yet another office'. The *bagh* did, indeed, become a metaphorical volleyball that was being bounced between one office and another, as different parts of the local state apparatus attempted carefully to carve out their own responsibility even whilst informing the others of what their job was. It became hard to keep up with the rapid-fire letter-based communication that went on *within* different wings of the district administration itself over the months of November, December, and January. While officials were passing the *bagh* around like a volleyball, the residents of Gopeshwar were accusing *sarkar* as a monolithic unity of 'doing nothing' other than indulging in their routine 'paper-games'. For instance, at a press conference that was held in the DM's office on 23 December, the increasingly hapless state was subjected to much public ridicule for its utter incapacity to regulate the *bagh* and was denounced by one and all for being a *kaghazi bagh* (paper tiger).

The emptiness of the state's pretensions of being in control or genuinely 'caring' about its citizens was evident not just in the long delays accompanying the declaration and capture/death of the *bagh*, but also in the process through which official figures were generated and compensation was paid to victims. The practice of maintaining statistics of attacks on humans by wild animals goes back to the British Raj. Thus, the *Garhwal Gazetteer*, which covers this part of present-day Uttarakhand, notes:

> From a return of inquests held in Garhwal between 1850 and 1863, the number of deaths from the attacks of wild animals was recorded at 276 during that period, and Rs. 13,784 were paid as rewards for the destruction of 91 tigers, 1,300 leopards and 2,602 bears. Taking the decade 1870-79, the returns show that 211 persons (123 males) were killed by wild animals and Rs 9,317 were paid as rewards for destroying 62 tigers, 905 leopards and 1,740 bears (Atkinson 2002 [1881]: 15).

Crucially, the *Gazetteer* admits that '[t]his return is avowedly imperfect, as it only includes the deaths reported to the authorities and the animals killed for which rewards have been claimed' (2002 [1881]: 16). In fact, Boomgaard has surmised that so strong were the misgivings of the British government that 'they discontinued the annual publication on killings – though not the data gathering – in 1927, owing to the unreliability of the data' (2001: 63). Under-reporting and generation of watered-down statistics of these incidences continues unabated till today, as does the practice of not publishing annual figures on fatalities.

The construction of dubious statistics on deaths and injuries caused by the *bagh* in the district is intimately linked to the convoluted and tortuous process of petitioning the state for compensation. Compensation for injury to self or property by the *bagh* or the death of a family member was to be issued on the production of – but of course – the correct documents. Awarding and receiving compensation is, again, not a straightforward case of submitting an application and receiving the established amount within a fixed time-frame. First of all, there is a complicated process that must be followed in order to be eligible to receive the compensation. This process, further, kept changing for no conceivable reason and the changes in procedure were poorly advertised. Having followed due process is not enough for, yet again, the unwrittens creep in. One must couch the request letter/petition (*prarthana patra*) to the state in a language of appeal, need, and rights, a delicate balance to be achieved by one who is proficient in these paper exchanges with the state (Bear 2005; Cody 2009). The vast majority of petitioners are, of course, not thus trained, which leads not only to failed documentary interactions with the state but also high levels of panic, anxiety, and despair in the very process of these interactions, generating 'nervous affectivity' of the form described by Navaro-Yashin (2007).

Once a petition has been written and submitted to the correct officer in the appropriate department, it is not as if one's job is done. One must '*maaro chakkar*' (go round and round) the offices to make sure that the document is not buried to be forgotten in some file or, even worse, lost altogether. Follow-up letters must be penned to serve as material reminders of the original issue, a key tactic of the Indian state's paper games. In the rare event that the compensation was released, its pitiable amount added to the sense of inferiority of human lives. The death of anyone under the age of 18, for instance, would lead to compensating the victim's family with Rs 50,000 or $1,000. Compare this with the $20,000 that every single tiger in India is currently being allocated on an annual basis by the state. With Rs 50,000, said one grieving father, you can barely buy two horses. 'Is the life of my dead 7-year-old daughter worth only two horses to *sarkar*? How does one make *sarkar* understand what the value of my daughter's life *really* was? What do they care anyway for they value the life of a *bagh* more than a human's', he asked as he ran around offices begging to get even this pittance released.

The end of the terror

On 28 January 2007, the reign of terror of the big cat came to an end with his hunting down by the local hero Lakhpat Singh Rawat. Residents of Gopeshwar and the nearby villages were jubilant. Bureaucrats heaved a sigh of relief and feted Mr Rawat with accolades and awards for his bravery. Proof of the death of the man-eater was published in the form of photographs that we all happily showed to each other.[15] Newspapers ran front-page articles proclaiming 'the end of the terror: the man-eating leopard has been killed' (*atank ka ant: mara gaya adamkhor bagh*). At first glance, the case of the man-eating leopard of Gopeshwar would seem to attest to the systematic production of indifference within the large, haphazard bureaucratic apparatus that underpins the Indian state (Herzfeld 1992). If not viewing it as a product of bureaucratic indifference or the realization of a Weberian nightmare of the iron cage of modernity, one might choose to focus on the wait involved in events related to the *bagh*, be it his hunting down or the eventual payment of compensation to his victims. Following Bourdieu (2000), it might be read as an assertion of state power. A Foucauldian lens, by contrast, would lead one to consider the act of making subjects indefinitely wait as an exercise aimed at disciplining them into becoming patients of the state, *pace* Auyero (2012). However, the ethnography that I have presented here allows us to draw out a different interpretation, both on what delays or waiting can lead to – a searing critique of the state in this case[16] – and why this seemingly bizarre wait occurred in the first place.

The ethnography presented above presents a scenario where a variety of forms of social time were at play simultaneously with the bureaucratic apparatus of the state struggling to reconcile them. In the first place we have the long-term strategy of averting the risk of the extinction of big cats that emerges from the global 'save the tiger' project. This powerful global and national-level conservationist agenda has coalesced in the framing of a legal regime that stipulates extreme caution before a big cat can be legally killed by the state in contemporary India. These legislations are interpreted and translated through the everyday social discipline of office life or by the enactment of slow and tedious documentary practices of various branches of the Indian state bureaucracy before the vital clause 11 (1) (a) can be enforced. Thus, we had the Forest Department, the Police Department, and the District Magistrate's Office within the district itself and various departments in Dehradun that were involved in exchanging letters and making phone calls before the permit could be 'won'. The slow pace of the bureaucratic practices compared to the urgency of dealing with the menace of a hungry big cat is another, particularly chilling, example of the ubiquitous 'clash between technocratic and lived time' (Abram & Weszkalnys 2011: 14). Once the document was won, there were the practical considerations of finding hunters and/or of possessing the required material such as guns. Further complications were brought on by the disadvantageous location of Gopeshwar on India's 'remote' Himalayan borderland. Gopeshwar is far away literally, in terms of physical distance from the state capital, and metaphorically, in terms of figuring as a meaningful space in the national and regional imaginary. In the context of this failure of the state to act swiftly, tied as it was to differing temporalities – that of long-term risk to animals and that of immediate threats to human life – a particular representation of time emerged. In this, citizens of the town nostalgically reminisced about the past, a past in which the state acted immediately to protect its populace. Bureaucrats were faced with residents who loudly proclaimed them to be ineffectual and uncaring. Even as they waged a documentary war within the labyrinthine and hierarchical Indian state structure, these bureaucrats fretted about what unpredictable events might occur in the near future. The fear of a violent insurrection against the state by an increasingly terrified and furious citizenry was constantly contemplated and discussed. Then there were the rhythms and movements of the hungry big cat itself, which were feared by everyone precisely because he remained entirely outside the realm of predictability. The reign of terror of the big cat led to a variety of affects, ranging from extreme fear to anger to the generation of nervous laughter among town residents, even as they formulated compelling critiques of the very peculiar functioning of the Indian state. A close focus on this episode ultimately allows us, I suggest, radically to reimagine bureaucracy as animated, as a space in which life unfolds within and at the intersection of conflicting orientations, disciplines, and affects of social time. Bureaucratic time should no longer be thought of as a Foucauldian social discipline that subjects citizens to its force, making them wait in order to disempower them. Nor can its qualities be captured by an analysis of risk projections, scenario planning, or states of anticipation or preparedness alone. Instead we must think through the various labours that are necessary within bureaucracies and between bureaucrats and citizens to make the state machinery work. Bureaucracy is revealed as a site for the mediation of heterochronies that is vulnerable to the critique that its failures to achieve this produce.

NOTES

Versions of this paper have been presented at seminars in Brunel, Cambridge, Durham, and Michigan Universities. I am grateful for these invites as well as for the comments from the audiences at these events, especially Matthew Hull's close reading for *Kitabmandal* in Michigan. I am indebted to David Sneath for kindly ploughing through my voluminous writings on man-eaters of the Indian Himalaya and to Laura Bear for her brilliant suggestions on how one might think through the literature on time.

[1] Gopeshwar is the district headquarters of Chamoli district in the North Indian state of Uttarakhand. I lived in Gopeshwar and worked out of the district office for close to a year over 2006-8.

[2] Throughout this paper I refer to human-eating big cats as man-eaters as this is how they are referred to popularly and in the literature.

[3] Historically, this is also the phrase used to write about events involving man-eating tigers and leopards in colonial accounts (e.g. Corbett 2007; see Pandian 2001).

[4] This understanding of waiting is particularly salient in studies of the state and bureaucracy. Thus, Schwarz notes that 'waiting is patterned by the distribution of power in a social system' (1974: 843) and that '[p]owerful clients are relatively immune from waiting' (1974: 848). A study of welfare waiting rooms in the US in the 1980s, however, dismissed the claim that all these spaces were 'dismal' or that waiting constituted a 'degradation ritual' of bureaucracy. Instead, it found marked difference between waiting rooms, with some, indeed, being 'most unpleasant' and some 'blandly functional and even pleasant' (Goodsell 1984: 476).

[5] Guyer describes the 'near future' thus: 'the process of implicating oneself in the ongoing life of the social and material world that used to be encompassed under an expansively inclusive concept of "reasoning" ' (2007: 409).

[6] For an excellent history of big cats on the Indian sub-continent, see Rangarajan (2005).

[7] Richards (1992) notes a 'profound cognitive gap' between local understandings of the future of tropical rainforests in West Africa and those of conservationists who want to 'save the forest'.

[8] I adopt this gendering and refer all through this paper to the *bagh* as a male in order to remain as faithful as I can to the manner in which this event unfolded.

[9] The cunning, unreliable *bagh* was also described, in English, as being 'gender-biased' for his attacks were largely directed at women. As a category, women are more vulnerable to attacks by wild animals in the mountains as they are the ones who gather and fetch water, fuel, and fodder for their households. This aspect was acknowledged, but it was simultaneously said that he liked women's blood and he knew that women were weaker, which made him gender-biased. The *bagh*, then, was stereotypically gendered as a male and his victims as female. The cunning and unrealiable, gender-biased *bagh* was also described by residents of Gopeshwar, especially by children, as shaking hands, smiling, winking, leering, thinking, soliloquizing, sunbathing, and visiting his neighbours in Kund colony where he was believed to have taken up residence along with senior state officials. Further, this complicated creature liked the taste of certain bloods in the same way as we like certain teas, grimaced when he licked some petrol by the petrol pump, was capable of prophesying (as was evidenced from the pre-emptive moves he made), and, even, worshipped the Hindu god Shiva, given his circumambulation of the town's Shiva temple.

[10] While the Indian state places the *bagh* and the tiger in the same category, in the International Union for Conservation of Nature's 'red list', which classifies species by the level of their imperilment, the tiger, along with the snow leopard, figures as an 'endangered species': that is, they both face a very high risk of extinction in the near future. The leopard, on the other hand, is 'near threatened': that is, it may be considered threatened in the near future (*http://www.iucnredlist.org/*).

[11] There were cases of leopards being shot down but on their post-mortem it was found that this particular one was not a man-eater and, therefore, not the one for whom the permit had been taken out. It is impossible, in practice, for a hunter to be sure that the *bagh* he spots is indeed the correct one, for it is not as if he has the opportunity to inspect him/her before going for the kill. The death of an 'innocent *bagh*' on the basis of a state-issued licence by an accredited hunter is not really covered by the law. The fuzziness of the law allowed for such (unfortunate) incidences to be 'papered over', according to the CWW.

[12] This was the official tally of deaths by the *bagh* thus far. Unofficially (i.e. unvalidated by governmental measures), the death count was by now between six and nine.

[13] The minimum sentence for the killing of a big cat in India, according to the Wildlife Protection Act of 1972, is three years in prison and a fine of $220, and the maximum sentence is seven years in prison and a $550 fine.

[14] The phrase by which this period was described was: '*Gopeshwar mein bagh laga hua hai*', or, roughly, 'There is a leopard stuck to Gopeshwar'.

[15] Rawat has emerged as the 'native' heir to Jim Corbett, who became a *shikari* after a sedulous study of the habits of his prey. Much like Corbett, Rawat, too, refuses to accept an honorarium from the government for his successful tracking down of man-eaters in Uttarakhand. A school teacher by profession, he took to hunting down man-eaters after three of his students were killed by a *bagh*.

[16] In a similar vein, Jeffrey shows how the experience of limbo amongst unemployed educated youth in northern India 'seemed to act as a seed-bed for the generation of somewhat novel youth cultures and political protests' (2011: 187).

REFERENCES

ABRAM, S. & G. WESZKALNYS 2011. Introduction: anthropologies of planning – temporality, imagination, and ethnography. *Focaal – Journal of Global and Historical Anthropology* **61**, 3-18.

ADAMS, V., M. MURPHY & A.E. CLARKE 2009. Anticipation: technoscience, life, affect, temporality. *Subjectivity* **28**, 246-65.

ATKINSON, E.T. 2002 [1881]. *The Himalayan Gazetteer or the Himalayan districts of the North Western Province of India*, vol. II. Delhi: Low Price Publication.

AUYERO, J. 2012. *Patients of the state: the politics of waiting in Argentina*. Durham, N.C.: Duke University Press.

BEAR, L. 2005. *Lines of the nation: Indian railway workers, bureaucracy, and the intimate historical self*. New York: Columbia University Press.

BOOMGAARD, P. 2001. *Frontiers of fear: tigers and people in the Malay world, 1600-1950*. New Haven: Yale University Press.

BOURDIEU, P. 2000. *Pascalian meditations* (trans. R. Nice). Cambridge: Polity.

CODY, F. 2009. Inscribing subjects to citizenship: petitions, literacy activism, and the performativity of signature in rural Tamil India. *Cultural Anthropology* **24**, 347-80.

CORBETT, J. 2007. *The man-eating leopard of Rudraprayag*. New Delhi: Oxford University Press.

CORBRIDGE, S. 2004. Waiting in line, or the moral and material geographies of queue-jumping. In *Geographies and moralities* (eds) R. Lee & D.M. Smith, 183-98. Oxford: Blackwell.

CRAPANZANO, V. 1985. *Waiting: the whites of South Africa*. London: Random House.

DAMANIA, R., J. SEIDENSTICKER, T. WHITTEN, G. SETHI, K. MACKINNON, A. KISS & A. KUSHLIN 2008. *A future for wild tigers*. Washington, D.C.: World Bank (available on-line: *http://documents.worldbank.org/curated/en/2008/01/9515307/future-wild-tigers*, accessed 16 January 2014).

GOODSELL, C.B. 1984. Welfare waiting rooms. *Journal of Contemporary Ethnography* **12**, 467-77.

GOVERNMENT OF INDIA 1972. The Wildlife (Protection) Act, 1972. New Delhi: Government of India (available on-line: *http://envfor.nic.in/legis/wildlife/wildlife1.html*, accessed 16 January 2014).

GREENHOUSE, C. 1989. Just in time: temporality and the cultural legitimation of law. *The Yale Law Journal* **98**, 1631-51.

GUHA, R. 2005. The authoritarian biologist and the arrogance of anti-humanism: wildlife conservation in the Third World. In *Battles over nature: science and the politics of conservation* (eds) V. Saberwal & M. Rangarajan, 139-57. New Delhi: Permanent Black.

GUYER, J. 2007. Prophecy and the near future: thoughts on macroeconomic, evangelical and punctuated time. *American Ethnologist* **34**, 409-21.

HERZFELD, M. 1992. *The social production of indifference: exploring the symbolic roots of Western bureaucracy*. Chicago: University Press.

HUSSAIN, S. 2012. Forms of predation: tiger and markhor hunting in colonial governance. *Modern Asian Studies* **46**, 1212-38.

JALAIS, A. 2005. Dwelling on Morichjhanpi: when tigers became 'citizens', refugees 'tiger-food'. *Economic and Political Weekly* **40**, 1757-62.

——— 2008. Unmasking the cosmopolitan tiger. *Nature and Culture* **3**, 25-40.

JEFFREY, C. 2008. Waiting. *Environment and Planning D: Society and Space* **26**, 954-8.

——— 2011. *Timepass: youth, class and the politics of waiting in India*. Stanford: University Press.

JHALA, Y.V., Q. QURESHI, R. GOPAL & P.R. SINHA (eds) 2011. *Status of the tiger, co-predators, and prey in India, 2010*. Dehradun: National Tiger Conservation Authority and Wildlife Institute of India (available on-line: *http://www.projecttiger.nic.in/whtsnew/tiger_status_oct_2010.pdf*, accessed 16 January 2014).

KAFKA, F. 2000 [1925]. *The trial* (trans. M. Brod). London: Penguin.

LAKOFF, A. 2006. Preparing for the next emergency. *Public Culture* 19, 247-71.

——— 2008. The generic biothreat, or, how we became unprepared. *Cultural Anthropology* 2, 399-428.

MACKENZIE, J.M. 1988. *The empire of nature: hunting, conservation and British imperialism*. Manchester: University Press.

MATHUR, N. 2010. Paper tiger? The everyday life of the state in the Indian Himalaya. Ph.D. thesis, University of Cambridge.

MAY, J. & N. THRIFT (eds) 2001. *Timespace: geographies of temporality*. London: Routledge.

NAVARO-YASHIN, Y. 2007. Make-believe papers, legal forms, and the counterfeit: affective interactions between documents and people in Britain and Cyprus. *Anthropological Theory* 7, 79-96.

ORWELL, G. 1948. *Burmese days*. London: Secker & Warburg.

——— 2009 [1950]. *Shooting an elephant and other essays*. London: Penguin.

PANDIAN, A. 2001. Predatory care: the imperial hunt in Mughal and British India. *Journal of Historical Sociology* 14, 79-107.

RANGARAJAN, M. 1996. The politics of ecology: the debate on wildlife and people in India, 1970-95. *Economic and Political Weekly* 31, 2391-409.

——— 2005. *India's wildlife history*. New Delhi: Permanent Black.

REITH, G. 2004. Uncertain times: the notion of 'risk' and the development of modernity. *Time & Society* 13, 383-402.

RICHARDS, P. 1992. Saving the rain forest? Contested futures in conservation. In *Contemporary futures: perspectives from social anthropology* (ed.) S. Wallman, 138-53. London: Routledge.

RILES, A. 2006. [Deadlines]: removing the bracket on politics in bureaucratic and anthropological analysis. In *Documents: artifacts of modern knowledge* (ed.) A. Riles, 71-92. Ann Arbor: University of Michigan Press.

SABERWAL, V.K., M. RANGARAJAN & A. KOTHARI 2001. *People, parks and wildlife: towards coexistence*. New Delhi: Orient Longman.

SCHWARZ, B. 1974. Waiting, exchange and power: the distribution of time in social systems. *American Journal of Sociology* 79, 841-71.

SSORIN-CHAIKOV, N. 2006. On heterochrony: birthday gifts to Stalin, 1949. *Journal of the Royal Anthropological Institute* (N.S.) 12, 355-75.

STOLER, A.L. 2009. *Along the archival grain: epistemic anxieties and colonial common sense*. Princeton: University Press.

THE TIGER TASK FORCE 2005. *The report of The Tiger Task Force: joining the dots*. New Delhi: Project Tiger, Government of India.

La terreur du grand félin : bureaucratie et médiation des temps sociaux dans l'Himalaya indien

Résumé

Le présent article décrit l'irruption d'une panthère mangeuse d'hommes dans un village de l'Himalaya indien et la lutte des autorités locales contre le grand félin. En se concentrant sur ce qui s'est passé au sein de l'appareil d'État pendant cette période, il se veut une contribution à l'étude du temps moderne dans la bureaucratie. Le manque saisissant d'efficacité et d'efficience dans les mesures de contrôle et de régulation du grand félin résulterait, selon l'auteure, d'un conflit entre différents temps sociaux déployés simultanément. L'article identifie cinq formes distinctes de temps social en jeu pendant cette période, qui ont causé de longues périodes d'attente et suscité de féroces critiques des villageois envers l'État indien. En définitive, l'auteure contribue à repenser les théories actuelles du temps bureaucratique, qui se concentrent sur la production d'attentes impuissantes, d'analyses de risque et d'anticipations. Au lieu de cela, selon elle, l'étude des bureaucrates des échelons les plus bas et des citoyens montre qu'une tâche centrale de la bureaucratie est de tenter une médiation entre des formes contradictoires de temps social. Prenant ses distances avec les analyses en termes d'indifférence bureaucratique, l'article décrit l'échec comme l'impasse de tentatives visant à faire concorder des formes et représentations du temps sans commune mesure. Ces échecs mettent gravement en péril la légitimité des bureaucrates et peuvent susciter une critique radicale de l'État.

8

A wedge of time: futures in the present and presents without futures in Maputo, Mozambique

MORTEN NIELSEN *Aarhus University*

A series of recent anthropological studies on time emphasize the crucial importance of the future as a guiding trope in the present. Although located beyond an immediate temporal horizon, the future is consequently taken as connected to the present in a meaningful way through a sequence of chronological moments and hence potentially accessible. This paper takes its point of departure from the growing body of anthropological work on time and futurity, but challenges the inherent assumption of linearity characterizing the relation between present and future. Based on fieldwork carried out in Maputo, Mozambique, it examines the non-linear temporalities of house-building. According to house-builders living on the fringes of the city, the future constitutes a temporal position from where the present might be properly illuminated. However, when seen from the present, the future surprisingly seems to reflect its own inevitable collapse, thus making it crucial to maintain appropriate distance between the two. Whereas the imagined perspective from the future suggests an immediate readability of the present, the inverse temporal gaze (i.e. from the present) reflects the radical uncanniness of the future. Still, although prefigured as a failure at the end-point on a linear scale, the future asserts itself by opening up the present. It wedges itself within the present moment and establishes temporal differentiations without indicating a progressing trajectory. In a peculiar inversion of conventional linearity, the present becomes the effect of the future rather than vice versa.

Anthropological studies of time often seem to be caught by an insoluble paradox. As Roy Wagner tells us, '[T]ime could never be perceived without the distinctions we impose upon it' (1981: 73), and so the devices we use to predict time (calendars, rituals, etc.) also produce its particular characteristics. 'We know time', Wagner continues, 'by its stealthy habit of creeping up on us. We *make it* creep up by assuming that we are able to predict and prepare for it' (1981: 74, italics in original). Classic anthropological studies, such as E.E. Evans-Pritchard's explorations of ecological and structural time among the Nuer (1940) or Clifford Geertz's analysis of punctuated life in Bali (1973: 391-409), suggest that temporal succession may be understood as a relationship between inherently exterior moments following each other like beads on a string. In *The Nuer*, Evans-Pritchard describes how structural and ecological time both 'refer to successions of events which are of sufficient interest to the community for them to be

noted and related to each other conceptually' (1940: 94). Succeeding events are registered in terms of a yearly calendar that structures the mutually dependent relationship
between a cycle of activities and a conceptual cycle, where the latter derives its meaning
and function from the former. As if commenting directly on Evans-Pritchard's analysis
of time among the Nuer (which he probably was!), Wagner reminds us that,

> We create the year ... in terms of events and situations that make them significant and worthwhile, and
> we do so by *predicting* them and then seeing how the events and situations impinge upon our
> expectations. Calendars, schedules, time-tables and seasonal expectations and routines are all 'pre-
> dictive' devices for precipitating (and thereby predicting ourselves with, and not *predicting*) time.
> They are a means of setting up expectations, which in their fulfillment or nonfulfillment become 'the
> passage of time' ... (1981: 73-4, italics in original).

By allowing the devices we use to predict time also to account for its particular
modalities, time is recognized only to the extent that it presents itself in the geometrical forms afforded by (invented) time-reckoning devices (cf. Gell 1992: 235). This
doubling of time was recognized already in Émile Durkheim's seminal treatise *The
elementary forms of religious life*, where it is suggested that '[a] calendar expresses the
rhythm of the collective activities, while at the same time its function is to assure
regularity' (1965 [1912]: 23). As such, time-reckoning devices afford a regulatory mechanism by which any social occurrence will find its natural location in a series of
unrepeatable moments (Meyer 2012). In his influential studies of changing temporal
orientations in eighteenth-century working-class England, E.P. Thompson (1967)
unpacked how this synchronization of time involved a fundamental transformation in
the work ethic and the orientation to labour. Although initially orchestrated as con-
certed ways of organizing work tasks, new systems of time-discipline came to function
as internal regulatory mechanisms for the structuration of social life as such.[1] Time
became spatialized, as it were. Hence, as a crystallization of what the editor of this
special issue of *JRAI* aptly coins 'modern times', the planning and synchronization of
a wide variety of human activities does, indeed, constitute a primary technology by
which time has been made present in social life (cf. Abram & Weszkalnys 2011). Even
so, as I will shortly argue, the (quantitative) planning of social life made possible
through linear chronology makes it difficult – if not outright impossible – to capture
the (qualitative) temporal modulations and rhythms that give to social life its different
forms of directionality and pace.

As if heeding Johannes Fabian's succinct critique that 'much of the study of "cultural
transformation" of human experience remains sterile because it is not capable (or
unwilling) to relate cultural variation to fundamental processes that must be presumed
to be *constitutive* of human Time experience' (1983: 42, italics in original), a recent body
of work has challenged the 'spatialization of time' by emphasizing the fluidity of
socio-historical change. Inspired by social philosophers, such as Henri Bergson (1913;
1965), Alfred North Whitehead (1978), and, particularly, Gilles Deleuze (1988; 1994;
2005), this work examines how time erupts as 'durations': that is, convergences of
different temporalities within one rhythmic configuration (Das 2007; Hodges 2008;
Kapferer 2005; Nielsen 2010b; Turetzky 2002). In *Art and agency* (1998), Gell examines
the temporal 'thickness' of Maori meeting houses. During the latter half of the nineteenth century, the Maori found themselves no longer capable of engaging in combat
using traditional warlike methods. Instead, Maori communities tried to outdo each
other through the construction of elaborately carved and painted meeting houses

designed to serve as objectifications of their wealth, technical skill, and ancestral endowment. Although, as Alfred Gell describes, to enter a meeting house was to 'enter the belly of the ancestor', its physical space was equally filled up by the anticipated future moment when the efforts invested in its construction would eventually materialize as a 'political triumph' over an opponent. The Maori meeting house therefore did not belong to a 'now' as the datable moment on a chronological scale when it was constructed, but to an extended temporal field (*durée*) 'reaching down into the past' while 'probing towards an unrealized and perhaps unrealizable futurity' (Gell 1998: 258).

In Nancy Munn's work on Gawan value creation through long-distance kula-shell exchanges, we find parallel accounts of 'extended temporal fields' that seem to defy conventional chronological linearity (1983; 1986; 1990). Through transactions with valuable shells, Gawans engage with a wider milieu beyond that of the present, which is both spatial and temporal. All high-valued kula shells are potentially of interest to more than the persons involved in a given transaction. Reciprocal exchanges therefore involve not merely the actual transfer of valuables but, equally, the possible (albeit unrealized) pasts and futures which were *not* activated through the event. If, say, a person's illness is believed to be caused by witchcraft attacks associated with ongoing transactions, the cause might be elicited by searching backwards from the presently visible (negative) signs towards a past which was hitherto only a dormant potentiality (e.g. rather than the activated transaction A<>B, the unrealized transaction A<>C emerges as the possible cause of the present problems), while simultaneously unfolding a 'negative future', as it were, implying the death of the unfortunate person having fallen ill (Munn 1990: 4-8). Hence, although Gawans obviously make connections between discrete moments and events, these procedures cannot be understood as entailing linear time (Munn 1990: 14). As the temporality of social life 'is developed from the action of situated agents who are actively creating the relations of particular events at various moments, that is, in a given "present"', the meaning of the event is contextualized as 'of the moment' while the moments themselves emerge gradually through the ongoing and intermittent assembling of discrete events (Munn 1990: 14).

By emphasizing the coexistence of different events within one durational configuration, time is treated not merely as a series of discrete moments following each other like beads on a string but, rather, as a continuous multiplicity. This qualitative conceptualization of time as 'duration' (*durée*) was first formulated by the French philosopher Henri Bergson and subsequently served to orientate the seminal work by Gilles Deleuze on virtual multiplicity and becoming as univocity (Bergson 1913; 1965; 2001; 2005; Deleuze 1988; 1993; 1994). Inspired by the mathematician G.B. Riemann, Bergson distinguishes between a discrete (quantitative) and a continuous (qualitative) multiplicity or manifoldness. Discrete multiplicities are those that contain their own metrical principles (denumerable), whereas continuous multiplicities are those in which the metrical principles are located in the forces that act on them from the outside (non-denumerable). Given that a multiplicity is distinguished by a mark or boundary, we are therefore essentially dealing with a certain form of 'quanta'. As Keith Ansell-Pearson explains in his insightful discussion of durational flows, '[I]n the case of a discrete magnitude we make the comparison with quantity by counting and in the case of a continuous one by measuring' (2002: 16). Taking as a point of departure Riemann's elaboration of the geometrical principles of space, what Bergson did, then, was to transform the distinction between the two multiplicities by linking the continuous with the sphere of duration:

[F]or Bergson, duration was not simply the indivisible, nor was it the nonmeasurable. Rather, it was that which divided only by changing in kind, that which was susceptible to measurement only by varying its metrical principle at each stage of the division ... In reality, duration divides up and does so constantly: That is why it is a *multiplicity*. But it does not divide up without changing in kind, it changes in kind in the process of dividing up: This is why it is a nonnumerical multiplicity, where we can speak of 'indivisibles' at each state of the division. There is *other* without there being several; number exists only potentially. In other words, the subjective, or duration, is the *virtual*. To be more precise, it is the virtual insofar as it is actualized, in the course of being actualized, it is inseparable from the movement of its actualization (Deleuze 1988: 40, 42-3, italics in original).

In order to explain how different durations are mutually implicated, Bergson (1913) gives the example of mixing a glass of water with sugar and waiting until the sugar dissolves. Although it is perfectly possible to calculate how long it would take for the sugar to dissolve, this 'mathematical time' coincides with an impatience that constitutes a crucial segment of the duration of the person doing the mixing of sugar with water and which is impossible to protract or contract at will. The experienced duration is therefore not really singular but always implicated with others; it is one and many at the same time.[2] As such, duration constitutes the virtual coexistence of time with itself. It is, as Deleuze describes, a becoming that endures by incessantly differing from itself (1988: 37).

This paper builds upon this recent body of work that seeks to go beyond the 'spatialization' of time and argues for an approach to the study of social transformations that takes seriously their durational fluidity. Rather than merely outlining the linearity of a particular process, we need also to pay attention to the ways in which a given temporal configuration may come together as a 'radical plurality of durations' (Deleuze 1988: 76). Still, despite the obvious benefits of broadening the analytical scope, we should not throw the proverbial baby out with the bathwater, and it might therefore be relevant to consider how temporal moments assert themselves as differentiated singularities even when erupting within durational flows (cf. Grosz 1999: 28). Returning to Munn's work on Gawan exchanges, it could be argued that the past and future occurrences being actualized through an event in the present maintain or even acquire their discrete qualities (i.e. they can be distinguished from other coexisting temporal moments) precisely because they erupt within a durational flow. Although we might concur with Deleuze that any temporal moment asserts itself as a provisional contraction of the durational flow as such (1988: 51-72; 1994: 70-6), its singular qualities are immediately recognizable as being different from those of other coexisting moments, say, as the datable cause leading to a person's current illness. Hence, in contrast to the (calendric) differentiations, which, Wagner told us, in their fulfilment constitute progressive linearity, we have here a radically different form of temporal singularization. As a way of addressing the 'praxial requirements of the present', certain pasts and futures connect and come to constitute a durational flow that has no ground outside itself. Whereas time-reckoning devices, such as the chronological calendar, essentially establish a quantitative 'spatialization' of time, durations give rise to qualitative expansions of time simply because the repertoire of images and moments is increased and intensified (Ansell-Pearson & Mullarkey 2002: 17; Deleuze 1988: 63).

In this paper, I shall consequently focus on the process of durational differentiation as a 'becoming without ground, without foundation' (Colebrook 2002: 50). As I shall argue, by focusing on the singularization of time that is established through durational flows, it becomes possible to challenge conventional understandings of time as a

forward-moving progressive chronology without, however, having to give up the idea
of temporal differentiation (i.e. that different moments might be distinguished from
each other). I will therefore suggest that durational differentiations may manifest
themselves in non-linear ways, and I qualify this perhaps counter-intuitive argument by
analysing the significance of the future among house-builders living on the outskirts of
Maputo, Mozambique. Although prefigured as a failure on a linear scale, the future
asserts itself by opening up the present. It wedges itself within the present moment as
a transversal movement and establishes temporal differentiations without indicating a
progressing trajectory. In a peculiar inversion of conventional linearity, the present
becomes the effect of the future rather than vice versa.

Presents without futures

According to residents living in Mulwene on the outskirts of Maputo, the future exists
as an unstable transformative potentiality which needs to be concealed from the
outside world. Any exposure of desired things to come is considered as an unwanted
premonition which threatens to collapse the distance between present and future and
thus make the properties of the latter accessible to outside forces. While interviewing a
local healer (*curandeiro*), I asked whether she had discussed her plans of extending her
house with some of the nearby neighbours. 'Ihhh! Do you want me to hand over my life
to another person? You really can't do that!' She shook her head several times before
continuing: 'It's not a good thing to expose what is at the bottom of your heart ... here
we wish for bad things to happen to others (*nós desejamos mal de outras pessoas*)'. Unless
the 'content' of the future is properly concealed, it will eventually be appropriated by
some malignant force in the outside world. During a conversation on inherited land,
Boavida Wate,[3] a stout-hearted former community chief in Mulwene, warned against
the excessive exposure of desired future gains: for example, by purchasing farming
equipment based on expectations for the coming harvest. 'We can't take our riches
outside (*não podemos levar a nossa riqueza para fora*)', Wate told me. 'Other families will
try to take possession (*apoderar-se*) of my belongings', agreed 'Old' Guambe, Wate's
friend for more than four decades: 'We are constantly worried about what the reactions
might be. Therefore we act with caution (*andar com cuidado*) and don't tell much about
what we'll be doing next'. Apparently, concealing the 'content' of the future was a
widespread strategy even within the highest political echelons. During the campaign
for the 2004 national elections, I noticed that the candidate for the governing Frelimo
party, Armando Guebuza, only sparsely advertised the location and precise time for
upcoming campaign activities. I asked Gabriel, a municipal architect working in
Mulwene, what might be the reason for this lack of information. 'Today (*hoje em dia*)
you don't trust anyone. So Guebuza will make it publicly known that he will show
himself but not when it will happen ... he won't tell the exact time because someone
might take advantage of that information'.

It thus seems likely that concealed or even negated plans serve as exterior surfaces, as
it were, protecting those desired futures which so easily become appropriated by
malevolent outside forces. As temporal buffers, they deflect unwanted attention while
simultaneously enabling the experimentation with alternative temporal trajectories.
Still, although this is undoubtedly true in many situations, the relationship between
negated and desired futures should not be seen merely as a distinction between form
(negated future) and content (desired future). Paradoxically, by actualizing that which
should not be realized, the former serves as a vehicle for the coming into being of the

Journal of the Royal Anthropological Institute (N.S.), 166-182
© Royal Anthropological Institute 2014

latter. In Paulo Granjo's lucid account of divination practices in southern Mozambique (2012; see also Granjo 2011; Honwana 1996), he thus describes how alternative futures might be accessed by manipulating the probabilities for the likely, albeit unwanted, (future) outcomes of current actions. Through divinatory practices, the productive potentials of the future are elicited by actively altering the conditions (in the present) for what lies ahead. Desired outcomes therefore cannot be seen as detached from the unwanted but likely future from which they emerge almost as excrescent temporalities. In a peculiar inverse manner, the transformative potentials lodged in the future are accessible only through a reversal of its form: that is, by initially acknowledging its inherent impossibility as an end-point on a linear scale. Indeed, among residents living in Mulwene, future scenarios are typically unfolded through definite (rather than subjunctive) statements while also indicating that they will most likely never happen (Nielsen 2011a).[4] In order to have effects, the future has to manifest itself in particular ways, and this requires an initial inversion of its form that is then turned inside out so that the actual desired future effectively becomes an effect of the premonitioned but unwanted (future) reverberations of current acts. As we shall see below, without risking unwanted exposure, the 'inside' of the future could thus be publicly elicited precisely because it was brought forth in a negated form.

After this brief introduction to the dynamic relationship between presents and futures in the southern part of Mozambique, let me now turn to a case study which outlines how a particular collapsed future wedges itself in the present among house-builders on the outskirts of Maputo in order subsequently to discuss non-linear and non-progressive temporal differentiations.

'The unfortunate bricklayer'

'Is it them?' Alberto's question hung in mid-air without a proper addressee. I followed his eyes as he looked past me towards the white four-wheel drive Toyota crossing the square some fifty-odd metres from where we were standing. I replied by asking who he thought it could have been. Alberto started walking before responding: 'I don't know'; his voice was barely audible; 'someone who's coming to resolve my problems'.

During the last few months prior to our brief exchange at the square on 11 April 2005, Alberto's already difficult situation had taken a rapid downward-spiralling turn. For many years, Alberto and his family had rented his aunt's small plot in Mulwene, but after meeting Mafuiane, a local quarter leader,[5] it seemed likely that they would soon get their own piece of land in the neighbourhood. In return for building a cement house for Mafuiane, Alberto would be allocated a 15 × 30 metre plot by the community leader. In fact, a vacant plot had already been identified and, according to Mafuiane, Alberto could start building the much-desired house as soon as he had the necessary materials. After having informed his aunt of their imminent departure, Alberto bought as many stacks of reed and wooden pegs as he could afford and placed them in the vacant plot, where he would soon commence making a reed hut (*casa de caniço*) to serve as their temporary home while saving up for and gradually building a permanent cement house. Equally enterprising, his aunt proceeded to sell her plot and told Alberto (who was still living there) that he had to leave before 1 April 2005.

As Alberto soon was to discover, he was unfortunately not the only one having been allocated the vacant plot. In February 2005, Marta Mucavela, a primary school teacher from a nearby neighbourhood, acquired legitimate property rights to the plot through the Ministry of Education, which had parcelled out this section of Mulwene during the late 1990s in an attempt to provide land for the many landless teachers in Maputo. During a small ceremony in front of her new plot, Mucavela signed the formal transfer documents and immediately began contacting local bricklayers to arrange the building of a small one-room cement house. Before long, however, the propitious situation was radically changed and Mucavela was again potentially without a piece of land in Mulwene.

Although Alberto initially hoped that the prospects of a prolonged conflict would keep Mucavela from realizing the projected construction plans, the building materials being continuously unloaded by Mucavela's bricklayer suggested otherwise. Accompanied by Mafuiane, Alberto tried several times to convince the neighbourhood leader that the allocation had been both unfair and unjust, but without avail. The start of April was rapidly approaching, and as Alberto's frustration increased accordingly, he began thinking of alternative strategies; perhaps complaining to the Mayor's Office or even contacting the local media, as some neighbours had suggested to him. Come 1 April there was still no resolution. Fortunately, the new owner of his aunt's plot would not commence any building activities before the middle of the month, and so she allowed Alberto and his family to stay for a few days longer. Soon afterwards, however, on 10 April, her patience was apparently used up and Alberto was instructed to leave the plot within twenty-four hours.

Early next morning, my neighbour told me that Alberto had invaded the disputed plot and that he was already making his presence visible. I immediately went to see Alberto, and it was clear he had been busy. Along the left side, a reed hut had been erected on a stamped raised platform held in place by a row of cement blocks. Additional blocks were positioned on the zinc roof, and in the back left corner a small radio antenna was pointing towards the sky. Starting a few metres from the boundary line, a rectangular furrow had been dug reaching about halfway across the plot, and cement blocks had been placed along its edges. Nearly half of the plot had already been cleared, but the area right at the back was still covered by grass and wild thorny bushes (*espinhosa*). Alberto returned shortly after my arrival. He had been in the city centre trying to arrange a meeting with the municipal ombudsman (*provedor*), but after hours of waiting in a damp corridor outside his office, Alberto returned home empty-handed. I sat down outside the reed hut together with Alberto and his wife, Célia, to discuss recent developments in the dispute.

> I built a house because that's what the government wants. The neighbourhood leader came today to inform me that I have to stop the building project. But I really didn't start making the foundations to construct a house but, rather, to prevent her [Marta Mucavela] from building a house here. It's my land, but it's been usurped because I'm poor.

Célia nodded and said: 'She [Marta Mucavela] was the real intruder because we were the ones planting the *espinhosa*. She even tore up some of the plants. It's a lack of respect!' Alberto had to leave soon afterwards to go talk with Mafuiane about the situation and I followed along. We had just left the disputed plot when Alberto spotted the white four-wheel drive Toyota and asked, 'Is it them?'

Making a 'model neighbourhood'

Before continuing with the discussion of Alberto's invasion, we need briefly to contextualize the process. As I shall subsequently argue, by digging out a rectangular furrow, Alberto essentially wedged a particular but already collapsed future in the present and thus opened towards a reconfiguration of the social landscape.

Mulwene has grown significantly since 2000, when it was used as resettlement zone for the many disaster victims after the devastating flooding which hit Mozambique in the first three months of the year (Christie & Hanlon 2001). Prior to the flooding, the area had a population of less than 2,000, which consisted mainly of small-scale farmers and a small group of newcomers. A continuous influx of people reached its momentary peak in 2005 when the neighbourhood had 30,813 registered inhabitants (Nielsen 2010b). From the outset, the city council made it their overarching ambition to plan and built Mulwene as a 'model neighbourhood' (bairro modelo). In a municipal report on administrative and political aims concerning the resettlement process, it is stated that 'the city council intends to make Mulwene a bairro modelo with all the requirements that constitute adequate habitation'.[6] As is clear from this and other reports drafted during the initial resettlement phase, the making of a bairro modelo would entail that land parcelling and house-building projects were realized in accordance with a set of well-defined urban standards: for example, that cement houses had to be placed 3 metres from the boundary line towards the street in 15 × 30 metre plots. It was consequently envisioned that residents in the area could be allocated legal use-rights to formally acquired plots of land in correspondence to a legitimate urban plan comprising the entire neighbourhood. And, indeed, not long after the first families had been installed in tents in a section of Mulwene, the initial steps were taken towards actually creating the bairro modelo. Twenty-five donor organizations were active during the first months of 2000 building a total of 1,088 basic cement houses, making 460 drillings for individual and communitarian wells and constructing 1,100 latrines, a football field, 300 'precarious houses' (casas precárias) (i.e. reed huts), and two primary schools. The immediate result was impressive. After only a few months, rows of cement houses with corrugated iron roofs began to appear where previously tents or reed huts were the only housing possibilities (Nielsen 2008: 40-58). Although still unpaved, access was facilitated by the 12 metre-wide dirt road that connected Mulwene to the main EN1 highway, and in several sections of the neighborhood, rows of wooden pylons revealed that electricity was gradually being installed.

Despite the initial success, however, it was soon apparent that neither state nor international agencies were fully capable of realizing the ambitious project of creating a bairro modelo. Soon after the flooding victims had been transferred to Mulwene, the majority of international donor agencies began to lose interest in the project, and so it was up to state and municipal institutions to secure viable housing conditions for the growing number of residents coming to the area while also creating an adequate administrative structure that would respond to the needs of an emerging urban neighbourhood. With a weak state administration incapable of carrying out even basic urban development schemes, the project of creating a bairro modelo from scratch revealed itself as a utopian mirage whose ideological and practical weaknesses soon became apparent.[7] From the very beginning, architects and land surveyors in collaboration with members from the neighbourhood committee illegally parcelled out plots of land which were sold off to needy newcomers, who have subsequently acquired access to basic infrastructure, such as electricity and water, through informal transactions with local-level officials within state or municipal agencies. In this regard, the situation in Mulwene is similar to that of many other peri-urban neighbourhoods in Maputo and urban areas elsewhere in the country, where a burgeoning informal land market has been growing since the mid-1980s as a consequence both of the government's insuffi-cient administrative capacities and of the increasing liberalization of access to land, which often contradicts national legislation (Assulai 2001; Jenkins 2001*a*; Negrão 2004). Since Independence in 1975, all land has been nationalized and therefore cannot for-mally be transacted.

Considering the overt illegality of many occupations in the area, its physical homo-geneity is striking, with evenly structured blocks each consisting of sixteen 15 × 30 metre plots and laid out in a uniform grid separated by straight 10 metre-wide roads. From the outset, I consequently imagined that the physical environment reflected the initially stated ideal of creating a *bairro modelo* that adhered to a set of fixed urban norms. Based on the firm belief that some 'master plan' surely did exist, for several months I went from one municipal office to the next in order to find the document in which the evenly structured physical organization of the neighbourhood originated. As I would come to realize, however, the structured appearance emerged almost entirely through overlapping processes of informal parcelling authored by local leaders in collaboration with public officials (Nielsen 2007; 2011*b*). As transport facilities and basic infrastructure were gradually improved, people who were in no position to obtain land closer to the city centre took advantage of the opportunity to acquire a plot in the emerging neighbourhood. Through informal transactions, they were able to buy plots in Mulwene, which, although they had been informally parcelled out by civil servants, nevertheless imitated the 'fixed urban norms' associated with the *bairro modelo*. In many situations, then, the (formally) illegal residents acquire a form of pragmatic legitimacy through imitative building practices that might potentially be converted into legitimate property rights to their plots.[8]

In sum, people access land and build houses in Mulwene by imitating the aesthetics of an urban ideal that has already revealed its own collapse. According to current legislation on urban land, newcomers who occupy vacant land informally are consid-ered as illegal squatters and can potentially be removed with force by the government. However, by having their plots parcelled out and subsequently building their houses in accordance with the 'fixed urban norms' associated with the initial idea of making a *bairro modelo*, their status is potentially transformed from illegal squatters to legitimate citizens. As state and municipal officials working in the area often told me, urban governance tends to be guided by what is locally known as 'administration *ad hoc*', functioning simply to secure a 'minimum of urban order'. Provided illegal settlers build something which the state *could* have done, their occupancy is therefore generally accepted (Nielsen 2010*a*; 2011*b*). In this regard, the planning ideals associated with the initial aspirations of making a *bairro modelo* serve as an apt medium for securing property rights by informal residents coming to or already living in the area.

Futures in the present

In his discussion of the ritualized use of masked figures among the Foi people of Papua New Guinea, Weiner tells us that 'it is through the focusing of vision, through, say, the putting on of a mask, that the world *as a whole thing* in all of its analogic potentiality is made visible' (1995: 36, italics in original). In other words, the vision is expanded by narrowing the perspective in particular ways, such as when gazing at the world through a mask. Although the medium is radically different, I wish to suggest a similar line of reasoning regarding the case study introduced above. Indeed, it was by digging out a rectangular furrow 3 metres from the boundary line towards the street that Alberto

Journal of the Royal Anthropological Institute (N.S.), 166-182
© Royal Anthropological Institute 2014

suddenly found himself gazing at a potentially transformed world; a world where he might be seen by some outside force capable of disentangling his seemingly insoluble situation.

Let me begin to unpack the temporal layers of the process by returning to Alberto's statement that 'I built a house because that's what the government wants ... But I really didn't start making the foundations to construct a house but, rather, to prevent her [Marta Mucavela] from building a house here'. Seemingly a self-contradictory statement ('I built a house ...' and later 'I really didn't start making the foundations to construct a house ...'), it guides our attention towards the significance of the future as negated form in the present. In a nutshell, Alberto sought to actualize the full potentials of a future cement house (i.e. status as legitimate citizen in the neighbourhood with formal property rights to the plot) without converting its virtual reality into physical materiality. To be sure, Alberto was not at all interested in pre-empting the actual realization of a future house, as this would undoubtedly have exposed him to the erratic manoeuvres of outside forces. However, by wedging the future within the present and thus manifesting something that was already defined by its eventual collapse, it became possible to act on the inherent virtual potentials and thus carve out alternative socio-temporal trajectories. In many ways, Alberto's house was therefore surprisingly similar to those premonitioned futures elicited through divinatory practices described earlier that opened towards new temporal horizons through their eventual collapse. In both instances, the potential danger associated with excessive exposure was momentarily controlled by eliciting the desired future in a negated form. What the case study fleshes out with particular clarity, then, is how an active transformation of the conditions (in the present) for a premonitioned future occurs alongside the continued existence of the latter: that is, a collapsed future in the present − say, the ideal of a *bairro modelo* − constitutes the continued premise for carving out new temporal trajectories.

We find the perhaps most elaborate anthropological account of how differentiation − or discontinuity − is inserted into a continuous domain in Lévi-Strauss's seminal studies of myths (1955; 1963; 2005; see also Schrempp 1992). In *Totemism* (1963), he considers Firth's data on Tikopia and calls particular attention to the story of Tikarau. In ancient times, Lévi-Strauss recounts, gods and mortals were alike, with the gods functioning as the direct representatives of the clans. Tikarau, a god from a foreign region, visited Tikopia, and the local gods arranged a splendid feast for him that would take place after a series of organized trials of speed and strength. During one race, Tikarau slipped and declared that he was injured. While pretending to limp, he suddenly rushed towards the provisions, stole a heap, and ran to the mountains in an attempt to escape the hosts chasing him. While being chased, Tikarau fell, so that the clan gods were able to retrieve some of the foodstuffs: one coconut, one taro, a breadfruit, and a yam. In the end, Tikarau managed to return to the sky with most of the foodstuffs for the feast but four vegetable foods were saved for men (Lévi-Strauss 1963: 25-6). Hence, in this case:

> Totemism as a system is introduced as *what remains* of a diminished totality, a fact which may be a way of expressing that the terms of the system are significant only if they are *separated* from each other, since they alone remain to equip a semantic field which was previously better supplied and into which a discontinuity has been introduced (Lévi-Strauss 1963: 26, italics in original).

Discreteness is here introduced into a hitherto continuous system by eliminating certain fractions of the continuum. Foodstuffs were originally indeterminate in

Figure 1. Degrees of divisibility (adapted from Lévi-Strauss 1970: 54).

number, but after the reduction, a smaller quantity may spread in the same space, 'while the distance between them is now sufficient to prevent them overlapping or merging into one another' (Lévi-Strauss 1970: 52).

Although to claim an equivalence between the case study presented above and the Tikopian myth analysed by Lévi-Strauss would be taking the analogy too far, a tentative comparison nevertheless opens towards an exploration of temporal differentiations in a non-linear and non-progressive way. I will argue that Lévi-Strauss's succinct account of the transition from continuous to discrete reveals how an intensive flow may be differentiated in a qualitative manner. Essentially, the continuum maintains its limit-lessness but it is now held in place by a series of differential segmentations (see Fig. 1).

In the Tikopian account, it is the act of the stranger god that differentiates what was hitherto an undifferentiated virtual state of coexistence (*pace* Deleuze 2004: 176-7). In the case study described above, the differentiating act occurred through the negated future (manifested as a rectangular furrow) that wedged itself in the present and thus produced new temporal differentiations within a durational flow. At the moment when Alberto stood in the square and watched the white four-wheel drive Toyota pass us by, he was potentially (virtually!) a legitimate citizen.[9] With the furrow functioning as an imitation of the 'fixed urban norms' associated with the initial aspirations of creating a '*bairro modelo*', a future moment erupted in which Alberto was configured as having formal occupancy to the plot. Although its actual realization (in the future) was considered as being unlikely, it suggested a temporal horizon which defined a possible past (first meeting with Mafuiane, the quarter chief) and a consequential future (formal occupancy). In other words, with the suggestive future scenario of a cement house, past and future occurrences seemed to find their appropriate form *in the present*. No wonder, then, that Alberto believed it likely that some unknown outside agent would be aware of his existence and, he hoped, actualize what was already an existing (albeit virtual) reality.

Keeping in mind that we are here exploring how time erupts as a singular durational flow at the moment when Alberto watched the white four-wheel drive Toyota pass by – what was initially described as a convergence of different temporalities within one rhythmic configuration – it follows that the temporal differentiations being produced do not constitute a linear succession of moments. If we limit the discussion to the moments already mentioned ('first meeting with Mafuiane' and 'formal occupancy'), they may be understood in a non-linear manner as a confrontation between two contradictory terms, where the former implies relations of difference (i.e. informal access to land through ties with a local chief) and the latter implies relations based on similarity (i.e. formal access through citizenship).[10] This confrontation is, however, both actualized and momentarily resolved by the negated future wedging itself in the present. As a trace left in the present of that which will never be, the rectangular furrow both assembles and separates the two contradictory terms. Because the future is already prefigured as a failure, it operates in the present entirely as an intensive capacity for differentiation that persists across the diverging lines separating the two moments. Analogue to the trickster who is halfway between two polar terms and thus retains some of that duality (Lévi-Strauss 1955: 441), the future wedging itself in the present is identical to the differentiated moments while also maintaining an exterior quality by mediating their momentary assemblage. Paradoxically, the meeting with Mafuiane and the future acquisition of formal property rights seem to acquire significance through the making of the furrow. Whereas the present cannot serve as condition for the future, the inverse relationship is therefore more likely. In that sense, the temporal differentiations being produced here and now may be considered as what Cooper designates as 'the apparition of the after-effects of future possibilities in the present' (1998: 128).

Reverberations

It logically follows, then, that the effects of non-linear and non-progressive temporal differentiations cannot be gauged in terms of causal linkages. As Grosz tells us, durational time is 'braided, intertwined, a unity of stands layered over each other' (1999: 17), and so we need to examine how future eruptions in the present open towards new unfoldings of time without the former serving as a tool for anticipating a final destination. Let me therefore return once again to the occurrences that followed the encounter at the square in order to examine how the virtual coexistence of different pasts and futures in the present actualized a particular form of differentiation (or becoming) through which new social positions potentially became accessible.

Despite never having approached neither state nor municipal agencies regarding his housing situation, during the following days and weeks Alberto kept returning to the district administration in order to resolve the untenable situation. I was present at several meetings between Alberto, Mafuiane, Marta Mucavela, the neighbourhood chief, and Ussene, the district administrator, and the issue that was consistently brought up was the digging out of the rectangular furrow. On 18 April 2005, the district administrator made her first visit to the disputed plot and immediately noticed the furrow. 'This is wrong!' Her characteristically gruff voice made the exclamation sound almost like a threat. 'It's a lack of respect for the government that they have already made the foundation'. This statement is, of course, interesting particularly as no physical foundation had actually been made. According to local bricklayers, the foundation to a house consists of five layers of blocks poured in cement and all Alberto had done was to dig out a 30 centimetre-deep furrow and placed blocks along its sides. It is therefore, I suggest, as a (virtual) after-effect of the future in the present that it came to have considerable effects.

The after-effect of the future in the present was perhaps most forcefully expressed at a meeting between Alberto and the district administrator a few days after the initial invasion of the disputed plot. As he told me before the meeting, Alberto hoped for the administrator to acknowledge the legitimacy of his occupation and consequently allocate use-rights to the current plot, or, alternatively, relocate Alberto and his family to another plot in the vicinity. Without entering the debate on the possible legitimacy of Alberto's occupancy, the administrator stated that Marta Mucavela had been allocated the plot simply because Alberto had waited too long with commencing his construction project. When we were about to leave the administrator's office, however, Alberto gave a strong indication that his status might already have been transformed. Standing in front of Ussene while staring at the floor, he asked if she had considered the issue regarding the name for his still-unborn child. Ussene's response was brief, and it was apparent that her answer was negative. Outside the administration building, I asked Alberto what their brief exchange was about. As Alberto told me, he had previously asked Ussene if she would consider giving her name to his unborn baby. Although the administrator had originally agreed, for some reason she now declined the offer.

In the southern part of Mozambique, most living persons have a spiritual namesake (Portuguese *xará;* xiChangana *màb'ìzwenì*) (Junod 1962: 38). Name-giving constitutes an extension of the living person (xiChangana *nàvàlàlà*), whereby his or her person-hood is formed in a dialectical relationship between the living person and the deceased ancestor. Similar types of relationship are established between living persons with slightly different dynamics. If the child of *A* is given the name of *A*'s uncle (*B*), the latter is, so to speak, reconfigured as *A*'s child, whereby implicit reciprocal power relations between *A* and *B* obviously change accordingly. In other words, if the district admin-istrator had agreed to share her name with Alberto's baby, she would, in a symbolic sense, be (inferiorly) positioned as Alberto's daughter. Needless to say, if Alberto had succeeded in establishing this reciprocal relationship, problems regarding the plot would probably have become immediately manageable.

Although the brief exchange at the district administration seemed to indicate little change in Alberto's status, the ensuing encounters suggested otherwise. At the final meeting with all parties involved in the dispute, the district administrator commenced the discussion by lecturing Alberto about his wrongdoings. 'If you had only made a formal application instead of starting to build a cement house. The state cannot accept that!' In a subtle and oblique way, the negation of the house-building project here opens towards a consideration of Alberto as a legitimate citizen. To be sure, no illegal squatter would dare approach the district administrator with any application, formal or informal. Alberto therefore had to be (at least potentially) a legitimate citizen. And so, after many more meetings, Alberto was in fact allocated formal property rights to a piece of land located only a few blocks from where he initially invaded Marta Mucavela's plot. The rectangular furrow was soon covered and before long Marta Mucavela was busy making foundations for what is now a three-room cement house.

Conclusion

In Mulwene on the outskirts of Maputo, people engage with futures that will never follow the present. Through the recognition of its impossibility, the future moment is liberated, as it were, from its fixation on a linear scale while still maintaining the capacity to inform ongoing practices. As it wedges itself in the present, it effaces the boundary between the actual and the virtual, and that which will never be is already there. Past and future thus coexist in the present as interpenetrating singularities that destabilize or even bracket progressive chronology. What seems to emerge in its place is a cascade of virtual becomings that might be actualized as concrete possibilities, such as the described transformation from illegal squatter to legitimate citizen. It is therefore by approaching time as duration that we come to understand how social transforma-tions might occur in non-linear and non-progressive ways. In this paper, I have exam-ined this seemingly counter-intuitive process by outlining how an already collapsed future wedges itself in the present and through series of divisions and bifurcations has ramifying spatial and temporal effects. In a sense, its collapse produces an internal doubling so that the future not only exists as failure on a linear scale but also serves to open up the present in potentially productive ways.

Journal of the Royal Anthropological Institute (N.S.), 166-182
© Royal Anthropological Institute 2014

In *A thousand plateaus*, Deleuze and Guattari discuss the significance of being in-between positions. They consequently argue that:

> *Between* things does not designate a localizable relation going from one thing to the other and back again, but a perpendicular direction, a transversal movement that sweeps one *and* the other away, a stream without beginning or end that undermines its banks and picks up speed in the middle (1999: 25).

Through the analysis of the case study presented above, I have suggested that a collapsed future in the present may exhibit such transversal properties. It opens up time, as it were, and inserts itself within the differentiated moments without becoming completely equivalent to them. Not unlike the differentiation of intensive flows in the myth of Tikarau's visit to Tikopia, durational time thus maintains a virtual multiplicity while still undergoing continuous differentiations. Although moment 'A' might be identified as being radically different from moment 'B', the distinction does not imply directionality from one to the other. In a sense, durational time is movement without prediction; direction without destination. Returning again to the central question of how time is made present in social life, durational time in Mozambique might therefore be taken to afford a particular kind of planning scheme that brackets linear chronology without at the same time dissolving temporal differentiation. Here, the planned future does not necessarily constitute a promise of a forthcoming moment (Abram & Weszkalnys 2011: 9), but operates perhaps rather as a potent medium for differentiating the present in novel and potentially productive ways.

NOTES

This paper is based on fifteen months of ethnographic fieldwork carried out between 2004 and 2011 in Mulwene, a peri-urban neighbourhood on the northern outskirts of Maputo. I thank the Danish Research Council for Culture and Communication (FKK) for generously funding the three-year Ph.D. research project on which this paper is based. A first draft was presented at the ESRC 'Conflicts in Time' workshop in 2011, and I am grateful for the invaluable comments and suggestions given by the participants. In particular, I need to thank Laura Bear, the organizer of that workshop and the two anonymous reviewers for their challenging critiques and insightful comments.

[1] According to Thompson, this transformation dates from the end of the eighteenth century: 'Indeed, a general diffusion of clocks and watches is occurring (as one would expect) at the exact moment when the industrial revolution demanded a greater synchronization of labour' (1967: 69).

[2] For an ethnographic discussion of the qualitative (non-denumerable) aspects of numbering, see Strathern (1992: 11-13; cf. Verran 2001).

[3] All names used in this paper are pseudonyms.

[4] In this regard, the elicitation of futuristic potentialities among house-builders in Maputo may be seen as an analogue to the inversions of mythical images among the Salish-speaking people living along the Columbia River in Washington and Oregon. As described by Lévi-Strauss in 'How myths die', mythical images maintain their significatory fullness when adopted by other tribes by being inverted 'rather like a pencil of light rays passing through a pinpoint into a camera obscura, and being made to cross over by this obstacle – in such a way that the same image seen the right way up outside is reflected upside down in the camera obscura' (1974: 272).

[5] At the time when I was researching this case (2004-5), Mulwene was divided into fifty-six quarters (*quarteirões*) headed by individual quarter chiefs (*chefes de quarteirões*). All quarter chiefs referred to the neighbourhood leader (*secretário do bairro*) in charge of the local administrative unit co-ordinating official activities in the area.

[6] *República de Moçambique: 1 draft do projecto de reassentamento das populações em Mulwene* [Mozambican Republic: first draft of the resettlement project for the populations in Mulwene] (April 2000). Document in municipal archive, Mulwene.

[7] As argued by Jenkins (2000: 209), since Independence, urban land management has not been a political priority, and so the informal areas have rapidly expanded. Between 1990 and 1999, forty-eight plot layouts (smaller urban plans) were developed by the state and other institutions without overall co-ordination or land registration (Jenkins 2000: 209). Many of these plot layouts were subsequently used for illicit transactions between individual civil servants and different private agents. Finally, out of the 86,300 new housing units built from 1980 to 1997, it is estimated that as few as 7 per cent were provided by the state or private sector (4,000 and 1,500, respectively). The remaining more than 80,000 housing units were built without state assistance (Jenkins 2001b: 637).

[8] In 2009, the municipal department for management of urban land (Municipal Department for Construction and Urbanization [Direcção Municipal de Construção e Urbanização]) initiated a process of allocating legal use-rights to residents having formally occupied land illegally in selected areas of Mulwene.

[9] The concept of the virtual is, so to speak, a designation of the process of *becoming* detached from any physical actualization. In order to unpack how Alberto's utterance might be taken as a reflection of a virtual transformation, two brief discussions of coronations might be used as apt illustrations. First, Shields (2003) argues that the historical importance of the virtual can be detected from the various records of ritual events and ceremonies: for example, coronations of kings and queens. Thus, royalty were historically understood to be 'god-like beings', which is still apparent regarding the Japanese Emperor. Therefore 'coronations *actualize* the virtual, bringing the idea of "the King", for example, down to Earth in the form of an actual individual' (Shields 2003: 36, italics in original). Secondly, in Žižek's complex reading of Deleuze's work, the author describes the coronation scene at the beginning of Sergei Eisenstein's *Ivan the Terrible*, where Ivan's two closest friends pour gold coins on to his newly anointed head. As Žižek writes, 'Is it not the excess of the pure flow of becoming over its corporeal cause, of the virtual over the actual?' (2004: 3). In other words, it is at the precise moment of the crowning that the virtual potentials of the King's position are revealed in all their splendour. In the short time it takes to pour the golden coins over the anointed head, the King is connected to everything; or, rather, he *is* everything. Although it may seem far-fetched, I will nevertheless argue that the occurrence in the square bears more than a passing resemblance to the coronation scene described above. As the Toyota four-wheel drive passed by without the identity of the driver being revealed, its opacity, so to speak, connected with the furrow in Alberto's plot. Like the crowned King who is connected to everything at once, when connected to the passing Toyota, the rectangular furrow allowed for a series of (virtual) becomings that indicated a multiplicity of potential futures for the house-builder.

[10] The oppositional pair might fruitfully be described as a confrontation between 'alliance' and 'filiation' (Jenkins 1999: 23-4).

REFERENCES

Abram, S. & G. Weszkalnys 2011. Anthropologies of planning – temporality, imagination, and ethnography. *Focaal – Journal of Global and Historical Anthropology* **61**, 3-18.
Ansell-Pearson, K. 2002. *Philosophy and the adventure of the virtual*. London: Routledge.
———— & J. Mullarkey (eds) 2002. *Henri Bergson: key writings*. New York: Continuum.
Assulai, J.P.D. 2001. *Land market in urban areas*. Maputo: SARPN.
Bergson, H. 1913. *Creative evolution* (trans. A. Mitchell). London: Macmillan.
———— 1965. *Duration and simultaneity* (trans. L. Jacobson). Indianapolis: Bobbs-Merrill.
———— 2001. *Time and free will: an essay on the immediate data of consciousness* (trans. F.L. Pogson). Mineola, N.Y.: Dover.
———— 2005. *Matter and memory* (trans. N.M. Paul). New York: Zone.
Christie, F. & J. Hanlon 2001. *Mozambique and the great flood of 2000*. Oxford: The International African Institute in assocation with James Currey and Indiana University Press.
Colebrook, C. 2002. *Gilles Deleuze*. London: Routledge.
Cooper, R. 1998. Assemblage notes. In *Organized worlds: explorations in technology and organization with Robert Cooper* (ed.) R.C.H. Chia, 108-30. London: Routledge.
Das, V. 2007. *Life and words: violence and the descent into the ordinary*. Berkeley: University of California Press.
Deleuze, G. 1988. *Bergsonism* (trans. H. Tomlinson & B. Habberjam). New York: Zone.
———— 1993. *The fold: Leibniz and the baroque* (trans. T. Conley). London: Athlone.
———— 1994. *Difference and repetition* (trans. P. Patton). New York: Columbia University Press.
———— 2004. How do we recognize structuralism? In *Desert islands and other texts 1953-1974* (trans. C. Bush, C. Stivale, M. McMahon, A. Hickox & T. Eich), 170-92. Los Angeles: Semiotext(e).
———— 2005. *Cinema 2: the time-image* (trans. H. Tomlinson & R. Galeta). London: Continuum.

———— & F. GUATTARI 1999. *A thousand plateaus: capitalism and schizophrenia* (trans. B. Massumi). London: Athlone.

DURKHEIM, É. 1965 [1912]. *The elementary forms of religious life* (trans. K.E. Fields). New York: Free Press.

EVANS-PRITCHARD, E.E. 1940. *The Nuer*. Oxford: University Press.

FABIAN, J. 1983. *Time and the other: how anthropology makes its object.* New York: Columbia University Press.

GEERTZ, C. 1973. *The interpretation of cultures.* New York: Basic Books.

GELL, A. 1992. *The anthropology of time.* Oxford: Berg.

———— 1998. *Art and agency: an anthropological theory.* Oxford: Clarendon Press.

GRANJO, P. 2011. Trauma e limpeza ritual de veteranos em Moçambique. *Cadernos de Estudos Africanos* **21**, 43-69.

———— 2012. O que é que a Adivinhação Adivinha? *Cadernos de Estudos Africanos* **22**, 65-93.

GROSZ, E. 1999. Thinking the new: of futures yet unthought. In *Becomings: explorations in time, memory, and futures* (ed.) E. Grosz, 15-28. Ithaca, N.Y.: Cornell University Press.

HODGES, M. 2008. Rethinking time's arrow: Bergson, Deleuze and the anthropology of time. *Anthropological Theory* **8**, 399-429.

HONWANA, A. 1996. Spiritual agency and self-renewal in Southern Mozambique. Ph.D. dissertation, School of Oriental and African Studies, University of London.

JENKINS, P. 1999. Mozambique: housing and land markets in Maputo. Research Paper No. 72. Edinburgh: Edinburgh College of Art/Heriot-Watt University, School of Planning and Housing.

———— 2000. City profile Maputo. *Cities* **17**, 207-18.

———— 2001a. Emerging urban residential land markets in post-socialist Mozambique: the impact on the poor and alternatives to improve land access and urban development. Edinburgh: ECA School of Planning and Housing, Edinburgh College of Art/Heriot-Watt University.

———— 2001b. Strengthening access to land for housing for the poor in Maputo, Mozambique. *International Journal of Urban and Regional Research* **25**, 629-48.

JUNOD, H.A. 1962. *The life of a South African Tribe*, vol. I: *Social life*. New Hyde Park, N.Y.: University Books Inc.

KAPFERER, B. 2005. Situations, crisis and the anthropology of the concrete: the contribution of Max Gluckman. *Social Analysis* **49: 3**, 85-122.

LÉVI-STRAUSS, C. 1955. The structural study of myth. *Journal of American Folklore* **68**, 428-44.

———— 1963. *Totemism* (trans. R. Needham). Boston: Beacon.

———— 1970. *The raw and the cooked*, vol. 1 of *Mythologiques* (trans. J. Weightman & D. Weightman). New York: Harper Torchbooks.

———— 1974. How myths die. *New Literary History* **5**, 269-81.

———— 2005. *Myth and meaning.* London: Routledge.

MEYER, M. 2012. Placing and tracing absence: a material culture of the immaterial. *Journal of Material Culture* **17**, 103-10.

MUNN, N. 1983. Gawan Kula: spatiotemporal control and the symbolism of influence. In *New perspectives on the kula* (eds) J. Leach & E. Leach, 277-308. Cambridge: University Press.

———— 1986. *The fame of Gawa.* Chicago: University Press.

———— 1990. Constructing regional worlds in experience: kula exchange, witchcraft and Gawan local events. *Man* (N.S.) **25**, 1-17.

NEGRÃO, J. 2004. *Mercado de terras urbanas em Mocambique.* Maputo: Cruzeiro do Sul.

NIELSEN, M. 2007. Shifting registers of leadership: an ethnographic critique of the unequivocal legitimization of commmunity authorities. In *State recognition of local authorities and public participation: experiences, obstacles and possibilities in Mozambique* (eds) L. Buur, H. Kyed & T.C. da Silva, 159-76. Maputo: Ministério da Justica/Centro de Formação Juridica e Judiciária.

———— 2008. In the vicinity of the state: house construction, personhood, and the state in Maputo, Mozambique. Ph.D. dissertation, Department of Anthropology, University of Copenhagen.

———— 2010a. Contrapuntal cosmopolitanism: distantiation as social relatedness among house-builders in Maputo, Mozambique. *Social Anthropology* **18**, 396-402.

———— 2010b. Mimesis of the state: from natural disaster to urban citizenship on the outskirts of Maputo, Mozambique. *Social Analysis* **54**, 153-73.

———— 2011a. Futures within: reversible time and house-building in Maputo, Mozambique. *Anthropological Theory* **11**, 397-423.

———— 2011b. Inverse governmentality: the paradoxical production of peri-urban planning in Maputo, Mozambique. *Critique of Anthropology* **31**, 329-58.

Journal of the Royal Anthropological Institute (N.S.), 166-182
© Royal Anthropological Institute 2014

Schrempp, G. 1992. *Magical arrows: the Maori, the Greeks, and the folklore of the universe.* London: University of Wisconsin Press.

Shields, R. 2003. *The virtual.* London: Routledge.

Strathern, M. 1992. Writing societies, writing persons. *History of the Human Sciences* **5**, 5-16.

Thompson, E.P. 1967. Time, work-discipline, and industrial capitalism. *Past and Present* **38**, 56-97.

Turetzky, P. 2002. Rhythm: assemblage and event. *Strategies* **15**, 121-38.

Verran, H. 2001. *Science and an African logic.* Chicago: University Press.

Wagner, R. 1981. *The invention of culture.* Chicago: University Press.

Weiner, J.F. 1995. Technology and techne in Trobriand and Yolngu art. *Social Analysis* Special Issue **38**, 32-46.

Whitehead, A.N. 1978. *Process and reality.* New York: Free Press.

Žižek, S. 2004. *Organs without bodies: Deleuze and consequences.* New York: Routledge.

Temps imbriqués : futurs dans le présent et présents sans futurs à Maputo au Mozambique

Résumé

Une série d'études anthropologiques récentes consacrées au temps met l'accent sur l'importance cruciale du futur comme trope orientant le présent. Bien qu'il se situe au-delà de l'horizon temporel immédiat, le futur est considéré comme lié au présent d'une manière signifiante par une suite de moments chronologiques qui le rendent potentiellement accessible. L'auteur part du corpus de plus en plus conséquent de travaux anthropologiques sur le temps et la futurité, mais remet en question l'hypothèse de linéarité inhérente qui caractérise la relation entre présent et futur. À partir d'un travail de terrain à Maputo, au Mozambique, il examine les temporalités non linéaires dans la construction d'une maison. Selon les constructeurs de maisons qui vivent aux marges de la ville, le futur constitue une position temporelle à partir de laquelle on peut jeter un éclairage approprié sur le présent. Vu du présent, toutefois, il semble refléter son propre et inévitable effondrement : il est donc essentiel de maintenir entre les deux une distance adéquate. Bien que la perspective imaginée dans le futur suggère une lisibilité immédiate du présent, l'inversion du point de vue (à partir du présent) reflète l'étrangeté radicale du futur. Pourtant, alors même qu'il est envisagé comme un échec au bout d'une échelle linéaire, le futur s'affirme en ouvrant le présent. Il s'intercale dans le moment présent et établit des différenciations temporelles sans indiquer une trajectoire de progression. Par une inversion particulière de la linéarité conventionnelle, le présent devient l'effet du futur, et non le contraire.

Index